Society and Politics in Medieval Italy
The Evolution of the Civil Life, 1000–1350

NEW STUDIES IN MEDIEVAL HISTORY

General Editor: Denis Bethell

Society and Politics in Medieval Italy

The Evolution of the Civil Life, 1000–1350

J. K. HYDE

Macmillan

First published 1973 by
THE MACMILLAN PRESS LTD
London and Basingstoke
Associated companies in New York
Dublin Melbourne Johannesburg and Madras

SBN 333 11459 0 (hard cover)
333 11460 4 (paper cover)

Printed in Great Britain by
HAZELL WATSON AND VINEY LTD
Aylesbury, Bucks

For Maura

Contents

MAPS

PLATES

between pages 72 and 73

Acknowledgements

As the idea of this book first arose out of my teaching at Manchester, so my first debt is to the students who attended my classes on Italian history over the years whose questions and comments helped to shape the subject in my mind. The materials were provided by the diligent researches of many scholars, most but not all of whom are mentioned in the notes and bibliographies; in working their separate findings into a general pattern, I hope I have not distorted what they intended to say. I owe a special debt of gratitude to Professor Donald Bullough, who found time among many other commitments to read the early chapters; his expert observations saved me from many a blunder. From the editor of this series, Mr Denis Bethell, I have received more in the way of constructive guidance and encouragement than any author could expect or hope for; as this book has grown chapter by chapter, so has our friendship. Finally, I am aware that my family have had a lot to put up with while this book has been in preparation. I wish to thank them for their patience, especially my wife, who besides much support and encouragement gave time to read each successive draft as it appeared; her lay comments led to improvements on almost every page.

The author and the publishers wish to thank the following for permission to reproduce the illustrations appearing in this book: the Ministry of Defence (Air) and the Pitt Rivers Museum, Oxford, for Plates IA and IB; Dr Julian Gardner and the Courtauld Institute of the University of London for Plate II; Orlandini of Modena and Librairie Armand Colin: © *Naissance de l'Europe* by R. S. Lopez, published by Armand Colin S.A., Paris, for Plate III; the Bibliothèque Nationale, Paris, for Plate IV and Éditions d'Art Albert Skira, Geneva, for Plate VI.

The author and the publishers also wish to thank the Columbia University Press for permission to reproduce on pages 154–5 a passage from R. S. Lopez and I. W. Raymond, *Medieval Trade in the Mediterranean World* (1955), and C. T. Davis for permission to reproduce on page 165 a passage from his 'Il Buono Tempo Antico' in N. Rubinstein (ed.), *Florentine Studies* (1969).

Chronological Table

c. 235–68	Civil wars and barbarian invasions greatly impoverish western Roman Empire.
330	Foundation of Constantinople as second capital of the Roman Empire.
402	Invasion of Italy by the Goths; imperial court withdraws from Milan to Ravenna.
452	Huns under Attila destroy Aquileia and other cities of N.E. Italy.
476	Deposition of last emperor in the West; barbarian armies settled on the land.
493–526	Theodoric, king of the Ostrogoths, rules the Italians in the name of the emperor.
534–*c.* 54	Italy devasted by Justinian's Gothic war.
568	Lombards invade Italy.
653–61	King Aribert I: official conversion of the Lombards from Arian to Catholic Christianity.
751	Lombards finally capture Ravenna; collapse of Byzantine power in North Italy.
754, 756	Franks under Pepin raid Lombardy at request of Pope Stephen III.
774	Charlemagne, king of the Franks, conquers Lombard kingdom.
800	Charlemagne crowned emperor in Rome.
831	Saracens capture Palermo.
841–71	Saracens hold Bari.
875–962	Decline of the kingdom of Italy; power passes to local bishops and nobility.
876–*c.* 1025	Byzantine political hegemony over South Italy.
899–954	Intermittent Magyar raids on Italy.
915	Local forces under Pope John X destroy the Saracen stronghold on the Garigliano.
962	Otto I of Saxony crowned emperor in Rome.
c. 979	Archbishop Landulph enfeoffs *milites* with lands of the church of Milan.
983–91	Regency of the Empress Theophanu for her son Otto III; rights of the palace at Pavia alienated (?).

1143	Formation of the Roman commune; emergence of the council at Venice.
1151	Guido da Sasso first recorded podestà at Bologna.
1155	Frederick Barbarossa crowned emperor; execution of Arnold of Brescia.
1158	Frederick consults Italian jurists at the Diet of Roncaglia.
1167	Formation of the Lombard League against Frederick I.
1176	Lombard cities defeat Frederick I at Legnano.
1183	Peace of Constance; Frederick I recognises jurisdiction of the cities of the Lombard League.
1190	Death of Frederick I on crusade; succeeded by Henry VI who claims Naples and Sicily by right of his wife Constance and conquers them.
1197	Death of Henry VI; Frederick II king of Sicily, Germany and Italy contested between Otto of Brunswick (Welf) and Philip of Swabia (Waiblingen=Ghibelline) until 1208.
c. 1198	*Credenza di Sant'Ambrogio* formed in Milan.
1198	Innocent III becomes pope: virtual foundation of papal state in central Italy.
c. 1200	*Universitates* of law students formed at Bologna.
1204	Fourth Crusade dominated by Venetians captures Constantinople.
1209	First rule of St Francis.
1215	Fourth Lateran Council; Boncompagno's *Rhetorica Antiqua* read at Bologna.
1220	Frederick II crowned emperor; university of Padua founded.
1224	Frederick II founds the university of Naples.
1226	Death of St Francis.
1227	Rising of the *communanza* at Verona.
1228	Rising of the *popolo* at Bologna; Accursian gloss completed.
1231	Publication of Frederick II's Sicilian law-book, the *Liber Augustalis*.
1235	Frederick II undertakes subjugation of the Lombard communes.

1236-7   Frederick II captures Vicenza and Padua; *de facto*
          signoria of Ezzelino III da Romano in
          E. Lombardy established.

1240   Azzo VII d'Este captures Ferrara and establishes *de
          facto* signoria.

1245   Deposition of Frederick II by Council of Lyons.

1250   Formation of *Primo Popolo* in Florence; death of
          Frederick II.

1252   Gold genovins and florins first coined.

1259   Capture and death of Ezzelino III da Romano.

1260   Battle of Montaperti; beginning of Ghibelline
          hegemony in Tuscany.

1261   Michael VIII Paleologus captures Constantinople;
          end of the Latin Empire; Genoese gain access to
          Black Sea; election of Urban IV.

1264   Obizzo II d'Este elected signore of Ferrara.

1266   Battle of Benevento; death of Manfred; Charles of
          Anjou becomes king of Sicily; beginning of
          Angevin predominance in Italy.

1268   Death of Conradin, last of the Hohenstaufen, at
          Tagliacozzo.

1273   Rudolph of Habsburg elected king of the Romans;
          Napoleone della Torre imperial vicar of Milan;
          abortive reconciliation of Florentine parties by
          Gregory X.

1277   Battle of Desio; Visconti expel della Torre from
          Milan; Alberto della Scala elected signore of
          Verona.

1277-8   First Genoese galleys sent to Flanders and England.

1278   Nicholas III (Orsini) enforces papal claim to
          Romagna.

1279-80   Peace mission of Cardinal Latino to Bologna and
          Florence.

1282   Sicilian Vespers; French lose Sicily to Aragonese;
          Ordinamenti sacrati (anti-magnatial laws) at
          Bologna.

1284   Genoese defeat the Pisans at Meloria.

1290   Alberto Scotto elected signore of Piacenza.

1293   Ordinances of Justice at Florence.

1294–1303	Boniface VIII pope; who builds up the power of his own family, the Caetani; is a formidable enemy of the White party, and who is defeated and humiliated by the French king Philip the Fair.
c. 1295–1301	Conflict of Blacks and Whites in Florence.
1301	Mission of Charles of Valois and expulsion of Whites from Florence.
1302	Guido della Torre expels Visconti from Milan.
1305	Election of Clement V; beginning of the line of 'Avignon' popes.
1306	Fall of White stronghold of Pistoia.
1308	Clement V claims Ferrara for the papacy; war with Venice; Henry of Luxemburg elected king of the Romans.
1310–13	Henry VII in Italy.
c. 1314–21	Dante's *Divine Comedy* written.
1320	John XXII sends Bertrand du Poujet as legate against the Visconti.
1324	Marsiglio of Padua completes *Defensor Pacis*.
1328	Fall of Paduan commune to Cangrande della Scala of Verona.
1327–9	Lewis of Bavaria in Italy.
1329	Lucca sold by German mercenaries.
1332–3	Intervention of John of Bohemia in N. Italy.
1337	Taddeo Pepoli signore of Bologna; end of the last free commune north of the Apennines.
1342–3	Walter of Brienne signore of Florence.
1343	New regime in Florence; Peruzzi and numerous other banks fail; death of Robert king of Naples.
1346	Bardi go bankrupt.
1347–9	The Black Death in Italy.

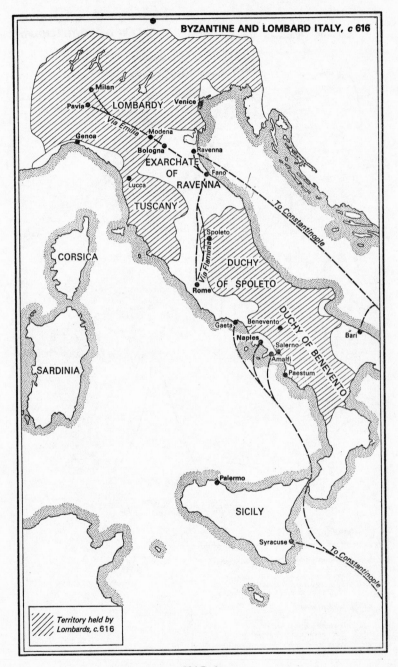

BYZANTINE AND LOMBARD ITALY, *c* 616

Milan
Venice
Pavia
LOMBARDY
Via Emilia
Modena
Genoa
Bologna
Ravenna
EXARCHATE
OF
Fano
RAVENNA
Lucca
TUSCANY
To Constantinople

CORSICA

Spoleto
Via Flaminia
DUCHY
OF SPOLETO
Rome

SARDINIA

Gaeta
Benevento
Naples
DUCHY
Bari
Salerno
Amalfi
OF BENEVENTO
Paestum

Palermo

SICILY

Syracuse
To Constantinople

Territory held by
Lombards, *c.*616

MAP 1

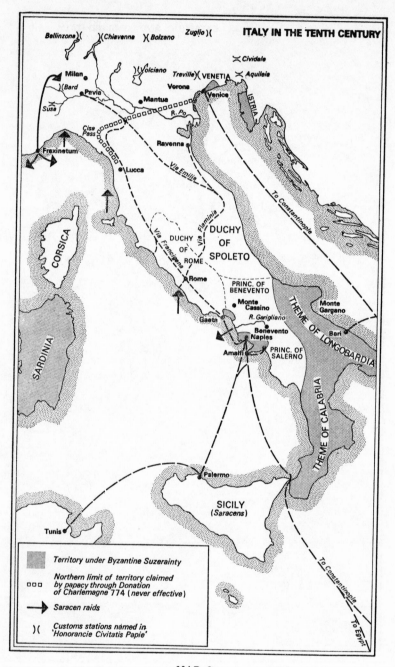

ITALY IN THE TENTH CENTURY

Bellinzona)( )(Chiavenna X Bolzano Zuglio)(

X Cividale

)(Volciano   Treville)(VENETIA   Aquileia

Milan

(Bard   Verona   Venice   ISTRIA

Pavia   Mantua

Susa   R. Po

Cisa Pass

Frexinetum   Ravenna

Via Emilia   To Constantinople

Lucca

CORSICA   Via Flaminia

Via Francigena   DUCHY OF ROME   DUCHY OF SPOLETO

Rome   PRINC. OF BENEVENTO

Monte Gargano

SARDINIA   Monte Cassino

Gaeta   R. Garigliano   THEME OF LONGOBARDIA

Benevento   Bari

Amalfi   Naples

PRINC. OF SALERNO

THEME OF CALABRIA

Palermo

SICILY
(Saracens)

Tunis

Territory under Byzantine Suzerainty

☐☐☐ Northern limit of territory claimed
by papacy through Donation
of Charlemagne 774 (never effective)

➔ Saracen raids

)(Customs stations named in
'Honorancie Civitatis Papie'

To Constantinople

To Egypt

MAP 2

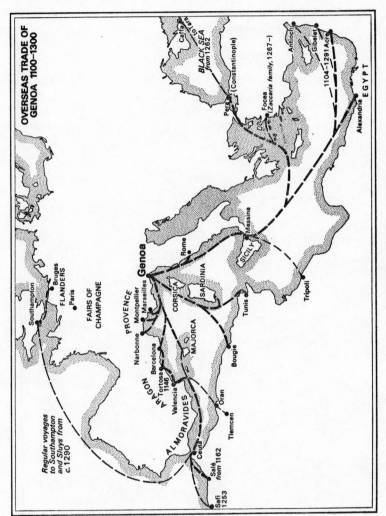

OVERSEAS TRADE OF
GENOA 1100–1300

Southampton

Bruges
FLANDERS
Paris

FAIRS OF
CHAMPAGNE

Regular voyages
to Southampton
and Sluys from
c. 1290

PROVENCE
Narbonne Montpellier
Marseilles
Genoa

ARAGON
Barcelona
Tortosa
1146
Valencia

ALMORAVIDES
Ceuta
Salé
from 1162

Safi
1253

Tlemcen
Oran

MAJORCA

CORSICA
SARDINIA

Rome

Bougie

Tunis

SICILY
Messina

Tripoli

BLACK SEA
from 1261

Caffa

Pera
(Constantinople)

Focea
(Zaccaria family, 1267–)

Antioch

Gibelet
1104–1291 Acre

Alexandria

E G Y P T

MAP 3A

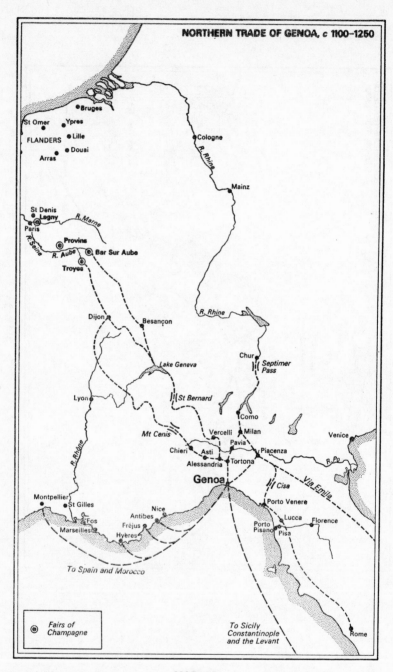

NORTHERN TRADE OF GENOA, c 1100–1250

Bruges
St Omer
Ypres
Lille
FLANDERS
Douai
Arras
Cologne
R. Rhine
Mainz
St Denis
Lagny
Paris
R. Marne
R. Seine
Provins
R. Aube
Bar Sur Aube
Troyes
Dijon
Besançon
R. Rhine
Lake Geneva
Chur
Septimer Pass
Lyon
St Bernard
Como
Mt Cenis
Vercelli
Milan
Venice
Chieri
Asti
Pavia
Piacenza
Alessandria
Tortona
R. Po
Via Emilia
Genoa
Cisa
Montpellier
St Gilles
Nice
Antibes
Porto Venere
Fos
Fréjus
Lucca
Florence
Marseilles
Hyères
Porto Pisano
Pisa

To Spain and Morocco

Fairs of Champagne

To Sicily Constantinople and the Levant

Rome

MAP 3B

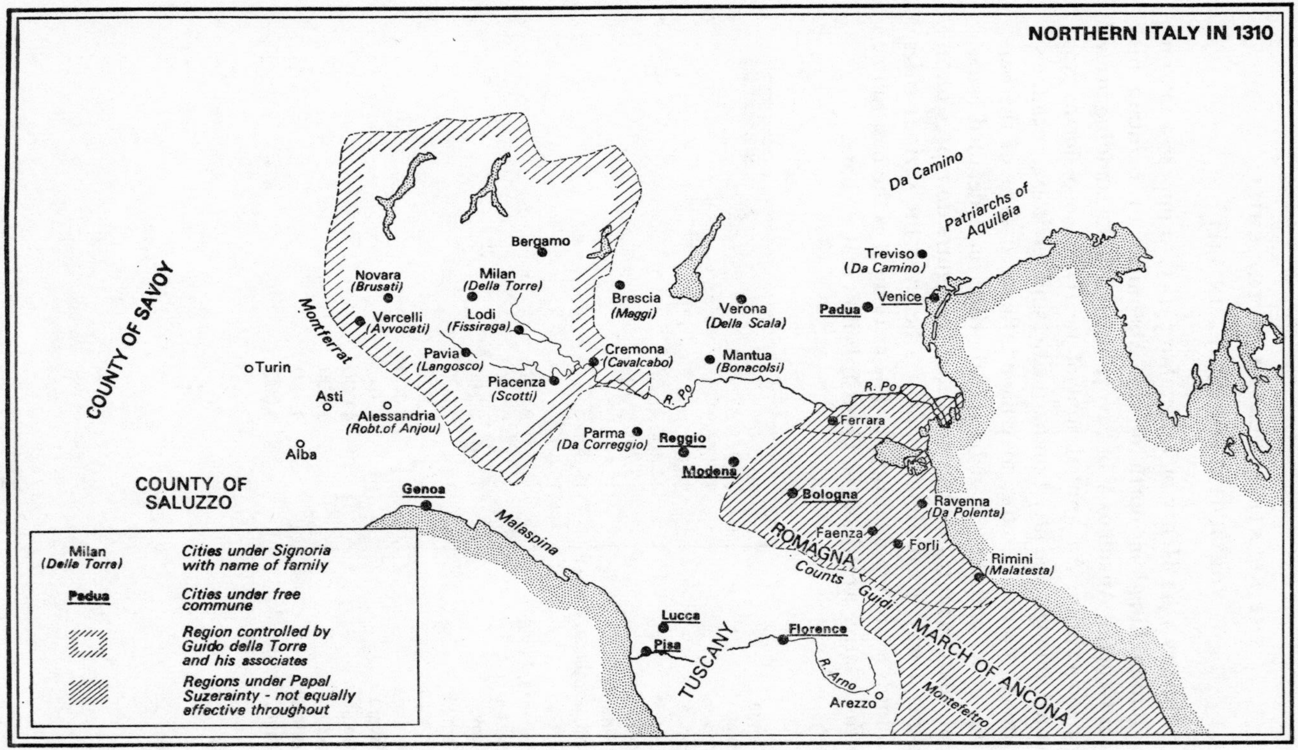

NORTHERN ITALY IN 1310

Da Camino

Patriarchs of
Aquileia

Treviso
(Da Camino)

Venice

Padua
(Da Camino)

Verona
(Della Scala)

Mantua
(Bonacolsi)

Brescia
(Maggi)

Bergamo

Cremona
(Cavalcabò)

Modena

Milan
(Della Torre)

Lodi
(Fissiraga)

Parma
(Da Correggio)

Reggio

Piacenza
(Scotti)

Pavia
(Langosco)

Novara
(Brusati)

Vercelli
(Avvocati)

o Alessandria
(Robt.of Anjou)

R. Po

Ferrara

Bologna

ROMAGNA

Counts Guidi

Faenza

Forli

Ravenna
(Da Polenta)

Rimini
(Malatesta)

MARCH OF ANCONA

Montefeltro

Lucca

Pisa

Florence

Arezzo o

R. Arno

TUSCANY

Malaspina

Genoa

Montferrat

Asti o

o Alba

o Turin

COUNTY OF SALUZZO

COUNTY OF SAVOY

MAP 4

Milan
(Della Torre)   Cities under Signoria with name of family

Padua   Cities under free commune

    Region controlled by Guido della Torre and his associates

    Regions under Papal Suzerainty - not equally effective throughout

THE RELATIVE WEALTH OF THE CHIEF
NORTH ITALIAN CITIES IN 1311

In February 1311 Henry of Luxemburg tried to impose a tax on his Italian kingdom north of the Apennines to maintain his Vicar-General, Amadeus V of Savoy, his staff and a standing army of 1,500 cavalry. An annual sum of nearly 300,000 florins was divided among some fifty Lombard cities and territorial magnates. Although political factors may have influenced some of the bargains made, and there had been little time for a detailed assessment, there is no reason to doubt that the figures do represent, in a general way, what Henry's advisers believed the various cities and lords could reasonably pay. The assessment is the best source for the relative wealth of the Lombard cities that we have.

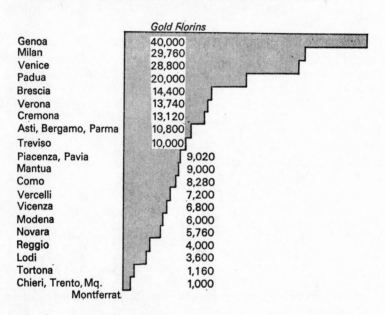

Gold Florins

Genoa	40,000
Milan	29,760
Venice	28,800
Padua	20,000
Brescia	14,400
Verona	13,740
Cremona	13,120
Asti, Bergamo, Parma	10,800
Treviso	10,000
Piacenza, Pavia	9,020
Mantua	9,000
Como	8,280
Vercelli	7,200
Vicenza	6,800
Modena	6,000
Novara	5,760
Reggio	4,000
Lodi	3,600
Tortona	1,160
Chieri, Trento, Mq. Montferrat	1,000

MAJOR ITALIAN CITIES c.1340

Novara
Como
Vercelli Bergamo
MILAN
Pavia
Cremona
Piacenza
Asti
Alessandria
GENOA
Brescia
Crema
Verona
Mantua
Parma
Reggio
Modena
Bologna
Faenza
Pistoia
Lucca
Pisa
FLORENCE
Siena
Arezzo
Orvieto
Viterbo
Rome
Vicenza
Treviso
Padua
VENICE
Ferrara
Ravenna
Forlì
Rimini
Ancona
Perugia
Capua
Aversa
Naples
Barletta
Bitonto
Trani
Bari
Monopoli
Taranto
Brindisi
Trapani
Palermo
Messina
Catania

APPROXIMATE POPULATION, c.1340

○	**MILAN**	80,000–100,000
●	**Palermo**	c.50,000
○	Verona	20,000–40,000
△	Ferrara	c.10,000
---		*Boundary of Kingdom of Naples*

MAP 5

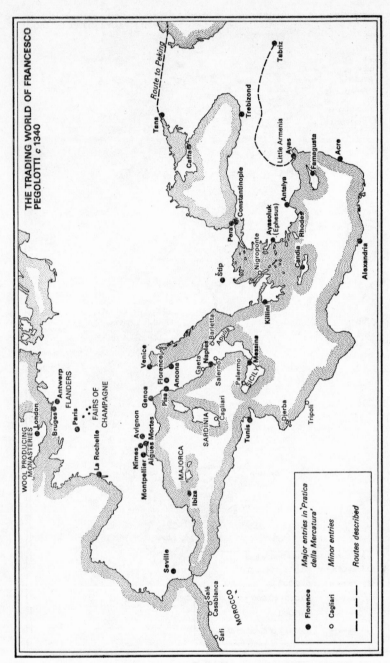

THE TRADING WORLD OF FRANCESCO
PEGOLOTTI c 1340

Route to Peking

Tabriz

Trebizond

Tana

Little Armenia
Ayas
Caffa
Famagusta
Acre
Constantinople
Pera
Antalya
Ayasoluk (Ephesus)
Rhodes
Štip
Nigroponte
Candia
Alexandria
Killini
Barletta
Apulia
Venice
Gaeta
Napies
Florence
Salerno
Ancona
Pisa
Genoa
Avignon
Cagliari
Palermo
SICILY
Messina
Nîmes
Montpellier
Aigues Mortes
SARDINIA
Djerba
Tripoli
MAJORCA
Tunis
Ibiza
WOOL PRODUCING
MONASTERIES
London
Bruges
Antwerp
FLANDERS
Paris
FAIRS OF
CHAMPAGNE
La Rochelle
Seville
Salé
Casablanca
MOROCCO
Safi

MAP 6

Florence   Major entries in 'Pratica
            della Mercatura'

Cagliari   Minor entries

- - - -   Routes described

Introduction

LAND of St Francis and of Dante, fragmented among tumultuous republics and unstable tyrannies, the repeatedly invaded spiritual and commercial nerve-centre of the Latin West, medieval Italy presents a mass of striking detail which cries out to be fitted into an overall pattern satisfying and meaningful to the present age. For the other major states of western Europe such patterns exist, established in the main by German, French and English historians of the last century who saw the history of their respective countries largely in terms of their national monarchies. The history of medieval France and England was represented as the story of how the crown and the organs of central government gradually extended their power, overcoming anarchy and local particularism; in medieval Germany the elements were the same but the outcome was different, with the monarchy finally losing the game after a brilliant opening, the victim of adverse fortune and mistaken choices. At first sight the fate of medieval Italy would seem to be similar to that of Germany, for here too the monarchy was eventually eclipsed by the local city-states and principalities, but there is a significant difference. In Germany both the monarchy and the forces which defeated it were authentic products of German society; Italy, on the other hand, lost her national monarchy in the mid-tenth century, and it was German kings who fought the losing battle to maintain imperial authority in the peninsula. They failed, not so much because they sacrificed Italian interests to those of Germany – rather the reverse was the case – but because, having grown up in a different kind of society, they always remained strangers and visitors to Italy, unable to comprehend the nature of the country which they were trying to govern. Failing to harness the dynamic forces in Italian life to their cause, they spent most of their energies trying to smother them; even Frederick II, though he was brought up in Sicily, pursued policies in northern Italy which were socially conservative. Thus, while the history of medieval Germany, when written from the point of view of the monarchy, becomes a tragedy, that of Italy emerges as a confused happening in which the centre of the stage is monopolised by minor characters, while the chief actors are either barely audible upstage, or are bound, gagged, and thrown into the wings.

The modern shift of interest towards administrative, economic and social history, while it has brought much greater understanding of particular aspects, has not yet led to the emergence of a distinctive profile of Italian society as a whole. In recent years, professional historians have tended to concentrate on local or specialised studies and have sheered away from any general interpretations. This tendency has already produced some undesirable results. For example, in general studies of the Middle Ages, the Italian contribution is often both greatly under-represented and poorly related to the whole. What are commonly represented as the main characteristics of medieval society – feudalism, manorialism, scholasticism and Gothic – are, in fact, generalisations of certain features found chiefly in parts of England, northern France and western Germany, and they are quite untypical of most of Italy, where commerce was more important, society more urban and culture more lay than in the other lands of the West. The carrying over of notions derived from other parts of Europe to Italy has resulted in some persistent misunderstandings, such as the view that because the patrician class lived largely in cities and was interested in trade it must necessarily have been non- or antifeudal. Italian society cannot be made to conform to the pattern of other countries, nor can it be properly appreciated as a local deviation from the norm. The city-based civilisation of north and central Italy was no marginal exception, but a central and, in some respects, a dominant component of the medieval world, which calls for understanding on its own terms. King John and his contemporary St Francis, the Sicilians who rose against their French masters in 1282 exactly one week before the Welsh took up arms against the English king, the great adversaries Edward I of England and Philip IV of France, and the Italian bankers who financed them both – all these need to be given their due weight in any balanced analysis of the thirteenth century West.

Without some general picture of medieval Italy, neither the Middle Ages nor Italy can be properly understood. No medieval country lived less exclusively unto itself. Throughout the medieval centuries, Rome remained the centre of the political and spiritual ideals of the West, and her law was a model for both church and state; the medieval papacy was overwhelmingly the work of

Italians and was always especially sensitive to changes in the Italian scene. The influx of students, suitors and soldiers into the peninsula was matched by the outflow of prelates, merchants and bankers who exerted their influence into the farthest corners of the Latin West. On an even larger scale of reference, Italy was the most important meeting place of the three great heirs of the ancient Roman world – the catholic, the orthodox-Byzantine and the islamic civilisations; for both trade and culture, she was the leading intermediary between East and West. Again, the present formlessness of the medieval period has the effect of cutting Italian history in two. Imperial Rome seems to peter out in darkness and chaos; renaissance Italy lacks an adequate background. One reaction has been to try and make the Middle Ages as short as possible; some historians have placed the end of antiquity so late and the beginnings of the renaissance so early that Italy appears to have had hardly any Middle Ages at all. Too often, criteria derived from north-western Europe are applied to Italy in such a way that features are deemed to be typical of antiquity or the renaissance which are, in fact, merely typically Italian. Many of the current disagreements about the nature of the renaissance, in fact, stem from divergent views of the character of the preceding period. Yet the idea of a dark or middle age originated in Italy; it is high time that some attempt was made to recover its meaning.

It was, above all, the politically orientated national history of the last century which made nonsense of the Italian Middle Ages, and it is necessary to go back to before the age of the Risorgimento to find the precedents for an alternative approach. Jean Charles Sismondi's *Histoire des Républiques italiennes au moyen-âge* which was completed in 1818 is, in many respects, a summing up of the work of eighteenth century historians who could accept Italian political disunity as something natural. Moreover, as a citizen of Geneva, Sismondi had first-hand experience of life in a city-state which his successors of the romantic school lacked. He saw clearly that the mainsprings of Italian medieval history were local and he sought to trace the story of Italian liberty in the setting of the city republic and regional principality. His political ideal was a middle-class oligarchy, which was good deal nearer to that of the medieval commune than was nineteenth century demo-cracy; Sismondi's chief failing in dealing with medieval political ideas, was to take Italian propaganda, and especially the myth of

Florentine *libertas*, too much at its face value. But he was also influenced by his experience as a Swiss in the Napoleonic era, and
this emerges in his emphasis on Italian liberty in terms of resistance
to the foreigner. His interpretation was, therefore, strongly nation-
alist and anti-imperial in tone, and this no doubt contributed to its
popularity during the hundred years or so after its publication.
Indeed, in the first years of the twentieth century, the Englishman,
William Boulting, took the view that only changes in detail were
necessary to bring Sismondi up to date. His revised edition does
not explicitly put forward any new pattern, but because it is much
shortened by the omission of a great deal of local detail, imperial
affairs bulk much larger in it. W. Butler's *Lombard Communes*,
which appeared at about the same time, is also strongly centred on
the theme of an Italian struggle for liberty against the foreign
emperors. It was this approach which, for example, led Butler to
misinterpret the Guelphs and the Ghibellines as, in some sense,
national parties; in fact, neither the empire nor anti-imperialism
were strong enough forces to give any real unity to the medieval
Italian political scene.

The fate of the Sismondi tradition suggests that no purely political history of medieval Italy could ever be really satisfactory, for
to correspond with the subject it would need to be a many-headed
monster. Certainly, some recent Italian textbooks, written with
much greater technical expertise than that of Boulting or Butler,
have conspicuously failed to square the circle of treating national
and regional history together, and to do justice to a situation where
the parts are so much greater than the whole. To find a wider
approach, it is necessary to go back behind Sismondi to the man
who, above all, made his work of synthesis possible. Lodovico
Antonio Muratori was the librarian of the Este dukes of Modena
during the first half of the eighteenth century, but his interest in
Italian history was far from local. His fame today rests mainly on
the vast storehouse of original sources from all parts of Italy which
he made available in the twenty-seven volumes of his *Rerum Italicarum Scriptores*. His *Annales* is a work of reference, little more
than a compendium of the various local chronicles. For Muratori's
outline of the nature of medieval Italy it is necessary to turn to his
Antiquitates Italicae, where he sets out to give a description of the
kingdom of Italy in the Middle Ages, which he likens to a great
house with various rooms, gardens and outhouses, chapel, picture

gallery and stables. For him, Italy was a cultural rather than a political entity, but his definition of culture was wide enough to include the political institutions of the individual Italian states. Most of the seventy-five dissertations which make up the *Antiquitates* are devoted to a single aspect of Italian life. Influenced by the antiquarians' approach to the much more limited sources relating to classical antiquity, Muratori cast his net very wide, and among the subjects he regarded as worthy of inclusion were currency, heraldry, knighthood, personal names and education, as well as the more usual materials of political history. Usurers, leper hospitals and mercenary companies are rather curiously grouped together in one section; a dissertation on superstitions includes evidence for the first coming of the gypsies to Italy. The breadth of Muratori's vision of medieval Italy, as a single culture existing with local variations in a multiplicity of states, has never been surpassed. Sismondi failed to do justice to Muratori's deeper insights into Italian society and institutions, and so the sketch-plan of the palace of medieval Italy contained in the *Antiquitates* was never translated into the solid wood and stone of a great history.

The unity of medieval Italian history is to be sought not in the state but in a culture supported by a distinctive form of society. Muratori sensed this, but modern research into the economic and social aspects has made clearer the special features of Italian society and the ways in which it differed from the rest of the medieval world. One side of this relationship is summed up in a remark by R. S. Lopez: 'Italy was never medieval, yet no medieval phenomenon left her unaffected.' For example, the manorial economy, characterised by estates divided into the lord's demesne and the serfs' tenures, appeared in Italy as in the rest of Europe, but it declined in all but the most backward areas much earlier than elsewhere, and so plays a much smaller part in the economy of the central Middle Ages. Again, the feudal bond between members of the knightly class holding fiefs from their overlords was widespread in north and central Italy from the ninth century onwards, and was propagated in the south by the Norman conquest, yet the survival of other kinds of property on a large scale meant that feudal tenure never came to dominate all other types of land-holding in the way it did in parts of north-west Europe. Two important features of northern medieval culture, scholastic logic and Gothic architecture, both of which developed in the Ile de France during the twelfth century, spread only slowly and sporadically to Italy, so that their full impact was not felt until the end of the thirteenth century, when the main lines of Italian culture were already fixed.

The positive features of the Italian scene which marked it off from the countries of the north may be summarised as a much closer relationship with antiquity. In part this was a matter of survival. Not only the road system but the network of cities went back in the main to Roman or earlier foundations; the rich deposits of Roman art made it difficult for Italian sculptors and architects to escape its influence for very long. In part, it was a matter of parallel development and conscious revival; as the medieval economy advanced, it followed tracks already beaten in Roman times and eventually extended them. As society evolved, it was able to draw on the preserved experiences of antiquity. By far the most important medieval revival was that of classical Roman law through the study of Justinian's codification, which began in the late eleventh century and was continued at a high level for the next three hundred years. The relics of antiquity were so imposing that they could arouse both admiration and antipathy, but they could never be ignored. All Italian culture in the Middle Ages was conditioned by the dialogue with antiquity; the Renaissance was a new phase in a conversation which had been going on for centuries.

Like that of antiquity, Italian society in the Middle Ages was highly urbanised; by the later thirteenth century it appears that in the more highly developed parts of Lombardy and Tuscany the proportion of townsmen to countrymen had risen as high as one in three. By that time there were numbers of large cities in northern Europe too, but there the urban population was mainly involved in some form of trade or industry which tended to draw it apart from the rest of society. In most of Europe, civic liberty meant the power of the leading burghers to manage the local affairs of their town without interference from the lay and ecclesiastical hierarchies which dominated the rest of the land. In Italy, by contrast, the cities regarded the right to rule the territory round about as an essential part of their birthright, and this claim had its counterpart in the different kind of society to be found in both the cities and the countryside. When the Italian friar Salimbene visited France in the thirteenth century, the chief thing that he noticed, along with the shortness of the summer nights, was the fact that the nobility lived in the country. In Italy, the nobility had been attracted to the towns from an early date, and by Salimbene's time there were few aristocratic families who did not have a town house where they spent at least a part of the year. In the cities they inevitably mingled with the wealthier merchants and intermarriages took place; merchants bought land, and in the greater commercial centres the nobles were drawn into trade, either as investors or even as direct participants. In medieval England, only one family of mercantile origin, the de la Poles of Hull, reached the ranks of the aristocracy; in thirteenth century Italy, some half dozen greater cities were dominated by merchant aristocracies where the cultural fusion between the nobility and the businessmen was all but complete. In such places, the governing class was equally at home in town and country, and one can detect the emergence of a townsman's attitude to the countryside as a place of peace and recreation. The fusion worked both ways; if Italian noblemen were relatively 'civilised', Italian merchants acquired many of the characteristics both good and bad of the landed aristocracy. In the less developed areas, a social distinction remained, but the classes were close enough for the gap to be crossed in the course of a generation or two. In the most prosperous cities, members of the same family, or even a single individual, might combine a wide range of occupations such as commerce, banking, learning, the law, and professional or part-time administration or soldiering; landowning and some involvement in politics were almost universal. In the urban milieu, education was obviously valuable and relatively easy to obtain, so that the distinction in northern society between the learned clergy and the illiterate laymen was almost non-existent. In every sphere except the political, Italy was the country where barriers were lower.

The characteristics of Italian society so far described were very similar to those in many cities in antiquity, and could be paralleled in its more prosperous periods by medieval Byzantium, where there was a town-dwelling landed aristocracy whose members could be involved in war or trade. They were still prevalent in the sixteenth century when William Thomas, the first Englishman to attempt a history of renaissance Italy, wrote in 1549 that the gentlemen of the country generally professed arms, love and learning: precisely the points upon which Dante and his circle had prided themselves in the later thirteenth century. One occupation, which had been an integral part of the full citizen's life for Dante's contemporaries, was, however, closed to the sixteenth century Italian, unless he happened to be a Venetian of one of a small number of privileged families – participation in the politics of a city-republic. Medieval republicanism was originally a pragmatic affair which made its appearance because Italian society outgrew the existing political institutions; the communes began as a form of political self-defence and self-help at the end of the eleventh century when the cities were sliding into a state of anarchy. The commune was a particular form of association for which the general legal term was *societas*. Other kinds of *societas* were formed to administer family property or commercial ventures. Trade and professional guilds, the universities and political parties based on class or other interests were also *societates*. The clash of these associations within the commune and their struggles to control it produced an extreme political instability which was cured eventually only by the establishment of despotisms. In its heyday, medieval Italian society was never far from anarchy. In this it was at the opposite pole from that of Byzantium, whose empire was upheld by religion and a centuries-old tradition, where the emperor was regarded as God's representative on earth. The city-state of antiquity, too, was supported at many points by religious sanctions. The Italian communes, on the other hand, were essentially secular contrivances whose particularism flourished in spite of a universal religion and the claims of a universal empire. Throughout the medieval period, Italian political ideas generally lagged behind political facts, and the social and political ideals of the communes were only fully expressed when they were on the point of extinction. The ideology articulated with a new elegance in early fifteenth century Florence was, in all essentials, the one which the governing classes of the communes had professed for the past three centuries, and the life of the model citizen, governing his own affairs in town and country and dutifully participating in the affairs of the state, was described in the 1430s by Matteo Palmieri in a book called *Della Vita Civile*.

The aim of the pages which follow will be to trace the development of the medieval Italian *vita civile* from the first stirrings of economic revival in the tenth century until the economic setbacks of the mid-fourteenth, which also mark the point at which despotisms had been established in all but a few of the city-states and at which Italian culture seems to have paused to broaden and deepen its roots, as it were, in preparation for the great leap forward in the early fifteenth century. They are, in no sense, intended as a narrative history, though chronological divisions have been introduced in order to bring out the dynamic nature of Italian society and emphasise the distinctive flavour of the various stages in its evolution. In particular, I have tried in Chapters 2 and 3 to bring out the special characteristics of the century 1150–1250, when the Italians to some extent turned their backs on antiquity and created the political institutions and administrative machinery which were to last them for the rest of the medieval period and even beyond.

Naturally, the attempt to cover so large and complex a subject in so short a space has involved some difficult problems of selection. On the whole I have preferred to deal at some length with a few chosen examples, rather than flit about trying to build up a picture of that pale abstraction, the average city. Thus, for the tenth century I have concentrated on Pavia rather than Milan, and I have used Genoa rather than Pisa to illustrate the consequences of the twelfth century revival of trade. The growth of the *vita civile* is the centre of interest throughout, and for this reason the South largely drops out of the picture after the Norman conquest. There has been no space to deal with art, literature or intellectual movements except in passing; I have highlighted the revival of law and rhetoric because this seems to be the point where the intellect was brought to bear on the practical problems of the civil life. It has proved impossible to give an account of the *vita civile* of the age of Dante without saying a good deal about Florence. On the other hand, I have tried to avoid giving the impression that the Florentines were always the first and best at everything; Padua was ahead in the field of civic humanism, and the first family to combine banking with a *signoria* were the Scotti of Piacenza. Finally, an ideal book on this subject would have contained much more about the church and the complex role which it played in every facet of life; the research for such a book would have taken at least ten years, and the reader must be content with some suggestions and observations which are intended to do little more than suggest the lines along which further inquiries might proceed.

1. The Social Foundations of Medieval Italy

The Slow Death of Roman Italy

AMONG the first impressions likely to be formed by a visitor to Italy, especially if he comes from northern Europe or North America, is of the abrupt transition between mountain and plain and between city and countryside. In most parts of Italy the sharp outlines of the mountains, which provide the background to countless Italian paintings, fall directly into the plain as if into a green sea, and only in a few regions, notably Umbria, is there anything resembling the rolling hills of Germany, France or England. Foothills are rare, and so until the last decade or so, were suburbs; even today, with the vast growth of building in favoured rural areas, like the Lombard plain or the Arno valley, the break between town and country is usually clearly discernible. Moreover, the social distinction between citizens and country people still persists, and can be observed in any Italian town or city on market days, when the urban environment is invaded by the people of the surrounding region, who stand out with their distinctive ways of dress and speech.

These two contrasts are of the greatest importance for the understanding of Italian society and civilisation, to which they are related in very different ways. The division between mountain and plain is a fact of nature to which man has had to adapt himself. As barriers to easy communication, the mountains have obviously contributed to the intense regionalism of Italian life, though the history of the Lombard plain where local loyalties have been hardly less strong than elsewhere, suggests that other factors must have been at work too. More subtly, the close juxtaposition of mountain and plain in almost every region, by creating areas of contrasting economic challenges and potentialities has at all periods impeded the emergence of uniform social and political structures even within the restricted territory dominated by a single city. From ancient times, the dominant roles in Italian history have been played by peoples who learned how to exploit the immense resources of the plains and valleys. Starting from the banks of the Tiber, the Romans went out to develop the economic potential of the low lands of Italy, and it was there that they left their most conspicuous marks on the land in the shape of cities, aqueducts, roads and centuriation, the marking out of reclaimed land on a regular grid-pattern which is still plainly visible in several parts of the peninsula. The cities of the plains, especially of the Arno and the Po, were by and large the pacesetters of medieval Italy, and as such, it is right that most attention should be focused on them. But the mountain regions, although of secondary importance, should not be entirely forgotten. While it is true that the higher peaks are extremely inhospitable, the slopes, between 1200 and 600 feet above sea level, well-watered and enjoying a more temperate climate than the rest of the country, can be made extremely fertile. Being more easily cleared and drained, the higher lands were settled before the plains; easier to defend and maintain in cultivation, they were more resilient in times of trouble. The Etruscans were a people of the hills, and in central Italy cities built at a thousand feet or more above sea level, such as Siena, Perugia and Orvieto, continued in the first rank throughout the Middle Ages and into modern times. While in other regions the mountain zones fell under the economic and political hegemony of the plains, the regions of the middle hills were still intensely cultivated and, at least until the economic crises of the fourteenth century, they supported a surprisingly dense population. In these areas, the hills with their castles, which were not merely military strong points but fortified towns, presented a constant challenge to the cities of the plains; in the high mountains, the problems of law and order on which city governments expended much effort and expense were virtually insoluble under medieval conditions. In short, it should always be remembered that bordering the rich Italian plains there loomed the mountains where the tempo of economic and social development was much slower, so that half a day's journey and a climb of a few hundred feet could take the traveller back to a form of society which had vanished from the more developed regions some fifty or a hundred years before.

At first sight, the distinction between city and countryside in Italy seems to present a man-made parallel to the natural division between mountain and plain, with the cities cast in the active and dominant role and the rural areas in a largely passive one. The relationship has, in fact, been portrayed very much in this way in many books about Italy, the work both of Italians whose education imbued them with an outlook which equates cities with all that is civilised and worthy of study, and also by non-Italians misled by appearances and, perhaps, by preconceptions formed in their own countries. The view of the medieval city as essentially dedicated to commerce and industry, even if it is not the whole truth, is serviceable enough as an approach to the towns of northern Europe, but when it is applied to Italy it obscures one of the most distinctive features of Italian society. In the Mediterranean world until the most recent times, the great majority of cities have lived as centres of consumption and distribution of the surplus produce of the rural areas around them; apart from a few important exceptions, they have been dominated not by merchants and manufacturers but by landowners. The dependence upon agriculture, not only for subsistence but also for the whole livelihood of the greater part of the governing class, has had a profound effect on every aspect of Italian civic life right up to modern times. The links between the cities and their territories have taken many forms but they have never been a matter of marginal importance; at most times the rise and fall of the urban communities has depended on them more than on any other factor. The apparent self-sufficiency of the ancient or medieval city, cut off from the fields by its walls and gates, is, in fact, an illusion, and any treatment of Italian civilisation in which the countryside is passed over as insignificant is bound to be wide of the truth.

The civilisation of ancient Italy had been founded on the fusion of each city with its subject territory which together made up the *civitas*, and while these units were preserved the country could undergo the most far-reaching changes and vicissitudes without any fundamental break in continuity. Thus, the Italy of the fourth and fifth centuries was very different from what it had been in the early days of the Roman Empire. For reasons which are still mysterious, the population appears to have been falling, while the increasing pressure of the barbarians along the frontiers caused heavy demands to be made on an economy of limited resources. The spacious open cities, which had flourished in the heyday of the *pax Romana*, were now reduced in area and population and confined within hastily constructed walls which did not always save them from capture and pillage during the civil wars of the fourth century and the barbarian invasions of the fifth. Yet, although there were local disasters, the cities proved immensely resilient as long as they retained their function as the centres of a sophisticated administration. It is significant that the withdrawal of the great landowners to their country estates, which took place in Gaul, did not happen to anything like the same extent in Italy. Indeed, some of the key cities of the north achieved a new importance under the embattled conditions of the late Empire. Aquileia, in the north-east, prospered as the rear base for the armies defending the upper Danube, while greater proximity to the frontiers led to Milan replacing Rome as the centre of imperial administration in the west until 402, when the court was transferred to Ravenna for reasons of defence and easier communication with Constantinople.

The Dark Ages came late to Italy, for even the assumption of political control by barbarian leaders and the settlement of their armies on the land brought no revolutionary change. The abolition of the western line of emperors in 476 had little significance at the time, for the barbarians who took over had too great a respect for the Roman way of life to wish to sweep it away. Indeed, the Gothic king Theodoric who ruled in the name of the emperor at Constantinople from 493 to 526, is credited with important public works in the Roman tradition; in particular, his reconstruction of the imperial palaces at Verona, Pavia and Ravenna foreshadows the leading role to be played by these cities during the next few centuries. Paradoxically, it was the policy of reconquest adopted by the emperor Justinian which plunged the country into twenty years of bitter warfare from 535 to 554 that heralded the breakdown of Roman civilisation in Italy. The destruction and impoverishment caused by the Gothic war seems to have been very great; recovery had hardly had time to begin before the Lombards burst into the peninsula in 568. This new wave of Germanic invaders, unlike the Goths, had been hardly touched by Roman influence before they entered Italy and their attitude to the imperial government was one of unmitigated hostility. Wherever they established their control, written records cease for a time; when they resume they reveal that the Roman world has died and a new culture, much poorer and more primitive but strongly influenced by Byzantium, has arisen in its place.

In the rural areas, the coming of the Lombards probably did little more than accentuate the regressive tendencies which had been at work for a long time. A regime of large estates, with a subject peasantry owing dues and labour services in the lord's demesne, had evolved under the empire, and had probably been reinforced by the pressure of war and high taxation ruining the small proprietors during the last two centuries of the Roman system. The Lombard chieftains had every incentive to keep these estates in being, but being used to a pastoral economy, they tended to convert the demesnes to animal husbandry and leave the cultivation of crops to the conquered Roman population. The scale of values of the new aristocracy is reflected by the Lombard laws of the mid-seventh century under which a master swineherd with two or three assistants was protected by a *wergild*, worth more than twice that of a peasant with his own holding.[1] Under these conditions, the elaborate drainage and irrigation works created by the Romans fell into disrepair, and great tracts of country even in the most favoured areas like the Po valley, reverted to marsh, forest and waste. In the cities, however, the impact of the Lombards was much more immediate and disastrous. Although valued as sources of pillage and strong points of defence, the Italian cities under the Lombard occupation lost for a time their vital functions as administrative centres, for at first the political institutions of the invaders were so primitive that any kind of sophisticated administration was impossible. The break hardly lasted more than a generation or so, but it was decisive in interrupting the traditions of city life in north and central Italy; significantly, no historian has succeeded in proving the continuance of civic institutions from late Roman to medieval times for any city north of Rome.

It was crucial for the recovery of Italy that the Lombard occupation never extended over the whole country, so that the lights were not put out everywhere at the same time. In the twenty years following 568, the Lombards not only occupied the inland areas of the north, where they settled most thickly, but they moved over the Apennines to establish a stronghold at Spoleto and, bypassing Rome, went on to seize Benevento and the port of Salerno. But the Byzantine emperors, Justinian's successors, did not give up the struggle easily, and with their command of the sea they managed to hold on to most of the coastline for a considerable period of time. Thus the Ligurian coast in the north-west did not fall until the 640s, and the eastern part of the Lombard plain, which the Byzantines administered from the old imperial capital of Ravenna, was not finally conquered by the Lombard kings until 751. When the rest of the Exarchate collapsed, the scattered settlements in the Venetian lagoon continued to hold out under Byzantine suzerainty, with the most far-reaching consequences for the future. Though frequently threatened, Rome, too, held out with the popes gradually assuming responsibility for local administration and defence; until the mid-eighth century they regarded themselves as subject to the emperor at Constantinople in temporal matters and only in 751 did they turn finally towards the Franks in the west for protection. (See Map 1.)

The Byzantines failed to preserve the political unity of Italy which was destined not to be restored until the nineteenth century, but by holding on as they did they helped to educate the Lombards so that in just over a century they had reached a level of civilisation comparable with that of the rest of the former Roman provinces of the West. The abandonment of the Arian heresy for Catholicism in the mid-seventh century opened the way for the fusion of the Lombards with the local population and seems also to have faciliated trading and other contacts with Byzantium. In 643 King Rothari promulgated the first written laws of his people, and by the early eighth century the Lombard kingdom in the north had developed a serviceable administration based on royal agents residing in a network of former Roman centres, while in the royal palace of Pavia the Lombard kings had built up a permanent administrative headquarters in a real capital city of a kind quite unknown in the barbarian kingdoms of the north. When the Franks under Charlemagne conquered Lombardy in 774, they found not only scholars superior to those of Francia but also a state at least as sophisticated as their own, and, in some respects, more so. It has recently been suggested that some of the legal innovations of Charlemagne's later years may have been based on the earlier practices of the Lombard kingdom.[2] Although the precise degree of the Byzantine contribution to the Lombard achievement is disputed, it is not unreasonable to conclude that it must have been very great, since in the later seventh century Greek influence was transmitted through the church even to far away Anglo-Saxon England. For despite all kinds of vicissitudes, including the whole upheaval associated with the emergence of Islam, Constantinople maintained a degree of wealth and civilisation during these centuries which overshadowed that of all the barbarian kingdoms of the West.

The Divided Society : The Seventh to the Tenth Century

Towards the middle of the tenth century, Abbot Odo of Cluny, the outstanding religious leader of the day, wrote the life of St Gerard, the pious founder of the monastery of Aurillac in Burgundy. Gerard had been Count of Aurillac and a nobleman of some importance, and in the last years of the ninth century he had undertaken several journeys to Italy, one of which provided his biographer with what he regarded as an edifying story. The count had been on a pilgrimage to the shrines of Rome, which for several centuries had been attracting clerics and devout laymen from all over the Latin West. While in the city he had bought several cloaks, one in particular being of great value, a luxury garment of a kind produced in Constantinople and greatly prized in the West. On its return, no doubt, the pilgrim caravan travelled by the Via Francigena (the Frankish road) which led up the western side of the peninsula, keeping a safe distance from the coast, as far as Lucca, and then crossed the Apennines by way of the Cisa pass. In Lombardy, the pilgrims encamped outside the walls of Pavia, and here they were visited by parties of Venetians selling oriental goods 'as their custom was'. One of these merchants, who impressed Count Gerard as a man of some standing, came to his tent and seeing the cloak which he had bought in Rome, inquired about its price. On being told, the Venetian exclaimed that even in Constantinople a garment of such quality could only be obtained for a much higher price than the count had named. It looks as if the merchant in speaking in this way was trying to flatter the distinguished foreigner, but according to the biographer, the effect of his words was quite different. Gerard, full of remorse for having cheated the vendor of a part of the just price, immediately sent a servant back to Rome with a sum of money to make up the difference between the price he had paid and the value put on the cloak by the Venetian.[3]

Although it was obviously not Odo's purpose, the story he tells throws quite a lot of light on the state of commerce in Italy in this poorly documented period. The materials of long-distance trade

were luxuries of eastern origin such as silks, spices, works of crafts-
manship in gold, silver and ivory, pictures and ornaments, all of
them objects of high value in relation to their bulk and weight.
The merchants, even those who were important enough to impress
a northern count, could be itinerants carrying their wares with
them, like the Venetians who met the pilgrims in their camp outside Pavia. Yet economically and morally, such men lived in a
different world from the agrarian simplicity of Gerard of Aurillac
and Odo of Cluny, whose belief in a just price reveals the attitude
of consumers in a largely subsistence economy; the Venetian in
the story was a professional merchant who regarded price in a
competitive light, contingent upon the place and the condition of
the market.

It would be interesting to know whether an Italian nobleman
of the time would have shared Gerard and Odo's point of view;
had he come from an inland region, the chances are that he would,
for one of the characteristics of Italy from the seventh to the tenth
century seems to have been a sharp contrast in the economic condition of some favoured ports like Venice, Naples, Amalfi and
Salerno and a few distributing points dependent on them, like
Rome and Pavia, and the bulk of the interior of the country which
was much more backward, like a dark cloud with a silver lining.
Like the political fragmentation of the peninsula, this economic
division had arisen as a consequence of the Lombard invasion,
but it was destined to disappear almost entirely as a result of the
broadly based economic revival of the eleventh century.

In the first century or so after the Lombard attack, the economic
contrast between the barbarian and Byzantine held territories
must have been very sharp. From about 690, however, there are
signs of increasing trade in the Lombard areas, and the establishment of a royal mint at Pavia, which struck gold *solidi* of Byzantine standard, suggests that the country was at last being opened
up to trade with the East. The process continued during the
eighth century, and in 750 a famous passage in the laws of King
Aistulf speaks of great and powerful merchants who are obliged
to maintain a horse, shield, breastplate and lance for service in the
royal host in the same way as quite substantial landowners. The
same edict sought to restore the customs posts on the borders of the
kingdom and to regulate contacts between Lombard and Byzantine merchants.[4] The effect of the Frankish conquest on this trade

is not easy to assess. On the one hand, north and central Italy became part of a vast continental empire whose relations with Constantinople were often far from good; after Charlemagne's imperial coronation in 800, a war broke out which was fought around the fringes of the Venetian lagoon. On the other hand, if the peace with Byzantium which was concluded in 812, whose terms have not been preserved, followed the same lines as the agreement between Charles' grandson Lothar and the Venetians in 840, then it must have included provisions to facilitate trade, as well as granting the Venetians privileges on the *terra firma*.[5]

Some writings of the Carolingian age suggest that the economic revival of the eighth century was a modest affair which was insufficient to restore civic life on any considerable scale. Paulinus, a poet of Charlemagne's court who was appointed patriarch of Aquileia in 787, lamented the fate of the metropolitan city of north-eastern Italy in the following terms:

> Once you were a city of noblemen, now you have become a den of rustics; once you were a town of kings, now you are only a collection of paupers' huts; formerly full of lofty houses decorated with wonderful white marble, now your land bears fruits, marked out by the measuring line of poor peasants.[6]

The case of Aquileia was a special one; stormed by Attila and his Huns in 452, the city had lost its *raison d'être* with the collapse of the Danube frontier and was never rebuilt. But even in the leading cities of Carolingian Italy which had recovered something of their commercial and administrative functions, the most impressive sights to be seen were the legacies of antiquity. This emerges most clearly from two descriptions, one of Milan and the other of Verona, both of which enumerate at length the massive remains of pagan times – the walls, temples, amphitheatres and market places – compared with which modern times can boast of no more than a few churches. Obviously overawed by these vestiges of vanished material greatness, the writers take refuge in an assertion of the moral superiority of their own Christian age, and vaunt the supernatural protection provided by the virtues of the saints whose bodies lie buried in the city. That these poems were written at all proves the re-emergence of some kind of civic spirit; at the same time, they reveal the limited material basis of the Lombard and Carolingian revival.[7]

The most important change in the Mediterranean world in the ninth century was the challenge to Byzantine supremacy presented by the Moslems of North Africa and Spain. The major Saracen attacks began on Sicily in 827; in 831 Palermo fell to them and in 843 Messina also. Although Byzantine strongholds held out in the island until 901, by mid-century the way was open for full-scale assaults on the mainland; around 852 a sultanate was established at Bari and for some years it seemed possible that Saracen fleets would succeed in closing the Adriatic to Christian commerce. Despite valiant efforts, the Carolingian kings of Italy failed to make any permanent headway against the invaders in the south, and they thus lost what was perhaps the last chance of re-uniting the whole peninsula under one rule. It was the Byzantines under the emperor Basil I (867–86) who drove the Moslems out of Bari and re-established Christian control in southern Italy. The boundary of the Byzantine province foreshadows, in its general line, the frontier of the future kingdom of Naples, which under Norman, Hohenstaufen and Angevin dynasties was to follow a course of development strikingly different from the territories further north. By the early tenth century, the worst of the Saracen danger was past. In 916 the local Roman militia under Pope John X destroyed the Moslem pirate base at the mouth of the river Garigliano, and in 972 a similar settlement at Fraxinetum in the south of France fell to a combined attack by a Byzantine fleet and land forces led by the count of Provence; by 960 the Greeks had begun a naval offensive which restored their supremacy in east Mediterranean waters. (See Map 2.)

The net effect of these unprecedented changes was to confirm the economic division of Italy along the lines already established. It was the areas in the Byzantine sphere of influence which, either by armed retaliation or skilful diplomacy, weathered the storm most successfully and even found ways to draw profit from changing conditions, while it was the already impoverished coasts of Carolingian Italy which were raided again and again. A North African Moslem, Ibn Hawqal, who compiled a handbook for merchants in 977, after describing the city of Palermo quarter by quarter, found nothing worthy of note on the whole arc of the Mediterranean coast from Andalusia to Naples, except for an unidentified Moslem settlement called Gabal-al-Qual. The Christian ports of south Italy, on the other hand, aroused his en-

thusiasm; Amalfi he considered the richest, but it was in Naples
that he saw linen cloth finer than could be found in any other
country.[8] The Campanian cities had the most varied origins and
histories. Naples was an ancient Greek foundation while Amalfi's
emergence in the sixth century suggests that it, like Venice, was
the creation of refugees who had left their homes during the
earlier barbarian incursions; while the others had remained under
Byzantine control, Salerno had fallen to the Lombards. Yet each
of them managed to flourish in the period of Moslem expansion.
Exposed to Saracen attacks after the fall of Palermo, they skilfully
avoided alignment with any major power and set about exploiting
their position as intermediaries between the Greek, Latin and
Moslem worlds. Their *duces* acknowledged a nominal Byzantine
suzerainty as a matter of convenience, but, in fact, acted as independent hereditary princes. That in order to survive they had to
make concessions to non-Christians does not seem to have troubled
their consciences overmuch; the offer of 10,000 silver *mancusi*
plus a year's relief from tolls in the port of Rome made by Pope
John VIII in 879 was apparently insufficient to detach the citizens
of Amalfi from the alliance which they had made with the Saracens four years before. Trading contacts with the Arab world
continued in the tenth century. In 996 over a hundred Amalfitan
merchants are said to have been killed in Cairo when their ware-
house was destroyed by the populace when they were suspected of
setting fire to some Egyptian warships in the harbour.[9]

The ninth and tenth centuries also saw the rise of another
nominal outpost of the Byzantine Empire, namely Venice. The
years following the treaty of 812 saw the emergence of the islands
of Rialto as the permanent centre for the scattered population of
the lagoon; it is thought that the pro-Byzantine *dux*, Agnello
Partecipazio (810–27), was the first to set up his residence on the
site now occupied by the doges' palace. During the brief reign of
his son Giustiniano, the remains of St Mark were allegedly stolen
from Alexandria and laid to rest in the palace chapel. The chance
survival of Giustiniano's will (829) shows that he had a considerable fortune made up of land, precious metals both coined and
uncoined, spices and 'money put to work', which seems to mean
some kind of commercial investment.[10] Unlike the equivalent
office in the ports of the south, the position of doge never became
hereditary but remained elective for life; it circulated among a

handful of families – the Partecipazio, the Candiano and the Orseolo – and no fewer than seven of the Partecipazio ruled Venice at various times between 810 and 942. The emergence of these early patrician families coincided with the establishment of Venetian hegemony over the sea-borne trade of north-east Italy. The political troubles which affected the mainland left them free to eliminate their rivals; for example, in 883 the Venetians captured Comacchio in the Po delta, whose prosperity had been built on the salt trade, and by 932 they had asserted their domination over the coasts of Istria. The carrying trade to and from Constantinople passed increasingly into their hands and the power of their fleet put them in a strong position to extract concessions from the emperor. The celebrated Golden Bull of Basil II in 992 nearly halved the rate of the toll which the Venetians had to pay at Abydos in the Dardanelles, giving them a considerable advantage not only over other foreign merchants but also over their rivals in southern Italy who were politically dependent on Byzantium. Headed by Bari, the ports of Apulia seem to have specialised in local trade, exchanging agricultural produce for the luxury goods of the East.

The economic conditions prevailing on the *terra firma* in the tenth century are illustrated by a memorandum drawn up by a Pavian writer about 1025 based upon records of the preceding century.[11] The economy of the city at this time was regulated by the chamberlain of the royal palace whose functions in this respect resembled those of the prefect at Constantinople. The urban guilds or *ministeria* were granted a monopoly of their various occupations in return for rendering specified services to the palace and the court when it was in residence. Foreign merchants were also licensed; the Anglo-Saxons had a special treaty, but the most valuable trade was in the hands of the Italian coastal cities. The men of Salerno, Gaeta, Amalfi and Venice were subject to a levy known as the fortieth *solidus,* and the leading merchants were individually obliged to render a pound of pepper, cinnamon, galenga and ginger to the chamberlain, and a comb, mirror and cosmetics to his wife annually for the right to do business in the city; in addition, the Venetians enjoyed the right to buy foodstuffs in any market in the kingdom in return for a payment of £50 made by the doge to the palace every year. Pavia had its own guild of merchants whose officials, described in the document as

great, honourable and very rich, held an imperial diploma per-
mitting the members to trade freely throughout the kingdom, and
no doubt there was a scattering of other substantial merchants
working along the main routes leading to the north and west. But
the degree to which a whole class or community, living only by
commerce, was regarded as something outlandish even in Pavia
is shown by a note added by someone to the passage in the
memorandum relating to the Venetians, which explains, with
some exaggeration, 'and that people does not plough or sow, or
gather the vintage'.

The plight of the inland cities of Italy which did not enjoy the
privileges of Pavia, during the years when the merchant oligarchies
of Venice and Amalfi were establishing themselves, can be illustrated by the vicissitudes of the middle-sized episcopal city of
Modena. A place of some importance in Roman times, the ancient
Mutina suffered heavily after the breakdown of the Roman order.
Captured by the Lombards in 570 and retaken by the Greeks
twenty years later, for nearly a century and a half, the city found
itself near the uneasy frontier between the Lombard kingdom and
the Byzantine territory of the Romagna. At some stage during this
dark period, the drainage system of the ancient city broke down
and the remains of its buildings were engulfed in marshes and
floodwater. In about 690, the Lombard king Cunibert is said to
have restored the partly ruined city, but fifty years later the region
was so insecure that his successors established a new fortified town
some five miles to the west to control the important crossing of
the river Secchia. The new settlement, which was known as Cit-
tanova (new city), seems to have flourished sufficiently to rival or
even surpass its ancient neighbour; the Lombard governor
(*gastaldio*) transferred his headquarters there, but the church
remained anchored to Mutina where the cathedral enshrined the
relics of St Gimignano, the patron of the diocese who had died in
the fourth century.

Sometime around the year 879, an outstanding cleric called
Leodoino became bishop of Modena. The death of Louis II in
875 had ended the best days of the Italian kingdom and ushered in
a period of ninety years in which the central power was generally
very weak. Local self-help being the order of the day, it is unlikely that Leodoino consulted any higher authority before putting in hand the building of walls and fortifications enclosing a

small area around his cathedral. An inscription explained that
the works were solely for the citizens' defence and were not
directed against peace-loving lords, but since by Roman law city
walls pertained to the state, the bishop found it prudent to legal-
ise his action by obtaining a diploma from the emperor Guido of
Spoleto soon after his coronation in 891. It is possible that this
privilege marked an early example of the take-over of civil power
within a city by its bishop, a state of affairs which became common
during the tenth century. In most cases, this meant that the jurisdiction over the city was divided from that of its territory, for it
was not until the time of the German emperors in the later tenth
century that grants of jurisdiction over a city and its district
were made to bishops, and then only in exceptional circumstances.

In the walls constructed by Leodoino there was a chapel dedicated to Christ, St Mary and St John, for which a cleric who knew
his Livy perhaps a little and his Virgil well composed the most
remarkable secular poem to come down to us from dark age Italy.
O tu qui servas armis ista moenia is addressed to the watchmen
on the walls and may have been chanted by the chapel clergy in
the evening at the time when the watch took up their posts.

> O you who guard these walls with arms
> Sleep not, I charge you, but stay wide awake.
> While Hector kept the watch in lofty Troy
> It was not taken by the crafty Greeks.
> Only when Troy was sleeping quietly
> Did false Synon ope' the traitor's door.

The poet goes on to remind the Modenese watchmen of the white
geese who saved the Roman capitol from the attacking Gauls, and
only after this does he invoke the protection of Christ and the
saints, before returning in his final stanza to 'the strong youth
brave with warlike courage' whose cries will sound from the walls
throughout the coming watch. The poem has often been described as expressing the steadfast spirit of the Italian citizenry
in one of their darkest hours, and it is significant that at least one
individual was conscious of the heritage of Rome and Troy and
the role of purely human courage at this crucial time. But there is
nothing to suggest that his ideas and feelings were widely shared.
A few years later, when Modena was threatened by the raids of

the nomadic Magyars, another poet added verses in a very different spirit, begging the patron St Gimignano to intercede for his poor slaves and save them from the spears of the Hungarians. In 899 this poet's worst fears were realised when the Magyars defeated the royal armies and swept down from the north-east. There is no contemporary record of what happened, but according to a later hagiographer, the entire population took to their heels leaving the city to be defended only by the saint; due to him, though the Hungarians occupied the deserted city for a time, they moved on without causing any serious damage.[12]

The Modenese sources underline the extreme fragility of city life around the turn of the tenth century, when the inhabitants of what had once been a major city did not even try to defend it against a horde of marauding horsemen. The period of the Magyar raids seems to mark the low ebb in the fortunes of the Italian kingdom; after the coming of the German emperors in the person of Otto I in 961, signs of recovery begin to appear, and by the end of the eleventh century not only a few favoured ports but the bulk of the inland cities of north and central Italy had recovered their population and prosperity. The wave of new cathedral and monastic churches begun at this time is evidence of the new wealth and self-confidence of the citizens; the Modenese, for example, began their great romanesque cathedral in 1099, to which the body of St Gimignano was translated in triumph seven years later.

While the end product is obvious enough, the origins of this great economic revival, which created the material basis for the rise of medieval Italian civilisation, remain extremely obscure. Clearly a growth in commerce, which would have benefited in the first instance only the sea ports and a few key inland centres, is inadequate to explain a change the most striking result of which was a steady rise in population not only in Italy but over the greater part of western Europe as well. The evidence points not to the towns but to the land as the vital sphere where the trend to a low or falling population which had prevailed since before the collapse of the Roman Empire was reversed. Yet the crucial period is not only badly documented but was one of intense localism. Detailed local studies involving intensive archaeological and topographical surveys can, in favourable circumstances, be expected to give firm if limited answers. Few such studies have been attempted in Italy up to now, but even if many more were available, the problem of generalising from their conclusions would still be considerable. For the present, any general view of the agrarian history of early medieval Italy must be partly based on conjecture and should be treated with some degree of reserve.

There can be little doubt that before the eleventh century the resources of the land in most of Italy were grossly under-exploited. The documents of the period relate mainly to the estates of the greater monasteries and the leading nobles, and they reveal huge estates which would have made their owners fantastically wealthy had they been intensively cultivated. The numerous references to marsh, forest and uncultivated land even in the most naturally fertile areas, suggest that they were not. For example, a donation made by the Marchesa Willa in 978 to the Florentine monastery known as the Badia shows that one third of an estate at Signa in the Arno valley only a few miles from the city was uncultivated; at another estate in the same region, the proportion of waste was five-eighths, while at Bibbiano in the Valdelsa, near the boundaries of Florentine territory, the uncultivated part of the estate was ten times the area where grain, vines and olives were grown. The lingering of wild conditions in the region of Mantua, naturally one of the richest parts of the Lombard plain, is shown by the charter of 1114 by which the monastery of Polirone released a village community from the customary obligation to participate in hunts for wild beasts in the forest at the lord's command.[13]

One of the first signs of the agricultural revival was the break-up of these vast underdeveloped estates into smaller, more intensively exploited units. One way in which this was done was through leases by which the tenant undertook to clear or improve the whole or a part of his holding in return for concessions on the part of the lord; a fairly typical arrangement was that the tenant was allowed three harvests from the reclaimed land free of all rent and dues except the tithe. Contracts of this kind can be traced back to the eighth century, but it seems to have been a long time before any permanent and appreciable gains were made. The most likely explanation is that the first assaults on the forests and marshes were carried out by small men: direct cultivators who might be obliged by the terms of their leases to reside on the land, and who might owe labour services to their lords. With their limited resources, the work would naturally be very slow, and where the swamps were malarial the reclaimed land must have cost many lives. Large scale land reclamation schemes requiring a high degree of organisation and control do not appear to become common until the twelfth century.

Even so, there are signs that some kind of a breakthrough was achieved in the late tenth and early eleventh century. A study of the area around Milan has shown that the price of land shot up fivefold during this period, and this evidence from a single region fits in well with the results of an analysis of some three and a half thousand land purchases taken from a wide area of north and central Italy between 962 and 1139. In 40 per cent of these contracts, something other than coined money was offered in exchange for land, and the use of money substitutes reaches peaks in the five-year periods 980–4, 1010–14, and 1045–9. These crises in the coinage supply were eventually solved by increased production and some degree of devaluation, but the fact that buyers were prepared to offer objects of gold and silver, valuable furs and cloths and even books, shows that they regarded land as a sure investment justifying the sacrifice of treasures which had probably taken a long time to collect. The advice given to churches to buy land, found in the writings of the eleventh century reformers Peter Damian and Atto of Vercelli, points to the same conclusions.[14]

The agricultural revival touched off far-reaching changes in the structure of Italian society. The general effect seems to have been an improvement in the condition of all classes, with the exception of those at the very top, a handful of great lay and ecclesiastical landlords whose position declined relative to other classes, if not necessarily in absolute terms. At the other end of the social scale, rural slavery declined steeply and serfdom, too, began to lose its *raison d'être* in the more advanced regions. As the manor ceased to function as a unit of agrarian organisation, demesne lands were leased out, and lords came to rely more and more on indirect exploitation through rents and seignurial rights and dues of various kinds. That these changes brought real advances for the lower classes is proved by the reactions they provoked. At the end of the tenth century the Emperor Otto III legislated against serfs who had taken advantage of their lords' absences on public service to deny their servile condition, and in the early eleventh century Bishop Leo of Vercelli inveighed against serfs on ecclesiastical estates who had won their freedom and become inflated with wealth, so that they now held the churches at whose expense they had grown rich in derision and disrespect.[15]

Legal emancipation placed a man in the large and varied category of free men which became the special characteristic of north and central Italy at a time when the society of north-western Europe was increasingly polarised, with a free military class on the one hand and a servile peasantry on the other. The free men of Italy can hardly be called a class, since the richest of them might be virtually magnates while the poorest could be starving. Some might be living on ancestral freeholds (alods); many would hold their land on long leases (livelli), paying fixed rents in cash, kind or a mixture of the two. Though the majority would be pinned to the land by poverty, there was no legal barrier to movement into the towns and cities; it is from this category of person – and not necessarily the poorest of them – rather than from the fugitive serfs beloved of the historians of northern Europe, that the growing urban population was recruited. That some individuals managed to make good is shown by the emergence in the region of Milan during the tenth century of a class of livellarii (leaseholders), who did not work the land with their own hands but lived from the rents of their own tenants. Even the anarchy of the tenth century played into the hands of some groups by giving the men on the spot an advantage over the absentee landlord who had more property than he could effectively look after in troubled times. For example, in about 922 the cathedral chapter of Verona granted to sixty-two men of Cerea freedom from all dues, except for an annual censum of four shillings and the obligation to entertain the chapter's representative when he called, in return for the completion of a defensive wall against the Hungarians around an existing tower.[16] The new fortified town or castello was to be garrisoned by the inhabitants who were, however, free to sell their houses within the walls at will. In the course of time, Cerea prospered so that by 1189 the adult male population had increased to over 200. With the return of more settled conditions in the eleventh century, many lords tried to reduce the privileges of such communities, but they were not always successful; many of the minor communes of the twelfth century were built upon the foundations of legal and financial concessions gained during the dark days of the tenth century.

In the eleventh century the key position in Italian society came to be held by the class immediately below that of the greatest land-owners. Of varied origins, these men were gradually caught up into the knightly class which came to embrace several ranks within itself. It is perhaps necessary to emphasise that in Italy feudal tenure never became universal as it did in England; alods and leases continued to form an important part of family holdings. Outside the Norman territories of Sicily and the South, feudalism spread piecemeal according to local conditions, the result of the desire of lesser men for more land, and especially church land, on the one hand, and of the need of greater men for supporters, and especially mounted troops in a period of considerable lawlessness, on the other. The process can be illustrated from the case of Milan. Here, in 983, Archbishop Landulph enfeoffed large numbers of his supporters and kinsmen with lands of the archbishopric, as part of an agreement by which he was allowed to return to the city after he had been turned out by a *coniuratio* which had been formed against him. The new church vassals were mainly men from outside the city, where the bishop's main strength lay, but in the characteristic Italian manner, they came to play a leading role in civic affairs. A generation later they constituted the class of tenants-in-chief (*capitanei*) in conflict with their own sub-vassals (*vavassores*) to whom they had in turn granted substantial bene-fices – a striking example of the ability of the land to support a larger and larger number of *rentiers* at this time. In 1037 the Milanese *vavassores*, after a long and bitter struggle, finally obtained from the Emperor Conrad II security in the tenure of their benefices and freedom to appeal to the emperor or his repre-sentative in cases of dispute.[17] This law, known as the *constitutio de feudis*, in effect abolished the feudal dependence of the *vavas-sores* on the *capitanei* and had wider and more lasting effects on Italian society than any other piece of imperial legislation. It con-solidated the various ranks of the feudal hierarchy into a single legal class, the majority of whom, as landowners of moderate wealth, naturally dominated the market towns and *castelli* and, attracted to the cities, built a bridge at a high social level between city and countryside which had immense significance for the future.

The Reopening of the Mediterranean by the Latins

AT the beginning of the tenth century the Italian ports outside
the Byzantine sphere of influence were still sunk in the poverty
and obscurity which had closed over them at the time of the Lombard conquest. Their recovery appears to have proceeded *pari
passu* with that of the other cities of the Italian kingdom; Genoa,
for example, received a royal diploma in 958 which confirmed
the right of the inhabitants to hold property according to their
own local customs. But it is not until after the year one thousand
that there are clear signs that Genoa and Pisa had grown sufficiently to try to break into the long-distance trade hitherto monopolised by the Saracens and Greeks and their clients. During the
first half of the eleventh century sporadic raids were undertaken
against the Moslems in various parts of the western Mediterranean. In 1004 and 1011 the chronicles tersely report the 'destruction' of Pisa by the Saracens, but they certainly exaggerate, for
the Christians were able to retaliate without much delay. In 1015–
16 the Pisans and Genoese launched their first recorded joint
expedition, against a Moslem pirate's lair on the island of Sardinia; 1034 saw the Pisan fleet extending its operations with a
successful raid on Bône on the North African coast.

About the middle of the century, a new factor began to appear
in the complex world of Mediterranean politics. Norman mercenaries, who had been employed by the various cities and princes of
South Italy in their wars against each other, had been seizing land
and making settlements in the inland areas since about 1030; now
their increasing power began to put serious pressure on both the
Greeks and the maritime cities. The appearance of these inter-
lopers must have helped the Pisans and Genoese, who were also
trying to break into a world hitherto dominated by the Greeks
and Campanians; when the Normans turned their attention from
the Greeks and Italians to attack the Saracens, the possibility of
direct co-operation soon suggested itself. The first Norman expedition to Sicily in 1061 met with no great success, but in the autumn
of 1064 the Pisans sent a fleet to eastern Sicily, proposing a combined attack against the Moslems. When it was found that the
Normans were not ready to move, the Pisans decided to go on
alone, and they carried out a successful raid on the harbour of

Palermo, carrying off six enemy ships. That spring, the Pisans had laid the foundations of a great new cathedral, proof in itself that the revival of the city was already well advanced; on the return of the fleet one of the ships and its contents was sold and the proceeds devoted to the construction of a wall of the new building, which, as it stands today, still bears witness to the spirit of the Tuscan seaport in the most dynamic period of its history.

No major offensive expedition is recorded as having been undertaken by the Italian cities for the twenty-three years following the Palermo raid; ominously, the Pisans and Genoese began to skirmish among themselves along the Tuscan and Ligurian coast. But great events which would eventually change the whole pattern of Mediterranean trade in their favour were taking place in Sicily and the South. During the 1070s the Normans completed their conquest of the mainland, including all the seaports on both sides of the peninsula except for Naples, which remained independent under its own duke until 1137. In the same period, the greater part of the island of Sicily was overrun by them, leaving the Moslems penned up in the south-east corner where they held out until 1091. Beyond Sicily lay Africa, where the Moslem emir Tamim launched retaliatory raids not only on the Norman-held south, but against all Italian ships and merchants in the western Mediterranean. The common danger brought the Pisans and Genoese together again, and in 1087 they organised a joint expedition with supporting contingents from Rome and Amalfi; the attack on Tamim's capital of Mahdia, near ancient Carthage, was almost completely successful, the port and most of the city being captured before the emir asked for terms. According to Arab sources, Tamim agreed to pay between 30,000 and 100,000 gold dinars to the Christians and granted Pisan and Genoese merchants free access to his territories; the Italian sources stress the great number of Christian prisoners released and the vast plunder in silver, gold and precious materials.

Ascendancy in the western Mediterranean had now been won by the Latins, and a Sicilian Moslem, Abu-l-Arab, reluctantly turned down an offer of hospitality and a prize of 50 gold dinars from a fellow poet, the ruler of Seville, on the grounds that 'the sea belongs to the Romans, and our ships circulate there only by exposing themselves to great risks; only the mainland belongs to the Arabs'.[18] With Sardinia and Corsica under Pisan suzerainty, the last major combined expedition against Saracen pirates took place in 1113–15, when a Pisan fleet with Spanish and southern French support, attacked and devastated the Balearic Islands, where and Arab dynasty driven from Sardinia had established a corsair state.

By comparison with their slow and often painful efforts in the West, the emergence of the Pisans and Genoese in the eastern Mediterranean has the appearance of a sudden and world-shaking coup. Here, too, the role of the Normans was indispensable. It was Count Roger's conquests in Sicily in the 1070s which opened the way to the East; in the same decade his brother Robert Guiscard began to develop his threat to the Greeks in the Balkans, which placed the Byzantine emperors, already engaged in a struggle for survival with the Turks in Asia Minor, in a desperate situation from which they could not escape by their own strength alone. The first to profit from Byzantine weakness were, as usual, the Venetians. In return for the services of their fleet against Robert, in 1082 they obtained complete freedom from all Imperial customs in the Aegean and Mediterranean; the western trade of the Empire was now entirely in their hands, the Greeks retaining only the Black Sea, Cretan and Cypriot trade for their own merchants. To solve the Turkish problem the Byzantine emperors resorted to appeals for mercenaries to the West which finally touched off the complex and massive movement known as the First Crusade. This was the moment of opportunity for the Pisans and Genoese, although they were slow to recognise the fact. Far from being in the forefront of the crusade, it was not until the autumn of 1097, nearly two years after Pope Urban's appeal to the city, that the Genoese sent a fleet to the East which helped the crusaders to occupy the port of St Symeon near Antioch. The Pisans were even slower to move, only stirring themselves in 1099 when they fitted out a fleet to escort their archbishop Daimbert, who had been appointed papal legate in the East. However, once they had seen for themselves, the Italian cities seized the chances which the crusade offered with both hands. Every port on the Levant coast which fell to the crusaders was taken with the help of an Italian fleet; in addition to immense booty, the Italians were rewarded with streets, quarters or thirds of the captured ports, in which they could build their own trading stations and warehouses and do business under the jurisdiction of their own officials. When the situation settled down about 1125, the Pisans were strongly established in the Norman principality of Antioch and in the county of Tripoli, and, to a lesser degree, further south in the kingdom of Jerusalem. The Venetians, who had entered late on the scene, had colonies in the south, chiefly at Tyre and Sidon. The Genoese colonies were the most numerous and were scattered along the whole coastline of the crusader states; they also had their own quarter in Jerusalem. In addition, the Pisans, though not yet the Genoese, had been granted a foothold in Constantinople which opened a small breach in the Venetian monopoly of trade with Byzantium.

Thus, by the early twelfth century, the pattern of long-distance trade of the time of Gerard of Aurillac had been entirely transformed. The Greeks and the Saracens who had dominated the Mediterranean in the ninth and tenth centuries had been eclipsed by the Latins, who now held the most profitable routes bearing silks, spices and dyestuffs to the West from Constantinople and the Levant firmly in their hands. The Norman expansion which brought the golden opportunity to the Pisans and Genoese, heralded the decline of the south Italian cities who lost their freedom of action by being absorbed in the increasingly powerful Sicilian Norman state. Amalfi alone sought to profit from the crusades through small colonies at Acre, Laodicea and Tripoli; the general tendency was for Sicilian and south Italian merchants to restrict their activities to the local trade of the central Mediterranean. Of the cardinal points in the old system, only Venice not only preserved but improved its position, not for the last time providing an outstanding example of continuity between two contrasting ages.

The passing of the old pattern of trade coincided with the gradual ending of the economic division of Italy which had begun with the Lombards. The trading centres of the new age were no longer bright points standing out against a background of poverty and depopulation, but were closely linked with their Italian and European hinterlands which were also riding a rising tide of growth and prosperity. In Italy the economic revival had achieved a pattern of cities not unlike that of late-Roman times. True, some of the Roman centres had disappeared or had shrunk into villages; this was the fate of some of the smaller cities of central Italy.

Generally, however, what happened was not a loss of population but a redistribution. Udine, for example, came to replace Aquileia as a regional centre in the North-east; in Tuscany Massa Marittima rose in the place of Populonia, Pisa took on the functions of Luni and further south Corneto grew close to the ruins of Tarquinia. Ferrara, drawing its sustenance from four great *massae* of reclaimed land in the lower Po valley, was a new creation of the medieval revival, but its growth was probably instrumental in preventing Adria and Ostiglia in the same region from regaining the importance they had had in antiquity. The geographical factors of mountain and plain, pastoral and arable, forest and waste, which had led to the division of ancient Italy into compartments of territory economically and administratively subservient to an urban centre, had not been changed by the Dark Ages, and with the rise of population they reimposed their former pattern with only minor variations. With the exception of the few seaports, long-distance commerce played a relatively minor part in the urban revival at this stage, and industry even less. The chief economic role of the cities was as markets for local produce as it had been in antiquity; the weekly *forum* was an integral part of the urban economy in a way that the occasional *mercatura* or *fiera* was not.

In these circumstances the economic contrast between the ports and the inland areas was fading. The monk Donizone of Canossa, who in 1114 described Pisa as a sea monster, filthy with pagans, Turks, Libyans and Parthians, and therefore quite unsuitable as a burial place for the Countess Beatrice of Tuscany, was expressing a conservative view. Twenty years before the biographer of Bishop Anselm of Lucca had ascribed the corruption of the clergy and the citizens to the inordinate wealth and luxury flowing into Lucca from distant places; foreigners bringing confusion of languages, and the swelling population had destroyed the old social order and harmony.[19] In Milan in the second half of the eleventh century, there emerged the Pataria, whose name may mean ragpickers; a party dedicated to the radical reform of the church, they gathered up the discontented elements of a society in ferment. The leaders were of mixed origins. The brothers Landolfo and Erlembaldo Cotta were laymen of the highest rank of the feudal hierarchy, the *capitanei*; one of the patrons of the movement was a rich moneyer, while the deacon, Arialdo, was probably a member of a lesser landowning family who, according to his biographer, had travelled in various lands and become a master of the liberal arts. Support came from no one class, nor was it restricted to the city; Arialdo began to preach the cause not in Milan but in the small town of Varese and the district round about, showing that even in rural areas there were people able and willing to understand his message.

The foundations of a new governing class had been laid by the fusion of landowners with a sprinkling of merchants and professional men. Compared with what was to come, the level of culture was modest, but it was quite widely as well as thinly spread. Italian society was already distinguished from that of northern Europe by the existence of significant numbers of literate laymen who, moreover, were not only to be found in the cities. Such higher education as there was for laymen was concentrated largely on the law. Indeed, the imperial chaplain Wipo went so far as to claim that all Italians sweated out their youth in legal studies.[20] Certainly he exaggerated, for he was urging the need for education among the German nobility on his master Henry III; yet the point would not have been worth making had it not reflected the impression which the Italians made on visiting Germans.

The lawyers of this period appear in the documents described as notaries, judges or *jurisperiti*. The significance of these titles is not easy to assess. The notaries were the successors of the Roman *tabelliones*, whose function of drawing up legal documents and records demanded a modicum of education; the church and the writing office of the royal palace of Pavia were important factors in the survival of this profession. Some of the judges, on the other hand, were probably quite untrained, simply royal or imperial nominees or members of the feudal courts of the bishops or lay nobility. But some at least were something more, men with some knowledge of written law, Roman or Lombard, the repositories of some kind of legal tradition. The judges of eleventh century Pavia are described as forming an *ordo* whose function was to preserve the rights and laws of the city. After the destruction of the royal palace in 1024 the lawyers of Pavia maintained their position as the leading interpreters of Lombard law; another former imperial capital, Ravenna, also had some kind of a law school with more than a local reputation. However rudimentary their learning may have been, the trained lawyers of this age had an importance out of all proportion to their numbers, for as a class they were the most highly educated laymen that there were. Moreover, unlike the merchants, who in this period would have been itinerant, they were normally to be found in the main centres of administration where their practical experience could be drawn on by the city communities in their search to provide more efficient and acceptable forms of government.

It was to the rapidly expanding society of north and central Italy, rough and raw as it was, that the future belonged. Yet a mature and sophisticated form of the *vita civile* did exist at this period, though to find it, it is necessary to look to some of the centres of the old-established network of commerce, to which the general revival of economic activity was bringing an Indian summer of prosperity. In Rome, for example, the powerful Frangipane and Pierleoni families, which became the local pillars of the reforming papacy in the later eleventh century, both had commercial origins and connections. Their palaces were in the commercial quarter of Trastevere and the Pierleoni were supposed to be converted Jews; in 1051 the head of the family, Leo, was described as *vir magnificus et laudabilis negotiator.*[21] During the eleventh century the influence of both clans was furthered by their ability to supply large sums of ready cash to the popes and their allies, but with the passage of time their outlook seems to have become more and more that of territorial magnates whose rivalry did much to prolong and embitter the papal schism of 1130.

For a true family of merchant princes in this period with interests stretching from Italy to the Levant and Constantinople, and with activities ranging from trade to international politics and the patronage of literature and art, we must turn to the little southern port of Amalfi, which in the second half of the eleventh century was enjoying the height of its precarious prosperity as an entrepôt of trade from Italy to the eastern Mediterranean. The origins of the Mauro or Pantaleone family seem to go back to the tenth century and the commercial rise of Amalfi itself. The first Pantaleone to concern us here is documented only in the last few years of his life, when he held the rank of *patricius* and was deeply involved in politics at the highest level. In 1062 he entertained Prince Gisulf of Salerno and his entourage at his own expense in his house in Constantinople, and at about the same time he acted as intermediary between the Emperor Constantine Dukas, the court of the western Emperor Henry IV and his anti-pope Honorius II, trying to build an alliance against the reformist pope Alexander II and the Normans of south Italy. Although obviously no friend of the Hildebrandine reformers in Rome, Pantaleone was clearly a pious man, who for the redemption of his soul gave a pair of bronze doors made in Constantinople to the cathedral of his native city, which were admired by Abbot Desiderio of Montecassino on a visit to Amalfi in 1065.

The patrician Pantaleone was dead by 1066, and it was his son Mauro who assuaged Desiderio's envy by presenting a similar pair of doors to Montecassino. Of him the chronicler Aimé of Montecassino said that his wealth and alms-giving were world-famous, and that he founded a hospital at Antioch and another for pilgrims at Jerusalem. He and his six sons also gave a valuable reliquary to the monastery of Farfa. Unlike his father, Mauro was a friend of Gregory VII and the papal reform party, and in later life he fell foul of Gisulf of Salerno who is alleged to have imprisoned his son, also called Mauro, and demanded an enormous ransom of 30,000 bezants. More fortunate and interesting is another of Mauro's sons, Pantaleone, distinguishable from his grandfather by his holding of the Byzantine dignity of *hypatos* (consul) twice. He kept up the family connection with the bronze foundries of Constantinople by giving bronze doors to the Roman church of S. Paulo fuori le Mura in 1070 and to the pilgrimage chapel of S. Michele at Monte Gargano in 1076. He also continued his father's patronage of the Latin monk John, who translated Greek works of hagiography for him at Constantinople. It was he who joined the Pisan expedition to Mahdia against the Saracens in 1087, in which year a kinsman called Pantaleone Viarecta presented yet another set of bronze doors, this time to the church of S. Salvatore at Atrani, a mile or so up the coast from Amalfi.[22]

The activities of this family over three generations would be noteworthy at any period; their passion for bronze doors was hardly equalled even during the Renaissance. With their palaces in Amalfi, Salerno and Constantinople, their contacts in Antioch and Jerusalem and their friendships with popes and emperors, the bare records of this family conjure up a style of life, a *vita civile*, far above the general level in the West at this time. Yet by 1100 isolated trading centres like Amalfi had had their day; in the long run there was no place for families like the Pantaleone in a south Italy dominated by the Normans. It was a long time before their like was seen again.

2. The Emergence of the Communes

The Old Regime

WHILE it was the economic revival that provided the driving force, the direction taken by Italian society was strongly influenced by the political conditions of the time. Throughout the peninsula during the eleventh century, the time-honoured imperial system of government – Byzantine in the south, German in the north – passed through a time of strain and weakness, ending in virtual collapse which handed the initiative to local forces. In the south the breakdown of the central government was relatively short-lived and a powerful Norman kingdom built upon Byzantine and Arab foundations emerged; in the north, on the other hand, the attempts to revive imperial power all ended in failure and local particularism triumphed all but completely. It was in this region, stretching from Rome to the Alps, that the characteristic Italian society of the Middle Ages was free to evolve most fully; here the communes became in effect city-states, so that the area may be conveniently described as communal Italy.

The weakness of the imperial regime in northern Italy had no single cause but was the result of a long and complex series of events. As we have seen, back in the eighth century the Lombard kingdom with its capital at Pavia had been, by contemporary western standards, a powerful and well-governed state. Having finally broken Byzantine power in the Romagna in 752, the Lombard kings were free to extend their power southwards and revive their long-standing threat to Rome itself. It is a measure of how formidable they seemed that the papacy was driven at once to seek the help of the Franks. Raids by King Pepin in 754 and 756 caused only temporary checks to the Lombard expansion; however, in 774 his son Charlemagne conquered the kingdom and added it to his numerous territories.

In the heartland of the Lombard kingdom the Frankish conquest brought no fundamental change. The administration continued under its new masters much as before, and such innovations as there were blended with the traditional system which, in any case, was very similar to that of the more romanised parts of the Frankish state. The palace at Pavia remained the centre of government, and only seven years after the deposition of the last Lombard king, it became once more a royal residence when Charlemagne set up an Italian sub-kingdom for his young son Pepin. But in the ex-Byzantine territories of central Italy and in the Romagna, where the recent Lombard conquest was not recognised by the popes, problems arose which had an immense significance for the future. The papacy had called on the Franks in order to preserve its independence in the new situation created by the collapse of Byzantine power; in the mid-eighth century there emerged in papal circles the idea that this aim could best be secured by the transfer of large areas of former imperial territory to the temporal power of the Holy See. The ideology of this ambitious scheme was expressed in the famous Donation of Constantine, which gave a pseudo-historical account of how the Emperor Constantine had resigned the sovereignty of much of the West to Pope Silvester at the beginning of the fourth century. The practical result of this dream was the advancement of the claim to much of central Italy and the former Exarchate of Ravenna, which was rashly granted by Pepin and confirmed by Charlemagne at the time of his first Italian expedition in 774. With the increasing Frankish involvement in Italy the impracticability of this settlement became obvious. Even before 800 Charlemagne is known to have exercised political rights in the Patrimony of St Peter which, after his Roman coronation, he was able to claim were justified by virtue of his imperial title. But the position remained confused, and important areas of Italy came, in effect, to recognise two masters.

The legal basis of the medieval Italian state was, therefore, unsound from the start. The *Regnum Italiae* was a Carolingian structure raised on Lombard foundations which were sound enough in themselves, but its extent was restricted by the recognition of the papal claims. To be king of Italy was not enough, for to justify the exercise of power in the Romagna, the centre and the south, it was necessary to be emperor also. So the two crowns became inseparably linked, with the result that the kingdom became overshadowed by the empire and was eventually reduced to a shadow, rarely remembered except in legal circles and on those occasions when imperial claimants were crowned as kings of Italy or Lombardy in Pavia, Monza or Milan. Yet even as emperors, the rights of the Italian rulers were not uncontested, for although the plan contained in the donations made little permanent headway until the end of the twelfth century, the latent papal claims, which were never forgotten for long, created a flaw in the very centre of the country, and the desire of the popes for freedom from intervention except on their own terms, aggravated the difficulties of the medieval Italian state.

There was no chance that the Italians would be left to work out their problems on their own. The fame of pagan and Christian Rome and the lure of an easy conquest would have brought foreigners to Italy even if the imperial title with its Carolingian associations had not invited powerful rulers from beyond the Alps to try to follow the example of the great Charles. In the late ninth century, Italy, like every other part of the Carolingian Empire, saw a decline in the power of the crown, which fell a prey to aristocratic factions. But while in France and Germany it was a native family which finally prevailed, in Italy control finally passed to an outsider; when the Saxon king, Otto I, became emperor in 962, he forged a link between the German and Italian crowns which was to last well into modern times. The Ottonian emperors and the Salians who succeeded them made tremendous efforts to make their rule in Italy a reality, and at times they achieved a considerable measure of success. Some chose to stress the religious nature of their office, and Henry II (1002–24) and Henry III (1039–56) came close to living out the contemporary ideal of a Christian emperor; for all that, they were not significantly more successful in their secular policies than the warrior-emperor Conrad II (1024–39), whose pragmatic measures left a permanent mark on Italy. Among the least successful was the idealist Otto III (983–1002), who tried to make the empire truly Roman again by taking up residence in the city; far from enlisting Italian pride in his support the move ended by provoking a rising against the emperor and his court. None of these emperors was lacking in ability and between them they tried a wide variety of approaches, but, in the long run, the task of ruling Italy proved to be beyond their limited resources. National differences which had mattered little in the time of Otto I, became more marked with the growth of Italian society and ended by making the emperors seem strangers in the land they were seeking to govern. The imperial system failed to adapt to the changing needs of Italy and after the premature death of Henry III in 1046 it was close to collapse.

The crucial problem for the German emperors, as for nearly all kings in the early medieval period, was how to get their orders carried out not only in their immediate entourage but in the distant parts of their huge territories, in the countless scattered communities whose interests were intensely local. A sophisticated state like the Roman or Byzantine empires could maintain a system of provincial governors, but during the invasions the Italian provincial structure had been entirely swept away, and even the metropolitan bishoprics, which were its ecclesiastical equivalent, had been much reduced in number. Charlemagne had used a makeshift system of *marchiones*, counts and *vassi dominici*, bringing many Franks with personal ties of loyalty to him into the peninsula, and his successors were committed to a constant struggle to try to retain the fidelity of families which were sinking deeper and deeper roots into the country and whose sense of obligation to the crown rapidly diminished. When the Saxon emperors tried to restore imperial control, they were faced with a powerful aristocracy, many of them descended from Charlemagne's men, who during the two generations after 875 had grown used to supporting royal claimants from the houses of Friuli or Spoleto, more or less at will. The new emperors strove to make alliances with the aristocracy as best they could, but not surprisingly they looked increasingly for a counterweight to the great families towards a group of powerful ecclesiastics, especially the metropolitan bishops of Milan and Ravenna and the patriarchs of Aquileia, whose appointment they controlled by virtue of their office. Indeed in many ways the greatest achievement of the German emperors in Italy was the introduction of distinguished and learned bishops, often of northern origin, into some of the leading Italian sees, including, in the times of Otto III and Henry III, the see of Rome itself. Yet the system, if it can be called one, always rested on a precarious balance of forces, and the excessive reliance on the church for secular government exposed the whole foundation of imperial rule in Italy to attack once the reforming papacy challenged the emperors' right to appoint archbishops and bishops. Nothing indicates the weakness of the imperial regime more clearly than its shaky structure at the provincial level; without the help of reliable intermediaries, the emperors struggled in vain to grasp the growing points of Italian society in the cities and their dependant territories.

Based as they were on the facts of economic geography, which ensured the survival of the cities, the Roman *civitates* have a continuous history through the Dark Ages in a way which the provinces have not. Roman society was built on the administrative and economic unity to each city with its surrounding territory which together constituted the *civitas*; in its heyday the empire resembled a federation of *civitates* under the hegemony of Rome. The government of the *civitates* was in the hands of an oligarchy of local landowners who formed the council or curia, sometimes flatteringly described by the higher Roman authorities as the local senate. This civilian and amateur regime, which left a good deal to local initiative, was gradually crushed out of existence by the harsh conditions prevailing during the last two centuries of the empire and the long years when Italy was divided between the barbarians and Byzantium. The paramount needs of defence and taxation, which the local councils proved unable to meet, led to a piecemeal transfer of all real power to officials nominated by the central government and the functions of the *curiae* dwindled away. By the eighth century the *curia* of Ravenna seems to have been reduced to doing no more than carrying out the legal formality of registering private contracts; usually only five or six members attended the council and some of the *curiales* were illiterate.

By the end of the eighth century the long process of transition in civic government was over. The Carolingians standardised a regime in which civil and military powers were concentrated in the hands of the count. There was generally a count for each *civitas*, though sometimes when the county formed part of a march the *marchio*'s lieutenant in an individual city took the title of *vicecomes* (viscount). In his judicial functions the count was supported by a number of *scabini*; later similar work was done by the city judges (*iudices civitatis*). The local bishop, too, had a prominent part to play in the Carolingian system. During the difficult centuries the bishops had come to be the moral leaders of the local community; they represented the saints who were the focus of civic patriotism. At a more mundane level, the bishops' control of the wealth, and especially the landed wealth of the church, which was usually considerable and was in some places enormous, brought them secular power and responsibilities which they were not slow to accept. They had acquired jurisdiction not only over their clergy and lands, but in many matters over the laity as well – powers that arose first by custom but which were later ratified and extended by pious emperors as a means of relieving pressure on the overburdened secular courts. Finally, the decline of secular education put such learning as the clergy and the bishop might possess at a premium. In Charlemagne's Christian *imperium*, where the aims of church and emperor were seen as one, it was natural that the bishops should be involved in secular government. Bishop and count were supposed to work together with the line of demarcation between their respective spheres none too clearly drawn; in practice, no doubt, they were also a check upon one another.

The delicate balance between the functions of the count and bishop could not survive the decline of the Carolingian state nor were the Saxon emperors able to restore it. As imperial power weakened, the offices of *marchio*, count and viscount became the prey of family interests which sought to secure the lucrative rights and valuable lands attached to them. In time the official and public nature of these posts was largely lost sight of, and they came to be treated as if they were no more than a special class of private property. Moreover, as the Italian feudal structure was never strong enough for the upper ranks to be able to enforce primogeniture, the natural desire of landed families to provide for more than one of their members in each generation was never checked. When the estates were divided between heirs, the title and the public rights were sometimes divided also, so that by the mid-eleventh century many comital families had split up into several branches. Although in some places they retained the vestiges of their office in the form of tolls or dues from city trades or markets, the main strength of the lay aristocracy was in the countryside. The comital families generally adopted the name of the most important castle of their estates, and landed families of ancient wealth generally alleged comital descent after a time, whether this was grounded in fact or not. Such families normally claimed immunity from the interference of royal officials on their estates, and from the tenth century such immunities were interpreted as conferring a positive right of jurisdiction over the inhabitants; the royal or imperial grant of a castle was also regarded as conferring jurisdiction. All these developments tended to break up the unity of the city and its territory which was the essential foundation of the *civitas*.

During the slow disintegration of the Carolingian system, the bishops showed a remarkable ability to adapt to the needs of the time. In a period of confusion and insecurity it was the bishops with their stronger sense of office, their deep roots in the history of the city and their access to the virtues of its saints and martyrs, who were often able to rally the frightened and impoverished citizens. Moreover, to kings and emperors seeking a counter-weight to the lay aristocracy, the celibate bishops were obvious allies, and so the policy of investing them with more and more secular authority, begun by the Carolingians, was continued and intensified by the German emperors. So, by and large, it was the bishops who prevailed, though to a degree which varied greatly from place to place. At one extreme were the counties where the bishop supplanted the count entirely and exercised all the functions of both offices in the city and its entire region. This arrangement, which was quite common in Germany, remained exceptional in Italy; of the seventeen dioceses where it is known to have been in force, the majority were in places of par-ticular strategic importance to the empire. More common was a situation where defence and the city walls, and justice and public works within the city and for a few miles around were in the hands of the bishop, whose lands outside would also be immune from the intervention of the count or any other royal official, while the rest of the region was controlled by the lay aristocracy. In the nature of things, however, it was difficult for the bishop to rule alone. Ancient custom gave the citizens the right to a say in the ad-ministration of church property, and the bishop's lay officials, such as the *vicedominus* and the *advocatus*, might on occasion be elected in the traditional general assembly of the inhabitants which generally met in front of the cathedral. The bishops also needed military support, not only citizens to man the walls but also knights to form the mounted elite essential to the armies of the time. During the wars of the tenth century bishops had been forced to buy military service by enfeoffing suitable men with church land, thus creating a body of episcopal knights whose assembly (*curia militum*) could be an important sounding board for local opinion on matters of all kinds.

There was thus no single system of government in the *civitates* of eleventh century Italy but a medley of different arrangements, many of them verging on anarchy, which varied widely from time to time and place to place. Sometimes a bishop, who was able to win strong local support, might achieve a position something like that of president in a city-republic, like Archbishop Aribert when the Milanese united behind him against the Emperor Conrad II in 1037. As Aribert's sudden fall in 1045 showed, such power was extremely precarious; in the long run imperially appointed bishops tended to identify themselves too closely with the upper feudal aristocracy, who formed their immediate entourage and consequently failed to conciliate the new classes of knights and citizens who found themselves outside the privileged circles of imperial and episcopal tenants-in-chief. By contrast, there were other regions where great families, like the marquesses of Tuscany, Montferrat or Saluzzo, ruled over great territories which were virtually sub-kingdoms. In the greater part of the country the situation was somewhere in between the two extremes, with power in the *civitas* divided between the bishop and his circle and a varying number of noble families who might be proud of their comital descent, genuine or fictitious, but who had generally lost sight of their functions as public officials. This was the heyday of the feudal nobility and a time when the jurisdiction of the cities over their territories was severely curtailed; indeed, many were probably moving towards an impasse from which they could escape only by recovering a fuller control over the surrounding region. Among other things, the commune provided the means for them to achieve this.

Some idea of the tottering state of imperial Italy in the eleventh century can be gained from a look at the city of Pavia. The decline of government in the historic capital of the Italian kingdom can be seen through the eyes of the writer of the memorandum known as the *Honorancie Civitatis Papie*, which in addition to details concerning the fiscal rights and guild organisation attached to the royal palace, gives a bitter account of the run-down of what had once been a great and powerful institution which the author regarded as an act of criminal folly.[1] In Lombard and Carolingian times Pavia had been a real capital city, a pale imitation of Constantinople, and the palace had been the principal royal residence and a centre of administration for the whole kingdom. Controlled by a specially privileged palatine count and a master chamberlain who acted as treasurer, the palace contained the notaries who staffed the royal writing office and the judges who heard the most important pleas; the city also contained the leading school of Lombard law. The mint attached to the palace was the most important in the kingdom. The decline began with the Saxon emperors who never really took to Pavia, Otto I preferring Ravenna and Otto III, Rome. According to the *Honorancie* the rights of the palace were kept intact and the office of chamberlain remained in the hands of the same family until the minority of Otto III (983–95), when a Greek councillor of the Empress-Regent Theophanu began the policy of selling off the various privileges attached to the institution. The process continued under Otto III and Henry II; writing shortly after the death of the latter, the author of the *Honorancie* seems to be making a plea to his successor to restore the palace to its formed state.

The *Honorancie* gives a very one-sided view of the case, for it is clear from other evidence that by the time of Henry II the existence of the palace had become irksome to many of the Pavians and its restoration was the last thing they desired. In 1004, after Henry II had received the Lombard crown in S. Michele, a riot broke out between his troops and the citizens; in 1024, when the news of his death became known, a rising took place and the palace was destroyed. Presumably, now that the fiscal rights which had brought money into Pavia had been alienated, the palace had become a dead weight on the economy of the city and an unwelcome check upon the freedom of the citizens. Within two years Henry's successor, Conrad II, had descended on Pavia. The terms of his settlement with the citizens have not been preserved, but it is clear that Conrad, who was not a weak emperor, had to compromise on the main issue; the palace was not restored and the royal residence was transferred to the monastery of San Pietro Ciel' d'Oro just outside the walls of the city. The place of coronation was moved to Milan, and the meadows of Roncaglia, just east of Piacenza, became the imperial rallying-point in central Lombardy. Pavia ceased to be in any sense the capital of the Italian kingdom, and in its most important functions it was not replaced. A centuries-old tradition of government came to an end.

It is difficult to know where the real power lay within the city after the settlement of 1026. The palatine counts seem to have withdrawn to the contado and their principal castle of Lomello; the chamberlains were no more. A new count appears in the city but his position as imperial representative cannot have been strong. The movement which destroyed the palace and first resisted and then negotiated with Conrad must have thrown up some leaders, but there is no sign that they were able to institutionalise their position. An episcopal document of 1069 shows the bishop acting with the support of the count, the *vicedominus*, the bishop's standard-bearer 'and a great part of our knights and of the civil population (*civilis populi*)'. The impression which this gives of divided authority is fully borne out by an extraordinary document of 1084 drawn up in the bishop's court by a notary who declares that he is acting on the orders of the *capitanei*, vavassors and citizens. Following a dispute between the convent of St Mary and the monastery of St Peter, the document makes it known that the monastery has been taken under the protection of the *populus* of the greater and lesser citizens; the witnesses include the bishop and his standard-bearer, and the instrument is signed by, among others, the viscount, the jurist Lanfranco, five judges, a doctor and several notaries. It is an open question whether the Pavian *populus* at this date had any corporate organisation; certainly there is no sign that it had its own officials or formal leadership. We have to wait until 1105 to find two men acting in the name of the community, who are said to have *ingeniose* shut out a recalcitrant abbess from her quarters in a convent. Although they are not so named, it seems that these two men were consuls, and with this unusual act the commune of Pavia becomes an undoubted fact.[2]

Insofar as it was a capital city Pavia was obviously unique and its decline had a significance for the whole of the Italian kingdom. Other aspects of the story, however, were paralleled elsewhere. In the Lombard period there were royal palaces in many of the major cities of northern Italy; by the eleventh century those which survived seem mostly to have been transferred to sites outside the walls. There are a good number of references to risings against bishops or imperial agents in Italian cities in the tenth and eleventh centuries. Information about most of these upheavals is very scarce; what is significant about them is that although they may have temporarily shaken the power of the old regime, none of them was able to put anything new and lasting in its place. So far from rushing into innovation the leaders of Italian society seem to have clung to the past until the old order, divided against itself, virtually abdicated and made reconstruction on a new basis almost unavoidable.

The Nature of the Commune

The next day . . . when the bishop and Archdeacon Gautier were engaged in collecting money after the noon offices, suddenly there arose throughout the city the tumult of men shouting 'Commune!' Then through the nave of the cathedral of Notre-Dame . . . a great crowd of burghers attacked the episcopal palace, armed with rapiers, double-edged swords, bows and axes, and carrying clubs and lances. As soon as this sudden attack was discovered, the nobles rallied from all sides to the bishop, having sworn to give him aid against such an assault if it should occur.[3]

This account portrays a revolutionary commune in its classic form as a rising of city burghers against their bishop and the nobility. Unfortunately for our purposes, it does not come from Italy but relates to the northern French town of Laon in the year 1112, and nothing quite like it has yet come to light giving a detailed eyewitness account of the birth of an Italian commune. In part this may be no more than accidental, for there is a good deal of less immediate evidence of violence accompanying the rise of the communes in Italy. Yet the lack of a clear description does, in general, reflect an important characteristic of the Italian scene, the absence of a clear-cut division between the old order and the new, which made the rise of the communes there a curiously muffled affair. In Italy it was rare for social and political divisions to coincide in such a way as to create a simple and dramatic confrontation like that at Laon; on the whole, the old political structure was too far decayed to offer any real resistance, and as for a social revolution, there was none, the commune representing only the resettlement of power within the existing ruling classes on a new basis. Though it was rationalised after the event, there is no evidence that the Italian commune was a political ideal to be striven for; rather it was the one among a series of expedients which happened to work and endure. Because it was a really new form of political association, it could hardly be reconciled with learned political ideas, yet it prevailed because it offered a workable solution to the impasse created by the breakdown of the imperial regime. And it survived as the political foundation of the Italian city-states long after the rise of despotisms and the passing away of the medieval society which created it.

The immediate background to the emergence of the communes is a series of disasters which shook the already tottering old regime from top to bottom. In 1056 the Emperor Henry III, the last to rule in the old style, died and for nearly twenty years Italy was left to its own devices without any strong imperial intervention from Germany. During this time the ecclesiastical reform movement which now aimed to disengage not only the monasteries but also the church in general from secular control, spread from Rome and Tuscany to most of the great cities of the kingdom, where it generally divided both the clergy and laity into two bitterly hostile camps. Then, in 1076, just as Henry IV began to pick up the reins of government in Italy, he came into headlong conflict with Pope Gregory VII over the crucial appointment of the archbishop of Milan. The general struggle which ensued, rather misleadingly known as the Investiture Contest, divided the old regime against itself, the imperialist nobility against the allies of the reformers, imperialist bishops and clergy against the supporters of the papacy. After nearly twenty years of civil war, there came Urban II's call to the crusade, which was answered not only by the maritime cities but also by large numbers of the ruling classes and many bishops. It is impossible to say which of these upheavals was the most important, only that out of the general turmoil the communes were born.

To try to catch a glimpse of an emergent Italian commune is a frustrating experience; so often the evidence seems to come just too soon or just too late. It has long been recognised that some of the best documented examples are provided by the maritime cities of Pisa and Genoa, where the young commune stands out against the background of overseas expeditions. It is not known how the early expeditions, up to and including the Pisan raid on Palermo on 1064, were organised. An imperial diploma of 1081 relating to Pisa is informative mainly for what it does not say. Henry IV, who was bidding for Pisan support in his struggle with the papacy,

agreed to limit his traditional rights of taxation and jurisdiction
in various ways, even going so far as to promise that he would
appoint no new marquess for Tuscany without the approval of
twelve elected representatives of the city.[4] The hereditary
Marchioness of Tuscany, Matilda, was one of the reforming party's
staunchest supporters, so it was natural that her rights should be
passed over; it is more significant that neither the viscount nor
any other local imperial representative is named in the document.
The local community seems to lack institutionalised leaders; the
privilege is addressed simply to the citizens of Pisa, and the only
officials referred to are a panel of twelve who are to be elected to
define the boundaries of the common pastures (communia pascua)
belonging to the citizens. Yet these, and the reference to the possibility of electing representatives in a collegium summoned by the
sounding of bells, suggest that the commune may have already
been in existence, although officers had not yet been created to
act in its name. Within four years, a Sardinian document refers to
the bishop, the viscount and all the consuls of Pisa. A verse account
of the Mahdia expedition of 1087 shows the combined force under
the leadership of the papal legate Benedict of Modena, but, at a
crucial moment, he takes advice from four Pisan leaders, two of
whom are described as principal consuls and two simply as noble
citizens.[5] The poem was probably written a generation after the
events described, but was based on accurate information. At
another point Ugo the Viscount is described as 'the head of the
city'; his heroic death is the dramatic centre of the poem, and
provides an opportunity for the poet to exhort his fellow citizens
to remain faithful to his descendants. That this plea had some
contemporary significance at the time the poem was written is
suggested by the more ambitious verse-history of the Balearic
expedition of 1113–15 which names among the leaders another
Ugo Visconte who was not one of the consuls.[6] Just as Archbishop
Daimbert had led the Pisan crusade in 1099, so his successor Pietro
is portrayed as the directing force of the Balearic expedition, supported by representatives of the clergy, among whom the author
of the poem was almost certainly numbered. A prominent part is
also played by the twelve consuls elected by the Pisans on their
departure; no fewer than three of these were members of the Visconti clan, and another of the consuls was also the bishop's vicedominus. The poet delights in reporting the debates and speeches

of the members of the leading circle of the expedition, whom he
calls the 'fathers'; but the rank and file, the *popolo*, is also given
some part in the direction of the enterprise. They are called to
hear the discussion and acclaimed the decisions made; on the
departure from Spain they joined the leaders in a mutual
oath.

Although the local background to the emergence of the
Genoese commune was rather different, its parallel development
fills in some of the gaps left by the Pisan evidence. At Genoa the
forces of the old regime were weaker than in the Tuscan port,
and the local community was strong enough as early as 1056 to
compel the Marchese Alberto to confirm, and in the process of
confirming, to define, certain aspects of the customary law of the
city. His oath was received on behalf of the inhabitants and their
descendants by three individuals who are described as *boni
homines* (good men), a common title for civic officials in the pre-
consular period. The Genoese contingent on the First Crusade
included seven *boni homines*, who promised the Norman prince
Bohemond to help defend his city of Antioch as a part of the
bargain by which the Genoese had received a church and a street
there.[7] According to the chronicler Caffaro, in February 1098,
about six months before this expedition set out, the Genoese
formed a *compagna* with six consuls for three years. There is no
evidence that this was the first time such an association had been
formed, but it was probably the first with consuls, for with the
next Genoese fleet, which set out for Palestine in August 1099,
we hear not of *boni homines* but of a 'consul of the army', suggesting that this more dignified and historic title was coming into
general use. Caffaro himself joined this force and gives an eyewitness account of its exploits in the East which, in a plain,
straightforward style which contrasts strongly with the rhetoric
of the Pisan poets, nevertheless portrays an enterprise organised
and led in much the same way as those of the Pisans. For example,
before Caesarea, Daimbert, now patriarch of Jerusalem, har-
angues a *parlamentum* summoned by the Genoese consuls urging
immediate assault on the city, and the rank and file acclaim his
words with cries of '*fiat, fiat!*'. There is a glimpse of the division
between the leaders and the *popolo* in Caffaro's statement that
after the fall of Caesarea, each of the rank and file received forty-
eight *solidi* and two pounds of pepper as their part of the booty,

but that the shares of the consuls and the 'better' men were much greater than this.

The Genoese sources give an exceptionally clear picture of the *compagna*, which was the local name for the commune. It was, at first, a temporary association, formed for a fixed term of three or four years. Although at the end of this time it was always renewed, as late as 1150 it was necessary for the consuls to make specific provisions safeguarding the rights of those who had entered into contracts with the *compagna*, in case the *compagna* should cease to exist in Genoa within the twenty-nine year period for which the contracts were to run. The essence of the *compagna* was the oath taken by all members, of which the earliest extant text goes back only to 1157, by which time its original simplicity had been obscured by many specific provisions. The main features were clearly to maintain peace and give help to fellow members of the *compagna*, to attend the *parlamentum* when summoned, and to obey the orders of the council and consuls in peace and war. Membership of the *compagna* was on a personal basis, and members were expected to pass on the names of suitable candidates for entry to the consuls; they also undertook not to participate in overseas voyages or even to accept investments in such enterprises from those who had been formally invited to join the *compagna* and had refused to take the oath. From 1122 the consulate was an annual office, but the number of consuls was subject to periodic reviews which did not always coincide with the renewals of the *compagna*. On taking office, the consuls took an oath the main features of which were a promise to uphold the honour of the city and its mother church, to maintain public order and to give justice to all members of the *compagna* in accordance with the customs of the city. As elected officials the consuls were regarded as the servants of the *compagna*, responsible to the members for their actions; for example, they were expressly forbidden to make war or impose taxation without the consent of the majority of the council.[8]

For no inland city is the infant commune as well documented as at Pisa and Genoa, but the case of Bologna will serve to show that the institution there was basically similar to that of the two great seaports. The situation leading up to the formation of the commune in Bologna is very obscure, but it seems that the conflict between pope and emperor played a decisive part in the collapse of the old order. In the imperial system, Bologna was attached to the province of Ravenna, which the emperors sought to control through the archbishops of Ravenna on whom they had showered privileges from the time of Otto III on. South and west of Bologna, however, began the territory dominated by the house of Canossa, marquesses of Tuscany, who also held important estates on the plain to the north-east, thus hemming in the city on three sides. So when Henry IV was excommunicated by Pope Gregory VII and the German Wibert, Archbishop of Ravenna, became his anti-pope, while Matilda, the head of the house of Canossa, took the papal side, Bologna found itself near the front line of the conflict. At first the bishop, and probably the local count also, were imperialists, but the reforming party put up a rival candidate, who by about 1084 had prevailed and carried the city on to the papal side. This probably meant that Bologna entered Matilda's sphere of influence and, though definite evidence is lacking, it is likely that the royal palace which still stood within the walls passed under her control. It must be no coincidence that it was only after her death without an heir in 1115 that the populace rose and destroyed the palace, as the inhabitants of Pavia and other cities had done before them. The next year, when the Emperor Henry V came to claim his rights as Matilda's overlord, it was in the interests of both parties that he should reach a quick settlement with Bologna. The formal diploma which he issued, granting the citizens their ancient legal customs, protection of their property and freedom for Bolognese merchants to trade in all parts of the kingdom, makes no reference to the commune or communal officials, though the existence of some kind of organisation is implied by the provision that fines for infringement shall be divided equally between the imperial fisc and the fellow citizens (*concivibus*). However, appended to the document is another of a less formal nature which is more revealing. Here the imperial pardon is extended to the Bolognese *popolo* and to those who helped them to destroy the palace; this specific wording suggests that *popolo* here does not mean the inhabitants at large but a particular body which may be identified with the sworn association of the commune. Moreover, in the two leaders named as responsible for the rising and in the eight Bolognese recorded as present at the reception of the document, it is tempting to see the chosen officials of the commune, to whom the title of consul will soon be given. The Bolognese consuls emerge into the clear light of history with an agreement with the *popoli* of two villages of the contado in 1123, in which they speak on behalf of their successors, the bishop and 'our whole Bolognese popolo', and promise to insert the agreement into 'the oath of obedience which our *popolo* makes to us'.[9] Clearly the *popolo* here, like the *compagna* in Genoa, was the local term for the commune, and the oath was the ancestor of the *sacramentum sequimenti*, which after many elaborations has survived in the Bolognese statutes of the thirteenth century.

We are now in a position to make some generalisations about the early communes. Firstly, they did not originate from above, from pope or emperor whose role was purely negative and permissive, but from the local situation and local initiative. The studied silence of the formal documents, and the confusion of terminology bear this out; only gradually did the term commune, which was originally applied to 'common' property and 'common council', come to prevail over local synonyms like *compagna* and *popolo*. Then they were personal, sworn associations and were, therefore, in theory terminable and potentially mobile. This possibility was clearly realised in the case of the maritime communes, which can be seen splitting amoeba-like, so that the overseas expeditions are in a real sense the commune on the move, with the consuls, senate and *popolo* all present and fulfilling roles similar to those they played when they were at home. The same characteristic appears from time to time in the inland communes, when the communal armies on campaign held councils and *parliamenta* in camp or in the field, and could legislate exactly as if they were meeting in the traditional council place in the city.[10] Finally, the communes show quite a high degree of participation in the making of decisions on behalf of the community. Not, of course, that they were democratic in either the ancient or the modern sense; the consulate was usually dominated in practice by a small group of families, and the role of the masses who attended the *parlamentum, concio* or *arenga* was limited to the simple act of acclamation. Yet the consular oaths spell out the responsibility of communal officials to the council very clearly; these councils, whose membership in major cities could rise to a hundred and more at quite an early date, enshrined the principle that authority was granted by the community. This was a major revolution after centuries during which power had been seen as radiating from above through a hierarchy of officials under the old regime. Although the governing class remained largely unchanged in almost every other way, the communes marked a sharp departure from the letter and spirit of the old regime, which was permanent, highly centralised and, with its marches and countries, and its royal palaces and castles to which rights and jurisdiction were attached, remarkably territorial in its outlook. The commune drew its origins from another world of less formal associations which had at the best been little more than tolerated at the lower levels of the old system. The most important element of continuity was the ancient assembly of all the inhabitants, known from Lombard times by such names as 'the gathering in front of the church', which was quickly adopted and revivified by the dominant minority who controlled the commune. On a smaller scale there are numerous traces of meetings of neighbourhoods (*vicinia*) in cities, towns and villages, whose functions included the administration of common lands. Again, although the church had been heavily infected with the hierarchical spirit of the late Roman state, there still existed areas of lay participation, ranging from the court of the bishop's knights, from which many of the leaders of the early communes were drawn, down to the parish level where the faithful claimed a say in the administration of church property.

In addition to these ancient institutions the commune was also influenced by certain more recent movements arising out of the turmoil of the eleventh century. One of these was the rise of politico-religious parties bound together by a series of solemn oath-takings, of which the best known example is provided by the Pataria of Milan. The leaders of the Patarini are several times described as administering oaths to their followers binding them to the aims of the party, and even putting pressure on those who were suspected of being lukewarm in the cause by insisting that they should swear their loyalty in public. The Pataria was far too much a sectional movement to provide the basis of a commune, but in structure and spirit it was clearly cognate with the early communes. The strife it created probably delayed the formation of the Milanese commune, which may well have arisen out of a peace settlement among the various classes and parties. This conjecture finds some support in the complex structure of the Milanese com-

mune as shown in a document of 1130; at that date, there was a
college of twenty-three consuls, ten of whom were *capitanei*, seven
vavassors, and six 'citizens' – figures which suggest bargaining and
compromise between the various classes. It may be added that
conjurations were not restricted to the reformist or more popular
parties, for in a similar situation in Piacenza, Pope Urban II, writing in support of the reformist bishop in 1088, mentions that many
of the clergy and laity had dissented from his election and taken
an oath against him.[11]

Another aspect of eleventh century society which throws light
on the commune is the aristocratic clan associations known as
consorterie or tower-societies. These bodies were formed to counter
the increasing anarchy of the period and the threat posed to noble
families by the excessive subdivision of their estates. They defended
the persons of their members by organising common defence and
the pursuit of the vendetta, and their property by the holding of
their possessions in common, avoiding the division of estates until
it was absolutely necessary. Both aims were united in the characteristic activity of building towers for common defence both in the
country and the town, which provided refuges and strong points
in case of private or party warfare. The administration of common
rights and property by the tower-societies makes an obvious
parallel with the similar activities of the early communes, which
in other ways may have arisen in many places as a means of curbing
the disruptive forces focused by the *consorterie*. We know, for
example, that Bishop Gherardo of Pisa, during whose period of
office the consuls are first documented in the city, took sums of
money from potential trouble-makers as a surety for good behaviour, and the text of a pacification carried out by his successor
Daimbert is still extant.[12] This shows the bishop supported by four
leading laymen imposing measures to enforce public order, including limitations on the height of towers and the destruction
of catapults and ammunition, on all the inhabitants of the city
and suburbs by means of an oath. Those refusing the oath or
breaking it are denounced with the words: 'He shall be excommunicated, and you shall have communion with him neither in
church nor in ship.' Because the guarantors of this peace cannot
be identified with the consuls, a direct affiliation between the
commune and the peace association at Pisa cannot be asserted, but
clearly the relationship must have been very close. One may hazard

the guess that the birth of the commune was more often the result of an act of reconciliation and compromise, rather than burning enthusiasm; the obstacles to its formation were as likely to be local dissensions among the potential leaders as effective resistance on the part of the representatives of the old regime, who in most circumstances probably found it safer and more advantageous to throw in their lot with the new order.

It follows from the nature of the commune that it was not restricted to major cities, the seats of bishops and the centres of counties, but could appear wherever the social and political conditions were propitious, which could mean not only smaller towns and fortified *castelli*, but even open villages or groups of them. It is remarkable that some of the earliest evidence of communes relates to smaller towns, like Biandrate in the territory of Novara, which had twelve leaders elected by the community as early as 1093. Nor were these lesser communes essentially different from those of the cities, though obviously the scope of their activities was generally more restricted; the village communes, for example, were largely concerned with the regulation of the local resources of land and water and the agricultural routine. Normally, too, the role of the overlord, either lay or ecclesiastical, was far more positive and decisive than that of the representatives of the old regime in the major communes. Many lesser communes can be seen to have stemmed directly from a charter of liberties granted by a lord, and others arose to fill the vacuum created when the lord surrendered some or all of his rights to the local community.

Another important consequence of the nature of the commune was that its claim to public authority was originally by no means exclusive. While it would be going too far to describe the early communes as private associations, for they must have been involved in public order from the start, it remains true that they were primarily concerned with the protection of their members and their common interests, and they had no organic connection with the public institutions of the old regime. Although they expanded their activities into the public sector very rapidly, at first this expansion seems to have been quite unsystematic and it could leave ample room for the older organs of government to continue to function. The formation of a commune and the establishment of a consulate did not involve any theoretical assertion of independence or sovereignty, and while communes were soon usurping imperial prerogatives in practice, there was no rejection of the emperor or his representatives in principle. Thus comital rights and jurisdiction, insofar as they were still effective, were not attacked, but gradually bypassed and undermined, an important factor in avoiding a frontal clash being the fact that many holders of comital rights were members of the commune and were frequently among the consuls. In Pisa, for example, the Visconti clan played a prominent part in the life of the city in the early communal period, constituting to some extent a separate estate within the commune; it was only in 1153 that a bundle of their rights, including tolls by land and sea and dues from the guilds, were finally confiscated by the consuls.[13] As this was the case with rights which had been public in origin, the early communes were even less likely to attack the private jurisdictions of landowners; so far from being anti-feudal, the Italian communes included many feudal landowners among their leaders.

The bishops occupied a unique and vital position in the period of the early communes. Here and there, no doubt, bishop-counts of the old school tried to defend their position as rulers of their cities on behalf of the emperor, and opposed the commune; such figures disappeared except in the more backward areas with the gradual triumph of the movement for church reform. However, the sooner the bishop lost or gave up his claim to formal temporal power, the more rapidly was he able to acquire wide-ranging, though less defined, influence over temporal affairs. With their belief in collective leadership, and a rather weak sense of their corporate identity arising from their lack of a long history and tradition, the early communes had a need for symbols to represent their unity and of impartial figures to preside over their more important activities. The bishop, who by his office represented the mother church and its patron saint, personified the city in a unique way, and his dependence on the pope, which was one of the results of the success of the reform movement, tended to give him a certain independence of local factions. The bishop was thus the most obvious candidate for the combined role of president and figurehead, such as was played by the Pisan bishops on the eastern and Balearic crusades. Insofar as the communes were soon trying to reconstitute the city regions on the lines of the ancient *civitates*, the bishop had a special importance, for the outlines of these regions had been preserved through the survival of the ecclesiastical diocese. When the bishop was a metropolitan, his rights over the province could provide a useful platform for the aggrandisement of the commune; for example, the claim of the archbishop of Milan to nominate the bishops of eighteen dioceses had great significance for the expansion of the Milanese commune. The hegemony exercised by the communes of Genoa and Pisa over the islands of Sardinia and Corsica had its legal basis in the attachment of the island dioceses to the ecclesiastical province of one or other of the mainland ports.

By the middle of the 1140s communes had been established in all the major cities of north and central Italy, though minor communes continued to be formed as the population grew. The last two great cities to swing into line were both exceptional in many ways. In the eleventh century Venice was still an essentially Byzantine city, ruled by a *dux*, softened by the Venetian tongue to doge. Centuries of isolation from Constantinople had profoundly altered the basis of the doge's power; no longer appointed by the emperor, he was elected by a general assembly of the population, and the nobility were able to ensure, by assassination or deposition if necessary, that the office never remained too long in the hands of a single family. It was, no doubt, a small circle of leading families who formed the council which first appears flanking the doge in 1143, 'created for the honour, utility, salvation and peace of our *patria*', to which council the *popolo*, that is the old general assembly, had taken an oath of obedience. Although the term does not appear in Venice until 1151, this was clearly a commune, though without consuls, the doge continuing to be the chief executive official of the state. In Rome, too, the older order with strong Byzantine influences lingered on, though here the most important factor in delaying the commune was the special position of the pope, who for many centuries had claimed sovereign power within the city and its district. Rome had a long history of risings against pope and emperor, but the scattered nature of the settlements, within the vast circuit of the ancient walls, made co-ordination difficult. At last, in 1143, the Romans succeeded in forming a commune of an unusual kind, though even then the inhabitants of the Trastevere on the right bank of the river were not included. The core of the Roman commune was a rather small council of about fifty members, which was called the senate; again, there were no consuls, though their role seems to have been filled by a

panel of about twelve *senatores consiliarii*, who were elected from
the senate for a short term of office. The examples of Venice and
Rome underline the point that the essential features of the commune were first the council, and second the oath; the consulate,
although it is usually much better documented, was by no means
indispensable.

The Mental Climate

THE pre-communal period was one of intense local patriotism,
stemming from the time when the cities had been small, weak and
threatened, so that their very survival had depended on the unity
of the citizen body. With the disappearance of external enemies in
the later tenth century, civic spirit began to manifest itself in
sporadic inter-city wars, generally between neighbours, which
opened up quarrels over territory and trade routes, some of which
were to persist for centuries. From the eleventh century, it is true,
there are signs of divisions within the growing cities on class lines,
like that between the *capitanei*, vavassors and citizens at Milan,
or the *milites* (mounted soldiers) and the *pedites* (infantry) in some
other Lombard cities. But it is striking that, at this stage of their
development, the inhabitants of the major cities generally succeeded in closing their ranks in the face of external attack, as Milan
and Pavia did more than once against imperial armies. Indeed,
without a reservoir of local feeling to overcome sectional differences, it is difficult to see how the communes could have been
formed at all. At Milan the most important symbol of communal
unity, the highly decorated ox-drawn cart called the *carroccio*
which served as a rallying point for the city's armies in battle, was,
in fact, pre-communal in origin, going back to the time of Archbishop Aribert's mobilisation of the men of the city and its territory against the imperialists in 1039.

In this period civic patriotism was most commonly expressed
in terms of loyalty to the local church and its traditions. The tenth
and the first half of the eleventh centuries were a great time for the
elaboration of legends about local saints and bishops whose stories
served to focus the sense of identity of the local community. For
example, from the fourth century the pride of the Milanese church
had been bound up with the renown of its great bishop St
Ambrose, but in the tenth or eleventh century someone wrote up

the legend of the apostle St Barnabas who was alleged to have brought Christianity to the city. The motive was undoubtedly to bolster the position of the metropolitan see against encroachments from Rome by playing off St Barnabas against St Peter and St Paul, but the story increased the prestige and self-confidence of the Milanese in secular affairs too. At Modena, the patron of St Gimignano, in real life a bishop who died in 397, was not only supposed to have saved the city from Attila and his Huns during his lifetime, but was also credited with the preservation of Modena from the Magyars by a miraculous intervention after his death.[14] Another fourth century bishop, St Zeno, is represented, in the lunette of the twelfth century west doorway of his church at Verona, standing with a group of fully armed infantry on his right and cavalry on his left. The inscription, which may be translated, 'The bishop with a serene heart grants to the people a standard worthy of defence', makes it seem very likely that the sculpture commemorates nothing less than the formation of the Veronese commune, which in this way was placed under the protection of a venerable figure from the past (See Plate II).[15] But ancient traditions were not indispensable to the expression of this kind of patriotism. Writers from among the Pisan clergy in the early twelfth century described the recent crusading exploits, in which they and their people had participated, as acts of God through the Pisans, to whom divine guidance was mediated by the bishops Daimbert and Pietro with the support and encouragement of the pope. The idea of the Pisan expeditionary force as the people of God stands out most clearly in an incident in the *Carmen in victoriam Pisanorum* which describes how, during the return from Mahdia, the Pisans succeeded in finding water miraculously on some barren islands, recalling the example of Moses and the Israelites in the wilderness.[16]

Reminiscences of classical literature provided the language, forms and an alternative set of images for the praise of the renewed medieval cities. The *Carmen in victoriam Pisanorum* opens with the poet pointing out the parallel between the Pisan conquest of Mahdia and the Roman victory over Carthage. The author of the poem on the Balearic campaign also states the equivalence of Pisa to the Rome of the Punic Wars; in addition, the idea of the Pisans as the new Romans may be said to permeate the whole work, which is strongly classical in tone and is intended to create echoes of

Virgil's *Aeneid* in particular in the reader's mind. It was commonplace to praise a city by calling it a second Rome. The writer
of the legend of St Barnabas prefaced his work with a short
description of Milan which stressed its heritage as the second seat
of the Empire in the west after Rome, while Moses de Brolo, who
wrote a poem in praise of his native Bergamo between 1112 and
1133, stresses the role of the Romans under the legate Fabius, who
conquered and civilised the city which had been founded by the
barbarian Gauls.[17]

While these works clearly show a conscsiousness that the
medieval Italian cities were treading a road of civic development
which the ancients had traversed before them, it would be a capital
mistake to regard them as thereby manifesting any specifically lay
or secular spirit. The Pisan poets draw as much on Biblical language and imagery as on classical, and although Moses of Bergamo's omission of any detailed description of the local church is
certainly odd, the explanation probably lies in the nature of the
literary model he was following rather than in his own secular
outlook, for he is known to have been one of the pioneer interpreters of Greek theology to the Latin world in this period. The
works of the clerical writers of this time show that classical authors,
particularly the medieval favourites, Virgil, Ovid, Suetonius and
Lucan, were studied in the cathedral schools where they received
their education, and the techniques borrowed from the pagan
authors were applied to Christian subjects without embarrassment,
as when the southerner Alfano da Salerno praised Pope Gregory
VII as a Roman hero who was defending the republic against the
barbarians. The most remarkable expression of a passion for pagan
antiquity is to be found in a work which achieved a phenomenal
success as a guidebook to the antiquities of Rome, the famous
Mirabilia Urbis Rome.[18] This book, compiled just before the
emergence of the Roman commune in 1143, contains a great deal
of older material including many legends about the more important Roman monuments and ruins connecting them in some way
with Christianity. But the most original part of the *Mirabilia* con-
centrates on pagan temples and shows a real, if quite unscientific,
curiosity about the purely secular and pagan aspects of the Roman
past. Yet it has been shown that the author was not an anti-clerical
partisan of the renewed Roman republic of 1143, but Benedict, a
canon of St Peter's.

The mental climate in the Italian cities during the formation of the communes was favourable to classical influence and even enthusiastic about antiquity, but, on the whole, appreciation of the Roman past remained at a superficial level; the pagan and Christian heritages were not reconciled at any depth but were simply aggregated together. The commune itself owed nothing to antiquity, or even to its most important survival, Roman law. With the exception of the revival of the Roman senate, the only debt to the past was the adoption of the title of consul to describe the leading officials of the early communes. The origin of this title looks like remaining an unsolved mystery. The survival of the term in an honorific sense in the Romagna and the Greek-influenced cities of the South may have provided a precedent; the Roman example, where the officials of some artisan guilds were known as consuls in the eleventh century, is less likely to have been followed. Another possible origin which has been suggested is a derivation from the verb *consulere*, which is found in the sense of 'to speak before an assembly'. Although the rapid spread of the title argues in favour of a central point of diffusion through pope or emperor, the conjectures attributing the revival of the title to Gregory VII or Henry IV are still unsupported by any conclusive evidence. The essential point, however, is that the consulate was new, and in no real sense a survival from the past; its adoption did not prove any deep understanding of antiquity but only a desire for a more prestigious title for the *boni homines*, who had emerged spontaneously out of the need of the communes for recognised leaders.

The main avenue towards a more profound appreciation of antiquity was provided by the study of Roman law which had never entirely died out, and which was being carried on in a number of centres during the eleventh century, of which the most important were Ravenna and Pavia. The basic structure of Italian secular education, consisting of grammar, rhetoric and law, had already emerged, and the *iudices* and *iurisperiti*, who had benefited from this training, were a vital element in the leadership of the early communes. The impact of individual jurists, however, is to be seen not in the service of the communes but of the empire. Lanfranco of Pavia advised Henry III, Peter Crassus of Ravenna defended Henry IV's inalienable right to the Empire against Gregory VII's claim that the pope had the power to depose him, and Irnerius of Bologna entered the service of Henry V and was excommunicated for his part in the election of the imperialist anti-pope Gregory VIII in 1118. What placed Irnerius in a different class from his predecessors was not his contribution to politics but his academic study of Justinian's *Corpus* and especially the 'Digest', which, in establishing a more detached and scientific method, placed the medieval study of jurisprudence on a new footing. Irnerius, who had begun as a teacher of grammar, achieved this great advance in Bologna precisely during the years in which the commune was taking shape there, but if he had any influence upon it, it is not discernible in the imperial diploma of 1116 to which he was a special witness, unless it was in the suppression of any direct reference to the commune which we have already noted as a significant feature of this document. To the academic Roman lawyer the commune could only appear as a highly irregular and probably illicit institution, unknown to classical Roman law.

For an unmistakable contribution from Roman law to the emerging communes of the twelfth century, it is necessary to turn to Rome where the new republic, founded in 1143, led a precarious existence because of the failure to reach a *modus vivendi* with the papacy. In the long deadlock both parties appealed to the emperor to exert force in their favour. In the exchange between the Romans and the imperial court in Germany, a new note is struck in a letter received by the newly-elected Frederick Barbarossa in 1152.[19] The writer, who conceals his identity under the pseudonym Wetzel, but who was certainly influenced by the ideas of the reformer Arnold of Brescia, introduces the idea that the imperial crown is bestowed not by the coronation by the pope, but by the election and acclamation of the Roman people. This claim was based on the view that the *Lex Regia*, by which the Roman people was held to have transferred its sovereignty to Augustus, was not, as most of the jurists held, valid for all time, but that it could be revoked and that emperors could be created without reference to the pope or the German princes. Naturally, this theory, which would have turned the emperor into a kind of Roman doge, found little support outside Rome and was violently rejected by Frederick, who three years later marched on Rome and put down the republic. The idea of an emperor who should be elected by the Romans continued, however, to haunt Roman and Italian visionaries for two hundred years.

3. The Century of Growth, 1150–1250

The Developing Economy

AT first sight, the hundred years from 1150 to 1250 might appear
to be an arbitrary division without any clear-cut characteristics to
distinguish them from those immediately before and after. The
distinctive persona of communal Italy is not easily perceived at
this period, for the revival of law and rhetoric centred on Bologna
which constitutes its greatest intellectual achievement is highly
technical and not easily appreciated. Although Italians played
some part in the transmission of Greek and Arabic writings, which
were an important element in the twelfth century 'renaissance',
the literary and intellectual flowering centred on northern France
largely bypassed communal Italy and had its counterpart only in
the courts of Sicily and the South. Although in architecture there
were some notable achievements both in Lombardy and Tuscany,
there was nothing to match the glories of early Gothic in north-
western Europe; until the mid-thirteenth century the Italians, on
the whole, remained faithful to the romanesque style, though in
places the influence of Byzantium was by no means dead. One
might say that the art in which the citizens of the Italian communes
made the most distinctive contribution was in the art of Christian
living; St Francis and his early followers expressed the highest
aspirations of their society, not in works of art or literature but in
their lives of voluntary poverty and holiness.

The friars are one sign of a society in turmoil; the age of St
Francis was also one of increasing conflict within and between
cities, and was the heyday of heresy when northern Italy had a
Cathar church which for a time looked like a serious rival to Catholicism. The keynote of the period is, in fact, rapid growth and
change, which dictated a concentration on practical affairs and
left little time for reflection and speculation. The voluntary root-
lessness of the friars mirrors the migration from the country to the
cities and the growth of the urban masses on a scale not seen in the
West since the decline of the Roman Empire. In politics the scene
seems to belong to the three great emperors, Frederick I, Henry VI

and Frederick II, yet in the background the communes were elaborating their political machinery to which the future belonged; they were so successful that, although there was room for development, there were few innovations in city government after 1250 until the later fifteenth century. It is in the economic field, however, that the century stands out most clearly as one of unparalleled growth. In long-distance trade it saw the full development of the system characterised by crusading enterprises and the fairs of Champagne; in the cities there was the rise of new forces characterised by the *popolo* and the guilds. After the mid-thirteenth century, the nature of the economy changes subtly, and questions as to whether all is well begin to press in; up to 1250, though the details may not be clear, the story of the economy of communal Italy is a success story.

The city which more than any other epitomises the surge of the Italian economy in this period is Genoa. On the eve of the crusades, when the position of Venice in the long-distance trading pattern of the Mediterranean was already well established, the main arteries of trade passed Genoa by. Hampered by the steep mountains to the north and lacking any foothold in Byzantium or the Levant, Genoese commercial activity was restricted to the European shores and islands of the western Mediterranean. The staples of this local trade were salt from Provence and Sardinia and grain from Sicily and southern Tuscany; it was the handling of these which enabled the Genoese to build up their fleet and seafaring skills so that, when the moment came, they were able to exploit their opportunities to the full. The crusades did for Genoa what the discovery of the Americas was to do for Cadiz; quite suddenly, the Ligurian port became the hub of a renewed and transformed trading system. Beginning in 1099 a series of successful expeditionary forces in the East won trading quarters for the Genoese in Jerusalem and most of the Christian cities of the coast; at Gibelet (Jubail) the whole town passed into their sole possession. These gains, obtained within the short space of ten years, enabled the Genoese to tap the eastern goods, particularly spices and dyestuffs, which were much in demand in the West. A surviving notarial register of contracts which gives a sample of the commercial activities of the port in the years 1154–64 suggests that by this time the direct trade with the Moslems through Alexandria was at least as great, and possibly greater than that carried on through the Christian states of the Levant.[1]

Although the premier trade with the East accounts for the greatest number of overseas destinations mentioned in the registers of Giovanni Scriba (92), Sicily, which is named 84 times and North Africa, which appears 73 times, were not far behind; even this small sample of the commercial contracts made in the city in these years indicates the way in which the Genoese were spreading their commercial activities over a wide area of the Mediterranean world. The African trade was particularly important and seems to have grown considerably during the period 1150 to 1250. In 1154-64 the chief centre of Genoese activity, according to Giovanni's registers, was Bougie in eastern Algeria, followed by Ceuta in Morocco. In 1161 the commune made a treaty with the Almohad ruler of North Africa which gave the Genoese the privilege of paying a tax of only 8 per cent instead of 10 per cent exacted from other foreign merchants;[2] a year later the Moroccan port of Saleh features for the first time in the registers. By the 1180s, when the registers of two more notaries throw some light on the question, the centre of Genoese trade seems to have shifted westward, with Oran newly opened up and Ceuta predominating over Bougie and Tunis as the favourite destination for trading ventures. In part this may have been due to the Moroccan port being named because it was the normal terminus for extended voyages along the French and Spanish coasts, but there can be little doubt that Genoese interest in Morocco was strong in the early thirteenth century, culminating in the first recorded sailing to Safi on the Atlantic coast, some three hundred and fifty miles beyond the pillars of Hercules in 1253. Besides its important function in spreading risks the African trade was complementary to that with the Levant in several ways. The contracts show that investors in Genoa could put their money into the shorter voyages in the spring and into the long voyage to the East in the autumn. Again, it seems probable that with the high prices of the dyestuffs and spices imported from the East the balance of trade with that region would tend to be unfavourable; with Africa, on the other hand, where the goods imported to Genoa included bulky commodities like hides and alum, it is likely that the balance was more favourable, thus cancelling or at least mitigating the effects of the drain of bullion to the East. Significantly, among the Genoese exports to Africa appear some eastern products such as silks, dyestuffs, paper and carpets, showing that by the end of the twelfth century the Genoese were acting as middlemen in the distribution of goods from one part of the Moslem world to another. (See Map 3A.)

The growth of trade in the Mediterranean demanded a corresponding proliferation of trade routes from Genoa to the north, by which Oriental imports could be distributed and European products brought south for export. The easiest of these made use of the natural gateway provided by the Rhone valley which was reached from Genoa by way of the ports of Provence. The chief power in this area was that of the counts of Toulouse and St Gilles, and this family's ambitions found that a principality in the East made it difficult for them to refuse Genoese requests for trading privileges. Thus, in 1108, a bargain was struck by which Count Bertrand promised the Genoese exclusive trading rights in the port of St Gilles in return for the services of a fleet of forty galleys in the Levant which joined the crusaders in the capture of the Moslem port of Tripoli.[3] In the following years working on the rivalries between the Provençal nobility and the southern French ports gave the Genoese a hegemony over the seaborne trade of the whole region. As early as 1138 the men of Marseilles, Fréjus, Hyères and Fos and the lord of Antibes were compelled to pay a tribute in corn and to follow the lead of the Genoese commune in their external relations; in 1143, when Alfonso Jordan of Toulouse quarrelled with William VII of Montpellier, William enlisted the support of the Pisans and Genoese. Their price was extensive privileges in Montpellier and they were able to force Alfonso Jordan to guarantee them special protection between Lunel and St Gilles, and at Narbonne.[4] Although the Italians never completely attained their aim of excluding the southern French from all overseas trade, their superior fleets and better diplomatic connections enabled them to restrict the Provençal merchants to a secondary role, and the communes of the French Mediterranean ports were unable to maintain either their commercial or their political independence.

In the early Middle Ages the difficult terrain had discouraged the use of the direct overland routes from Genoa to the north, but with the growth of commerce in the twelfth century it began to be worthwhile for merchants to carry their goods not only across the Apennines into Lombardy, but also to carry on by way of the western Alpine passes into France, Burgundy and the Rhineland. This development caused a radical re-alignment of the trade routes of western Lombardy and Piedmont, and whereas these had formerly led east and south-east to the river ports of the Po and its tributaries or to Parma and the via Francigena to Tuscany, they were now supplemented by a new network running southwards to the Ligurian coast. Cities controlling the key passes, like Alba, Chieri, Tortona and Asti, became the staging points of a new long-distance commerce; the new-founded city of Alessandria and the ancient river ports of Pavia and Piacenza alike profited from the new conditions. Most remarkable of all was the emergence of a group of local fairs in southern Champagne as the main centres for the exchange of oriental goods for the wool and woollen cloth of northern France, Flanders and England. Apart from their favourable geographical position, the fairs of Troyes, Provins, Lagny and Bar-sur-Aube owed their success to the special privileges and protection extended to them by the counts of Champagne. Between about 1180 and 1250 the greater part of the goods carried on the most important long-distance trade route in Europe changed hands in the tents and booths set up in the fields outside one or other of the fair-towns, and here, too, the Italian bankers carried out the bulk of the exchanges between northern and Mediterranean currencies, a function which the fairs continued to perform for some seventy years after 1250, when the commodities themselves began to be forwarded direct to the major cities and ceased to pass through the fairs. (See Map 3B.)

It would be misleading to give the impression that the growth of Genoese commerce was ever smooth. To an even greater extent than most Italian cities Genoa was liable to suffer from the effects of political changes within its own commune and in the lands with which it had trading relations. For example, we know that in the middle of the twelfth century, the commune was deeply in debt following the mounting of expensive naval expeditions to Almeria and Tortosa on the Spanish coast in 1147–8. Not only were taxes, monopolies and other sources of public income sold for ready cash to meet this crisis, but many of the commune's possessions in the Levant were granted to members of the Embriaco family for a long period, and the commune's third share of Tortosa had to be sold outright to Count Raymond Berenger of Barcelona. In the 1160s the Genoese backed Frederick Barbarossa's abortive plan for the conquest of Sicily and expended great efforts trying to install a puppet king on the island of Sardinia. There were destructive wars with Pisa and from time to time the city was rent by out-

breaks of civil strife. For a long time their Italian rivals prevented
the Genoese from taking much part in the profitable trade with
Constantinople. The trading quarter promised them by the Emperor Manuel in 1155 had hardly been set up before it was destroyed by the Pisans; after much diplomacy a new quarter was
assigned to the Genoese in about 1168, only to be destroyed by the
Venetians two years later. For a dozen years or so after this event
the Genoese enjoyed imperial favour, but from 1183 the power of
the Venetians began to increase once more, and finally, in 1201, a
body of crusaders with Venetian backing captured Constantinople
and established the ill-fated Latin Empire in which the Venetians
held the lion's share. Although it brought in enormous booty and
gave some leading members of the Venetian aristocracy the opportunity to satisfy their hunger for land and titles by establishing
principalities in Greece, the attempt to rule 'one quarter and one
half of the Roman Empire' imposed a severe strain on the Venetian
state which was forced to prop up the tottering structure of the
Latin Empire. It was, nevertheless, a bitter blow to Venetian pride
when Michael VIII Paleologus recaptured Constantinople in 1261;
the Genoese returned finally to the Bosphorus and before long
were sailing beyond into the long-forbidden waters of the Black
Sea.

In spite of many ups and downs, there can be no doubt about the
overall growth of the Genoese economy which continued its up-
ward trend until nearly the middle of the fourteenth century. The
population increased rapidly, especially in the twelfth century
when Genoa must have had many of the characteristics of a boom
city. As early as 1134 it was necessary to increase the seven *compagnie* which had made up the commune at the beginning of the
century to eight, four from the old *civitas* and four from the newer
burgus. In 1155 a new wall was laid out encircling both the city
and the burgus and enclosing an area of 53 hectares, which, in view
of the lack of open spaces and the known Genoese tradition of
building high, has been thought capable of holding a population
of up to 50,000. Despite the difficulties of the site, squeezed
between the mountains and the sea, expansion did not stop
here, but new suburbs were formed to the north and south
which in turn were walled in the first half of the fourteenth century, when the population is thought to have reached something
like 100,000.

This vast city was built upon commerce. Its contado was mountainous and poor, and the only industry of more than local significance was that of the *draperii*, who dyed and finished imported cloth, but not on a very large scale. A high proportion of the population, therefore, lived directly or indirectly by trade. This was facilitated by great improvements in commercial technique which from simple beginnings had achieved considerable sophistication by 1250. Starting from the partnership or *societas* with unlimited liability for all its members, businessmen evolved a number of devices to secure the spreading of risks and assist the division of labour. In the sea-loan, for example, the creditor shouldered the risks of the voyage by making repayment contingent upon the safe arrival of a particular ship; with the *commenda* contract, of which there were several varieties, one party advanced a sum to a travelling merchant who contributed his labour in return for a share in the profits. Another method was to sell shares in a ship and its cargo before it set out on a trading expedition. The foundations of modern banking were laid during this period. Beginning as money-changers who accepted deposits, by the mid-thirteenth century Genoese bankers were performing all the essential functions of their profession, such as extending credit and making transfers from one account to another. All these operations were frequently carried out by merchants too, and to keep pace with the growing complexity of business, methods of accounting were radically improved.

With these developments there went an increasing participation in business by men of widely differing classes and occupations. At one extreme there was the merchant oligarchy of five families, three of which claimed descent from the viscounts of the city, that appear to have dominated the Levant trade during the second half of the twelfth century. This participation in trade by the highest nobility of the region is exceptional and highly significant; the story of the rural counts of Lavagna who by the thirteenth century had become so much at home in the city that they dropped their title and became known as the Fieschi, underlines Genoa's power to attract the greatest landowners of the contado. At the other end of the scale notarial contracts of the mid-thirteenth century reveal a mass of shopkeepers, artisans or small *rentiers*, some of them women, who were placing quite small sums in the hands of professional factors for them to invest in trading activities of all kinds.

In between there were the merchants of moderate means, who in the twelfth century specialised in trade in the western Mediterranean, while the traffic to the Champagne fairs was largely handled by non-Genoese; from about 1225, however, native Genoese began to take over the northern trade and also moved with the Tuscans into banking, which had previously been dominated by Lombards and Piedmontese. Commercial activity was so diffused through the Genoese governing classes that the city had no need of a merchant guild, many of whose functions were performed instead directly by the commune; for example, only citizens or outsiders who had received express permission from the commune were allowed to invest in overseas trade. The current saying *'Genuensis ergo mercator'* – a Genoese, therefore a merchant – was only a slight exaggeration of the truth.

Subject to the ebb and flow of goods and capital, the Genoese business world was seldom stable for long. Wars, and especially crusading ventures, came to involve financial transactions on a very large scale. For example, the Genoese heavily backed the French King Louis IX's ill-fated attack on Egypt in 1249, and for a few years before and after this expedition set sail, the Genoese market was the scene of particularly intense activity which culminated in 1252 in the issue of the *genovin*, the first gold coin to be minted by an Italian commune and the immediate precursor of the more famous florin. As it happened, this pioneering attempt to establish a gold currency was not immediately successful, and the lead in this field passed to Florence; the next few years saw something of a trade recession which caused a number of businessmen in Genoa to go bankrupt.

A striking illustration of the vitality of the Genoese economy is provided by the number of outsiders who established themselves in the city so as to share in its exceptional prosperity. Until about 1225 when native merchants began to take over, the caravan trade over the Alps was mainly carried on by men from Piedmontese cities such as Chieri, Vercelli and above all, Asti. Other merchants came from further afield, from France, the Rhineland and Flanders. An outstanding role was played by the financiers of Arras, a group of families originating among the lesser feudal nobility, which, from about 1150, came to specialise in the export of northern wool and cloth to Genoa, an activity in which their descendants maintained an interest until at least the middle of the

PLATES

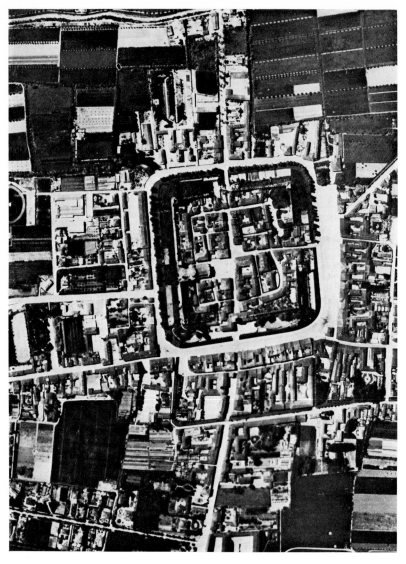

I   Two planned towns of northern Italy from the air
A. Castelfranco Veneto, founded 1195.

B. Cittadella, founded 1220.

II The Veronese Commune receives a standard from St Zeno – cavalry on the right, infantry on the left. Tympanum of the west door of the monastery of S. Zeno, Verona, executed by the sculptor Nicolao between 1135 and 1138.

III The crucial role of law in communal society. Twelfth-century capitals from Modena Cathedral representing Man oppressed by injustice (*above*) and the upright judge bearing the Code of Justinian (*below*).

IV The strong arm of the law in Genoa, 1190. The *podestà* leads his men to destroy the house of Fulcone di Castello.

V   The Signore triumphs over the Commune. Cangrande
della Scala of Verona (d. 1329), patron of Dante and
conqueror of Vicenza, Padua and Treviso.

VI The ideal of the Vita Civile. Citizens ride in the contado with hawk and hounds passing peasants bringing their produce into the city. Detail from the *Allegory of Justice and the Common Good* by Ambrogio Loren-

fifteenth century. Another especially important group were the men of Piacenza. The two cities had been drawn together early in the period of Genoese economic expansion, so that when the commune got into debt in the middle of the twelfth century, the Piacentine commune came to the rescue with a loan of £8500 which was repaid in 1154, partly in cash but mainly in spices and dye-stuffs. Relations remained close; a number of Piacentines are recorded as receiving permission to invest in the overseas trade of the port and also participated in the overland trade to Lombardy and beyond. In the mid-thirteenth century there was a flourishing body of bankers of Piacentine origin resident in Genoa, many of whom were involved in the trade with the fairs of Champagne. No fewer than fifty-seven Piacentines are known to have advanced loans to finance Louis IX's crusade, and some of them suffered bankruptcy in the slump after 1255.

It must be stressed that in its dynamism, its concentration on commerce and its dependence on distant markets, the Genoese economy was altogether exceptional, comparable only with its deadly rival Venice, where the roots of the commercial aristocracy were, of course, much older. Although Pisa was the third port of communal Italy, the economy was much more mixed, for the city was the marketing centre for a rich and productive hinterland and was the home of important iron and leather industries, the former based on the ore of the island of Elba and the latter depending partly on local and partly on imported hides. As a result the land-based economy exerted a much stronger pull in the Tuscan port, and it has been calculated that the interests of sea and land were roughly equal.

In the inland cities, the distribution and consumption of the products of the surrounding countryside generally played the dominant part in the urban economy, and the contribution of long-distance commerce varied greatly, depending upon each city's proximity to the main trade routes. An unmistakable sign of the presence of a substantial commercial class is provided by the emergence of merchant guilds of sufficient standing for them to be associated with the public affairs of their communes. As early as 1154 the Piacentines sent a consul of the commune and a *consul negotiatorum* to represent them in Genoa in discussions concerning the settlement of the loan; a merchant guild at Bologna, on the other hand, is not mentioned until 1194.[5] In

Florence the *consules mercatorum* first appear in 1182, but with the emergence of the Calimala guild of textile importers and finishers in 1192, the bankers and moneychangers in 1202 and the textile retailers of Por S. Maria in 1216, it is clear that the original merchant guild was breaking up into a number of more specialised associations, the first sign of the unusual commercial and industrial future which lay ahead of the city.[6]

Throughout communal Italy the century 1150 to 1250 was one of phenomenal urban growth. Although documentary evidence for total populations is almost non-existent in this period, it was the time when practically every major Italian city burst out of the narrow quarters which had sufficed during the bad times of late antiquity and the early Middle Ages; the new circuits of walls laid out between about 1170 and 1210 provide unmistakable evidence for relative development, even if the lack of information about the density of urban settlement makes translation into terms of population a hazardous procedure. For example, the port of Pisa increased in area from about 30 to 114 hectares, and the inland city of Bologna from 23 hectares to about 100; the growth of Florence at this period from 23 to 80 hectares was somewhat less. For a true picture of the size of Pisa about 1200, some allowance should be made for the trading quarter of Kinsica south of the Arno which was not walled until the early fourteenth century, but even if this is done, it is still clear that the curve of growth between the port and the inland cities was not radically different. At Milan, where the rhythm of development was hardly disturbed by the destruction of the city by the emperor Frederick Barbarossa in 1162, the fortified area in the early thirteenth century was somewhat over 200 hectares, considerably greater than the 185 hectares of Pisa at its greatest extent a century later. Yet Milan was not one of the major centres of international trade.

It appears that the size and rate of growth of medieval Italian cities was, with a few obvious and notable exceptions, only marginally affected by the opportunities for long-distance trade; the determining factor was the resources of the surrounding area which provided each city with its immediate reserve of foodstuffs, raw materials and men. Since we know that the population was increasing prodigiously, and that despite occasional dearths and famines the new urban masses were somehow fed, it follows that the period must have seen an enormous expansion in the productivity of the land. Yet in the present state of knowledge, it is impossible to speak of how this was achieved except in the most general terms, for while the agrarian history of the early Middle Ages has received some attention, and that of the later Middle Ages rather more, the twelfth and early thirteenth centuries have been relatively neglected. The evidence in the form of place names, references to land brought under cultivation and new rural settlements is quite abundant, but needs to be brought together and interpreted in a series of local studies before any general conclusions can be reached. All that can be attempted here is to suggest some of the more promising areas of inquiry.

Reference has already been made to the division of the Italian terrain into the regions of high hills, middle hills and valley bottoms; a marked trend of the period 1150 to 1250 seems to have been the intensive exploitation and settlement of the lowest areas, where drainage and possibly irrigation works would require the deployment of labour and capital on a considerable scale. The history of this achievement has yet to be written. The often repeated statement that irrigation in the region of Milan was initiated by the monks of Chiaravalle in 1138 seems to rest on little more than the misreading of an eighteenth century source. All that the contemporary document proves is that the Cistercians were interested in making a dam and diverting the course of the ancient canal known as the Vettabbia, but whether this was for the purpose of constructing a mill or for small-scale irrigation works is not clear; it was probably no more than many other landowners had done before them.[7] For the beginning of large-scale reclamation schemes, it is much more likely that the older religious houses or the large secular landowners were responsible rather than the new orders like the Cistercians, whose estates and resources must have taken some time to build up. A document of 1156 shows the abbot of the Benedictine monastery of Pomposa near the Po delta, making a systematic levy of forced labour on the dependants of the community for the building of a dike.[8] This example of the use of seigneurial rights to organise a major work of land improvement can hardly have been an isolated one; wherever a single landowner had virtual control of a suitable region, this would have been an obvious way of increasing his wealth and the yield of his lands.

In many areas, however, particularly near the major cities,

estates must have been so broken up that co-operation between the numerous proprietors must have been difficult to obtain. Here the role of directing public works had been a responsibility of the communes almost from the beginning; they had assumed the right of exacting forced labour and had the necessary authority to override the objections of local landowners if need be. In 1199 the commune of Verona, 'because of the great shortage of corn in the city', resolved to reclaim a marsh which was partly allocated to the neighbouring villages and partly retained as communal property. The commune's share amounted to 400 *campi*, of which 26 were kept as pasture for the city's warhorses, and the rest was leased to 400 men, who naturally formed themselves into a *consorteria* which elected two rectors and appointed a notary. Each shareholder paid the commune a tithe of the produce and 5s 6d *per campo* each year; by 1228 many of them had prospered sufficiently to buy their land freehold.[9] This is the kind of thing which ought to have happened frequently, but specific accounts of communally organised reclamation work at this period are few and far between.

Some of the best known records suggest that, in their public works, the city-communes were not always primarily concerned with increasing the productivity of the land. For example, the chronicles name a *magister* Guitelmo as the engineer employed by the Milanese commune to design fortifications, bridges and engines of war between 1156 and 1162. He also laid out the defensive ditch around the city which was being reconstructed after its destruction by Barbarossa, and he was probably also responsible for the canal leading into the river Ticino known as the Ticinello. Though both these works may have provided additional benefits in the form of land drainage and irrigation, the primary purpose of both was military, for the Ticinello ran along the boundary between the Milanese contado and the territory of the rival city of Pavia. Similar canals were dug, or at least projected, to divide the territories of some of the cities of the Romagna. Another motive leading the communes to invest in water courses was the provision of water mills; it was for this purpose, for example, that the Bolognese commune bought land along the river Reno in 1209.[10] Navigation by barges could be of secondary importance, as in the case of the Milanese Naviglio Grande running from the city to the Ticino, which is mentioned as early as 1187 but which does not seem to have been made navigable until 1271. On the other hand the Paduan canal system which ran for some forty miles from Monselice to the lagoon opposite Venice, with a branch to the salt pans of Chioggia, seems to have been designed primarily for navigation, although the water mills, which it fed at Battaglia, provided the commune with a useful additional source of revenue. Dykes and canals could have several uses and their economic significance is rarely as clear as it might seem at first sight.

The shortcuts towards a history of the agrarian economy are full of pitfalls. To take another example, the foundation of numerous new towns in north and central Italy between 1150 and 1250 would seem to provide evidence of growing population and, in a general way, perhaps it does. A classic case is that of Villafranca di Verona, laid out in 1185 on a rectilinear plan, with 179 agricultural holdings of 33 *campi* each provided for the inhabitants. In some regions of Italy such as Emilia and Piedmont the number of new towns (*borghi franchi*) founded by the major communes and endowed with fiscal and legal privileges, was considerable; between 1197 and 1255 about twenty were established in the district of Vercelli alone. However, when such foundations are looked at closely, it usually emerges that what took place was a gathering together of a population which had formerly lived in a number of separate settlements. In the episcopal city of Alessandria, founded in 1168 by the amalgamation of the populations of four villages, the citizens formed separate corporations which retained their own customary law down to 1221. The aims of the communes in creating *borghi franchi* were at least as likely to be political as economic, possibly more so. The new towns with their fortifications and privileged townsmen, who often enjoyed the status of citizens of the parent city, were intended to provide a bastion of communal power, either against the unsubdued population of the region or against a rival commune. A nice example of the latter is the new town of Castelfranco, established by the commune of Treviso near the borders of its territory in 1195; in 1220 the Paduans, having besieged Castelfranco without success, founded their own rival town of Cittadella seven miles away. As they stand today these two market towns bear the unmistakable marks of their planned origins, Castelfranco being laid out on a rectangular plan and Cittadella on a circular one (see plate I); their survival proves that they assumed a function in the economy of the region, but what this meant in terms of population and production is impossible to assess.

Although it is not yet possible to present a convincing picture of the process of rural development in this period, the earliest surviving tax assessments enable us to form some idea of its results. The book of hearths of the contado of Pistoia indicates that in 1244 there were about 34,000 persons living in an area of 350 square miles. Since this assessment excluded the city itself, but included a good deal of inhospitable high mountains, the average of nearly 100 inhabitants per square mile must be regarded as very high. A similar source for the territory of the little town of San Gimignano in 1290 suggests a somewhat lower density of around 80 persons to the square mile.[11] However, in such cases it is obviously unrealistic to exclude the population of the town altogether, since a good proportion of its inhabitants must have worked directly on the land. If the urban hearths recorded in 1277 are added to those of the contado, they indicate a total population for San Gimignano and its district of around 11,000 or 200 per square mile, a level which was not reached again in that area until the 1930s. Although the areas involved in these assessments are small, their position in central Tuscany makes it likely that they are typical of the more developed parts of Italy at that time. There is evidence that the small towns in these regions were also growing. For example, in the little *castello* of Pasignano, Plesner found the first reference to a *borgo* outside the original fortified area in 1129; in 1219 this was extended to form the *borgo inferiore*, which by the later thirteenth century contained some forty dwelling houses, including the towers of some of the more important families of the town.[12]

It appears then that, at least until 1250, the population of the cities, small towns and countryside of communal Italy was increasing considerably, though whether the rate was the same in all areas it is impossible to say. However, it is clear that the undoubted growth of the major cities could not have come about without immigration on a massive scale, for under medieval conditions of hygiene it is unlikely that the urban population would have been able by itself to keep its numbers stable, let alone expand at a formidable rate. The mass of these migrants must have been poor men who would leave little or no direct evidence of their passing.

The legal obstacles to movement from the country to the towns and cities were decreasing in all but the most backward areas as the large rural estates were progressively broken up by purchase and inheritance. By the middle of the thirteenth century it appears that, in the regions of the major cities, vast unbroken estates in the hands of a single lay owner had become a thing of the past; the holdings of the large landowners were commonly scattered over a wide area and were interspersed with the land of other proprietors, so that these 'pulverised' estates could be described only piece by piece and almost field by field. In these circumstances the manor must have ceased to function as a unit of agrarian organisation, labour services were commuted and the manor house became simply a centre for the collection of rents and dues in cash or kind. Landowners must, therefore, have had neither the desire nor the means to prevent their tenants or the surplus members of their families from going off to seek their fortunes in the towns and cities.

However, not all the immigrants to the cities were poor and others did not long remain so. One of the most important features of Italian society was the existence of a rural middle class consisting of families who had amassed enough property to live off their rents, helped out perhaps by the profits of some trade or profession. Some were wealthy enough to be assessed for mounted military service in the communal armies, others were judges or notaries employed in the administration of the rural communes and the collection of taxes; others, again, accomplished their escape from the land by setting up as artisans, craftsmen or shop-keepers. It was these prosperous and ambitious members of the rural communities who were particularly prone to the lure of the big cities; in 1246 the Bolognese commune was so alarmed by the flight of rural taxpayers that it tried to limit immigration into the city since it was alleged that only the poor remained on the land.[13]

In the major cities undoubtedly the most important social development in this period is the emergence of the guilds. Before the mid-twelfth century the evidence for guilds and confraternities is very scarce. In some places it appears that the old *ministeria* on the Byzantine and ultimately late-Roman model, through which trades were regulated in the interests of the state, lingered on though their property and the right to control their activities had sometimes passed from public officials to the church or private individuals. At the same time there are traces of religious confraternities apparently formed spontaneously on the initiative of their members, which met for worship and looked after the social welfare of the members and their dependants, but had no explicit connection with any particular trade or occupation. By the early thirteenth century this picture is completely transformed by the emergence of a whole range of guilds, which combine social and religious functions with the regulation of skilled crafts and professions of all kinds, together with commerce and shopkeeping, transport and even some kinds of agriculture, such as market gardening. The structure of these new guilds seems to owe little or nothing to the older *ministeria*, though the evidence for the latter is so slight that appearances could be misleading; on the other hand, the chance survival of the early records of the shoemakers guild at Ferrara prove that this had evolved from a religious confraternity whose regulations in 1112 show no connection with the craft.[14] However, if the guilds arose initially as private *societates* without official intervention, they were bound before long to come to the notice of the communes, which had taken on the public authority once vested in the imperial regime. In fact, the contacts between the guilds and the communes took two forms: on the one hand, the communes sought to harness the guilds to the regulation of trade, industry and the professions in the public interest, while on the other, the guilds banded together to defend their interests and exert a direct influence on the policies of the communes. It was in this way that, during the first half of the thirteenth century, the guilds became the backbone of radical political movements which sought the distribution of power within the communes on a wider basis than before; while in eastern Lombardy these political bodies were generally known as the *communanza*, elsewhere they appropriated the old name of *popolo* with its powerful democratic overtones. By 1250 the *popolo* had secured a dominant position in the constitutions of the major communes.

The precise social composition of the *popolo* varied considerably from place to place, so that each individual case needs to be carefully assessed. The guilds, for example, were never as 'democratic' as they tend to appear at first sight. In the first place they were essentially corporations of masters endowed with traditional skills and at least a little capital; unskilled and propertyless labourers, not to mention the great mass of the poor, were firmly excluded. Then, the grouping of various trade associations into a single guild for political purposes usually had the effect of placing the poorer sections under the dominance of those who were richer and who enjoyed a higher social standing. Indeed, some professional groups, such as the colleges of judges and guilds of merchants in some of the Lombard communes, stood aside from the *popolo* as being socially nearer to the old governing class. Meanwhile, the *popolo* drew much of its support from men who did not practise any particular trade or profession, but who were *rentiers* living on the proceeds of urban or rural property, possibly augmented by occasional moneylending or investments. Any landowner whose estates had been acquired too recently for him to be admitted to the circle of the knightly aristocracy would tend to gravitate towards the *popolo*; the differences between such men and the nobility would be social and political but not necessarily economic. Thus, although it was generally regarded as the party of the less well-to-do, of the infantry (*pedites*) of the communal militia as against the more wealthy mounted troops (*milites*), in practice the *popolo* was also the party of the newly rich. It drew much of its strength from individuals and families which were relatively new arrivals in the city; the names of guildsmen reveal a high proportion of men whose rural origins were still remembered. Among them there were many who had established their position by seizing the opportunities offered by the city, but there were others who had risen by way of the rural middle class, possibly passing through a stage in which they practised a trade or craft in a village or small town which acted as a bridge between the rural and the urban environment. The rise of the *popolo* is an index of the vitality of both the rural and the urban economy.

It would be a capital mistake to regard the urban expansion of 1150–1250 as being achieved at the expense of the countryside – the economy was much too closely integrated for that. Indeed, the period saw the forging of new and stronger links between each city and its contado. It was not only the great landowners who retained their roots in the countryside when they moved into the towns; modest members of the *popolo* and recruits to the guilds held on to their land when they left their villages, leasing it out but maintaining an interest in the yield of the harvests and the collection of rents. Again, many of the crafts and trades depended for their prosperity on the produce of the countryside. The victualling guilds distributed rural produce, the bulk of it from the city's own contado, and most of the artisan guilds drew on local raw materials such as timber, stone, wool, linen and leather. Many tradesmen were directly dependent for their business on rural connections. There were, for example, taverners who owned their own vineyards and gave credit to vinegrowers; there were drapers who advanced cloth on credit to retailers and travelling salesmen from up-country areas. Even the notaries, the bulk of whose professional activities were carried on in the cities, were to be found scattered in the countryside and small towns in increasing numbers during the thirteenth century, providing yet another bond between urban and rural society. All these links ensured that the typical Italian guildsman was not a burgher whose horizon was bounded by his city's walls, but a man who knew the contado and had a vital interest in its prosperity.

At the highest social level, the period 1150–1250 saw the increasing integration of the nobility into the life of the cities. The degree to which the great families were involved in moneylending and commercial investments seems to have varied greatly from place to place, and the role of urban rents in their continuing prosperity is disputed but was probably not very great. As landowners, however, all the nobility had a vital interest in the control of urban markets which could only be secured by political means. The rise of the *popolo* during the first half of the thirteenth century did not extinguish the power of the great landowners in the cities; at the most it only eclipsed it for a time. The triumph of the *popolo* was soon followed by the appearance of the first urban despots, who took the control of one or more cities into their own hands and established the first wave of the lordships (*signorie*) which were to dominate the political scene in the later Middle Ages and the Renaissance. It must be no coincidence that these early despots or *signori*, like Oberto Palavicino, Azzo VII d'Este and Ezzelino III da Romano, were all members of rich landed families of considerable antiquity, whose resources could give them a decisive grip on the crucial nexus between city and countryside. The two great political developments of the first half of the thirteenth century, the rise of the *popolo* and the appearance of the early *signorie*, both attest to a flourishing and expanding economy in the country as well as the town.

The Foundations of a Secular Culture

THE extraordinary growth of Italian society in the hundred years which culminated in the triumph of the *popolo* and the emergence of the first city despots, created a great hunger for practical knowledge. The building and feeding, policing and cleansing of the great new cities where both business and political activities went on with an intensity and on a scale never approached before, all threw up new structures and forms of association which cried out for expert definition and regulation; the inevitable conflicts generated within and between these more complex communities called for skilled advocates, mediators and statesmen, and even for a renewed civic morality to prevent the new society from tearing itself apart in internecine strife. To control destructive tendencies and to create order, the intellectual leaders of communal Italy put their faith in the deployment of law and rhetoric on a large scale, and in the end the essential needs were met, though with no great margin of safety. By about the middle of the thirteenth century, the groundwork of the practical political skills was more or less complete; the period of discovery and experimentation was coming to an end, and the universities and leading schools were taking up the work of dissemination and popularisation. The swarms of lawyers and rhetoricians, who played such an important part in the public life of the communes from the mid-thirteenth century, were the products of an educational programme, strongly secular and practical in tone, the main lines of which had been laid down during the formative century and a half leading up to 1250.

The sources of the new expertise were mostly very old. In the field of law, the study of Justinian's *Corpus Juris Civilis* became the training ground for the legal intellects of Italy, while for a time the rhetoricians looked beyond the textbooks of late antiquity to the doctrines of Cicero. Yet, although much of the material was ancient, the programme which evolved cannot be described simply as a revival of Roman law and classical rhetoric. The academics of this period saw the Roman past not as a unique golden age whose glories ought to be revived, but as the fountainhead of a continuing tradition in which they themselves were a living part; thus, almost without realising it, they moved from the examination of ancient authorities to the study of the glosses and interpretations of their own times, and, with growing self-confidence, created their own legal and literary culture which had little in common with the models from which they had started out. Paradoxically, the considerable renaissance of the twelfth century led in most fields not to classicism, but to something which may be characterised as Romanesque, that is, Roman details incorporated into a structure with a totally different style and spirit. In this respect, mid-thirteenth-century Italy stands in contrast both to the immediate past and to what was to come. In culture as well as in politics, there is much justification for calling the century from 1150–1250 the century without Rome.

Nowhere was the contrast between the picture given by the authoritative texts and the actual contemporary scene deeper than in jurisprudence, the big brother of all academic disciplines in Italy in the Middle Ages. This was the first great age of the medieval study of Roman law, which looked back to Irnerius as its founder; for a century after his death in 1130, his work was carried on by an unbroken succession of great jurists and teachers at Bologna so that, although many attempts were made, no rival school succeeded in establishing itself on a permanent footing until the university of Padua was founded by a group of dissident students from Bologna about the year 1220. By this time the Bolognese school had produced not only an unrivalled stream of *summae* and monographs on various aspects of the law, but it had practically completed the great work of supplying a detailed commentary to the whole text of the *Corpus Iuris Civilis*. Most of the contributors to this huge co-operative enterprise had been Lombards, with native Bolognese playing a leading role; but one of the secrets of Bologna's success was its ability to draw on the resources of Tuscany, and it was, in fact, a Florentine, Accursius, the first great mind to emerge from the growing city on the Arno, who cast the *glossa ordinaria* into its definitive form in about 1228.

The revival of academic jurisprudence was, by any account, among the greatest intellectual achievements of the Middle Ages, but this should not blind us to the limitations affecting the practical application of Roman law in the world of the communes. In matters of detail, such as legal procedure and the drafting of contracts, there were no serious barriers to the adoption of the practices taught in the schools, and these were gradually introduced without any great difficulty. But in private law, the movement back to Justinian met considerable resistance in the name of local custom which had evolved under barbarian and especially Lombard influence; the Pisan statute of the mid-twelfth century which declared that the city lived by Roman law while retaining something of Lombard law (*retentis quibusdam de lege Longobarda*) sums up well the situation which was common at this period. Feudal law survived without difficulty because, in the view of the jurists, it had been incorporated into the venerable body of Roman law through various edicts of the German emperors of the eleventh and twelfth centuries; thus, there was nothing incongruous in contemporary eyes about the Siennese, who had declared that they lived by Roman law in 1176, staging a judicial duel in 1225, since it was held that trial by battle had been made a part of the imperial law by Otto I in the tenth century. Eventually both Lombard and feudal law were tamed and domesticated by the prevailing Roman spirit, being codified and glossed as if they were a part of Justinian, and losing much of their distinctive character in the process.

It was at the highest level of public and constitutional law that the revival of Roman law created serious trouble. Committed as they were to the belief that the imperial and universal law was by nature superior to any local law or custom, whether written or unwritten, the academic lawyers had the greatest difficulty in dealing with the *de facto* self-government of the communes and its practical expression in communal statutes. The breakdown of the imperial system, which had made possible the emergence of the communes, was a scandal in the eyes of many of the jurists, for without an effective emperor as the fount of law and the ultimate source of political authority, the Roman legal structure lacked its keystone and seemed in constant danger of collapse. The civil lawyers tended to become imperialists almost *ipso facto*, and, despite the occasional voice warning that no good could be expected from the ignorant Germans, a number followed Irnerius' lead and entered the service of the medieval empire. The highpoint of this uneasy partnership came at the diet of Roncaglia in 1158, when Frederick Barbarossa asked the lawyers of the Italian cities to define the rights of the emperor in the kingdom of Italy. The answers they gave seem to have been an attempt to restore the position as it might have been before the Investiture Contest and proved unacceptable in the long run to the majority of the Lombard communes, which were not prepared to give up so many of the gains they had won at the expense of the imperial system during the previous hundred years. The lawyers of Roncaglia became widely unpopular, and, after years of bitter warfare, they saw Barbarossa forced at the peace of Constance (1183), to agree to terms which, in effect, marked the abandonment of their scheme for the revival of the imperial government in Lombardy. Yet the jurists did not entirely lose faith in the Empire, nor the emperors in them; both Henry VI and Frederick II made flattering gestures in the direction of the Bolognese school. It was only after Frederick II had founded his own university at Naples in 1224, and had reacted to the Bolognese commune's adherence to the second Lombard league against him by placing a ban on the *studium* there, that the lingering imperialist sympathies of the law school were finally extinguished.

Up to the end of the twelfth century the practical application of the new learning to civic life cannot be said to have proceeded very far; the case of Pisa, where something like a codification of local law and custom had been attempted, seems to have been altogether exceptional. It is true that rhetoric had been established as a separate discipline and adapted to contemporary needs to some extent; the first real Italian *ars dictandi* is attributed to Adalberto Samaritano, a member of an aristocratic Bolognese family of the same generation as Irnerius. Yet this civic rhetoric, which embraced the rules for the composition of the stylised rhythmic prose known as the *dictamen*, was virtually restricted to the writing of letters; what the handbooks offered was a series of exemplars of letters or parts of letters, from which the aspirant was expected to select something which would fit his need. In such books in the twelfth century not only were the rules and style of composition closely modelled on antiquity, but the social and political world they presupposed was often far removed from contemporary realities. A good example is the way in which a certain Goffredo in his *Summa de arte dictandi*, written in Bologna about 1188, attempted to translate the system of honorific titles which he found in Justinian into modern terms. 'Kings, provincial governors and Roman senators (*conscripti patres*) are *illustres*; dukes, counts and marquesses are *spectabiles*; barons, vavassors and perhaps the consuls of cities are *clarissimi*.'[15] From this one would hardly guess that provincial governors had been extinct for centuries, or that the consuls who are given such a humble place, were the rulers of the cities and, therefore, the greatest political force in the land.

About 1200, no doubt in response to social ferment outside, a change of emphasis becomes discernible within the schools, marked by a renewed attempt to grapple with contemporary problems. At this turn in the road, and pointing in the new direction, there stands the bizarre figure of a Florentine, older than Accursius and, to judge from their writings, about as different in character as it is possible to imagine. Boncompagno da Signa was not as great a man as Accursius, but from many points of view he is more interesting, for while Accursius summed up the achievement of the previous century, Boncompagno is associated with new departures. While the writings of the glossators were almost entirely impersonal, Boncompagno's personality, boastful, humorous and with a biting wit, bursts through everything he wrote. As a rhetorician he seems to reflect the currents of his age in an exaggerated form; none of his works was definitive, but most of them exemplify the new practical spirit which was to pervade the schools for the remainder of the century.

Boncompagno was born near Florence about 1165–70 and was teaching at Bologna shortly before 1200; his last work was written in impoverished old age after 1235. Although he raided the territory of the lawyers whenever he felt inclined, his home ground was rhetoric and most of his seventeen surviving works are concerned, at least in part, with the rhetorician's stock in trade – letter writing. The main characteristic of Boncompagno's letter material was the degree to which it was directed towards the actual needs of his pupils in specific contemporary situations; paying no more than formal homage to the time-honoured classifications and the out-of-date social hierarchy, Boncompagno empties before his readers a veritable cornucopia of arguments, anecdotes and witticisms suitable for all occasions. The *Rhetorica Antiqua*, for example, begins with a parody of a notarial document by which the author designates his book his residuary legatee, and there follows a short dialogue between *auctor* and *liber*. The main treatise is divided into six parts, of which the three shortest are concerned with letters to and from the pope, prelates and other ecclesiastical matters, while the parts devoted to the letters of secular rulers, nobles, citizens, communes and students are long and detailed. There are letters for rulers making peace and war, seeking alliances or exchanging captives; noblemen correspond about the education of their sons to knighthood or about tournaments; merchants exchange business news or ask for loans; and students pursue recommendations from their masters while trying to cheat them of their fees. The *Rhetorica Antiqua* is a baggy monster packed with digressions and anecdotes which range from a classification of popular songs and funeral customs from different parts of Italy to stories of the author's triumphs over rival teachers and complaints about student activists. In conclusion Boncompagno records how the book was read before the doctors of both laws in the presence of many other doctors and scholars at the church of S. Giovanni in Monte in Bologna in 1215 – the first recorded case of an approbation of this kind in Italy, symbolising the fact that rhetoric was leaving the tutelage of the ancient authorities and was beginning to make its home in the market-squares, lecture rooms and counting-houses of communal Italy.[16]

In the early years of the thirteenth century rhetoric was an expanding subject, and Boncompagno helped to extend its frontiers in more than one direction. In his *Rhetorica Novissima*, for example, he sought to provide the law students of his day with a complete guide to oratory to supersede Cicero. In this late work, the ageing teacher's cynicism is much in evidence; the strongest advocate in the courts is not eloquence but copious gifts, and although civil law is superior to canon law, both in the end depend upon money. In his view, all speeches, and especially political ones, are much inferior to the written word; nevertheless, by being one of the first to write specifically about them, Boncompagno made a vital contribution to what was to become the *ars arengandi* (the art of speech-making). Again, in the treatises which he devoted to the framing of privileges, testaments and statutes, Boncompagno helped in the groundwork of the *ars notaria*, which was in the process of establishing itself as a separate discipline aimed at the vocational training of notaries. His book on civic statutes, dubbed *Cedrus* because the authors of statutes shoot up everywhere like cedars, is remarkable for its realistic and practical approach, contrasting strongly with the more academic outlook of the professional jurists; the bold assertion that city statutes are made and enforced according to the general custom of Italy, notwithstanding any imperial legislation to the contrary, accurately reflects the mentality of the men who controlled the destinies of the communes at this time.[17]

Boncompagno envisaged a many-sided role for the rhetorician; on the one hand, he might be engaged in law or politics, while on the other, he could contribute to literature and moral philosophy. In his only historical work, *De Obsidione Ancone* (The Siege of Ancona) Boncompagno broke new ground by embellishing his account of an incident in the wars of the Italians against Barbarossa with long speeches which illustrate the character and motives of the main protagonists and serve to drive home the moral that Italy is the queen of the provinces of the Empire and can be enslaved by the lawless Germans only when divided against herself.[18] Although Boncompagno made no attempt to revive a classical style, the concentration on a single time and place to epitomise the whole conflict between the Italian communes and the Germans gives the work something of the quality of a classical drama. Boncompagno deserves to be remembered as the first university teacher to write a history and he founded a small but interesting school of academic historians who expressed through this medium the ideals of the thirteenth century communes. Finally, *opuscula* on such subjects as friendship, love and the ills of old age, though their dry classifications and moral commonplaces make tedious reading, do show that Boncompagno was groping towards the idea of the rhetorician as a practical philosopher, an ideal which was eventually revived in the very different atmosphere of the mid-fourteenth century by Petrarch.

Many of Boncompagno's ideas were quickly taken up and elaborated by others during his lifetime. For example, even more comprehensive letter collections were being produced in the 1220s and 30s by a Bolognese cleric called Guido Fava, who also introduced *précis* of occasional speeches in the vernacular which he called *parlamenta*; these marked another momentous step in learning's journey down into the city hall and market place.[19] Again, between 1223-45 the first known *summa artis notarie*, which set out to cover all branches of the notary's work, was compiled in Bologna by Ranieri da Perugia. The new discipline developed rapidly and the definitive textbook which served for centuries to come was written by Rolandino Passaggieri in 1255. About 1222 an unnamed writer drew together a number of leads

provided by Boncompagno and composed a new type of handbook
for civic magistrates. The *Oculus Pastoralis* combines practical
advice to the intending official, such as carefully to check the terms
of his appointment and adhere scrupulously to his oath of office,
with outlines of speeches suitable for all kinds of public occasions;
there is, for example, a long harangue addressed by the *podestà*
to the ambassadors of another commune in favour of an alliance
which draws heavily on Cicero's *De Amicitia*.[20] The *Oculus Pastoralis* initiated a *genre* of practical books for civic magistrates
and especially for *podestà*, which throw a lot of light on the actual
practice of government and the moral atmosphere in which the
public affairs of the communes were carried on in their heyday. It
is striking that, among Boncompagno's works, the *Cedrus* was not
imitated for many years; it represented an incursion by an amateur
into the territory of the professional jurists which was not to be
repeated lightly. The next known treatise *de statutis* did not appear until about 1284 and its author, Albertino de Gandino, was,
significantly enough, not a university jurist but a practising judge.

In Boncompagno's time the most momentous changes took place
in the organisation of the academic community. When he first
came to Bologna, it is probable that the law school was still a
loose-knit body under the control of the doctors. Each doctor
formed a little *societas* with his students, under a contract which
obliged the master to teach and the scholars to pay. There were
also a multitude of charitable guilds patronised by the academic
community, both doctors and scholars; in particular, those laymen
who were not Bolognese citizens tended to band together in confraternities for mutual protection and welfare. Around the year
1200 these guilds of non-Bolognese students sought to strengthen
their position by forming themselves into four (later two) federa-
tions or *universitates*, each with an elected rector at its head. The
rectors claimed jurisdiction over their fellow-students and this,
together with their desire to regulate many aspects of the academic
life brought them into sharp conflict with the doctors. Boncompagno describes bitterly the methods by which the students cowed
the doctors into giving way on most points; these included boycotts
of lectures and the refusal to pay fees. In the end the student universities came to control almost the whole of the academic routine;
even the content of lectures was prescribed, and doctors could be
fined for failing to cover the ground or for going on too long.

However, the granting of degrees remained at the discretion of the doctors. The dominant position of the students became a distinctive characteristic of the Italian universities, which with their officials, statutes and jurisdiction and – one might add – distrust of arbitrary power, closely resembled the self-governing communes of the cities where they made their homes. Relations with the communes of the host cities were not always smooth, but the cities had such a strong financial interest in the success of the university that, in the end, the academic community secured a privileged status, its members being described as enjoying the advantages of citizenship without the corresponding obligations.

The emergence of the universities does not in itself prove that student numbers were increasing in the early thirteenth century, though this seems extremely likely. The advent of the *popolo* and the expansion of political and bureaucratic activity created greater opportunities for law graduates throughout communal Italy, and the school of the post-Glossators, with their concentration on practical application of the law, who predominated at Bologna after Accursius, provided a kind of teaching which was well suited to the needs of the time. It is curious, however, that so many of the attempts to found further universities met with so little success. Apart from Naples, which was kept alive by the royal patronage of the Hohenstaufen and the Angevins, only Padua flourished, and even here the university passed through a difficult time during the tyranny of Ezzelino da Romano in the 1240s and 50s so that it had to be virtually refounded in 1264. The new secular learning spread all the same, and, in the absence of local universities, the notarial schools in the greater cities seem to have provided a focus for the dissemination of legal culture.

A good example of the way in which ideas were spread is provided by the career of another Florentine. Born in 1220, Brunetto Latini was a notary by training and profession, who as a translator and populariser did much to lay the foundations of a civic culture in the rapidly-growing city of Florence, which until his time had lagged behind the other Tuscan cities in the cultural field. Up to the age of forty Brunetto seems to have been no more than a highly successful notary, who had achieved the influential position of secretary and letter-writer to the governing council of the Florentine commune. Then, in 1260, the unexpected fall of the regime he served compelled Latini to enlarge his experience; six years of exile in France were probably decisive in opening his eyes to the possibilities of the vernacular. The fruit of his exile was an encyclopaedia entitled *Li Livres dou Trésor,* which was designed to give merchants and citizens who could read French a smattering of science, history, both sacred and profane, morals and politics in an easily digested form. Brunetto used the standard authorities of the time, for originality was not the aim; what was new was the strongly practical slant of the book, one-half of which was concerned with practical sciences. Prominent among these were ethics and politics, which, as one would expect, is largely subsumed under the heading of rhetoric; a great part of Book 4 is, in fact, a treatise for city magistrates in the tradition of the *Oculus Pastoralis.*

On his return to Florence in 1266 Brunetto took up his public career again, but he also continued to write, though now in the Tuscan vernacular; until his death in 1294, he exerted a strong influence on the intellectual development of his younger contemporaries, though whether this was done through formal as well as informal teaching is not certain. Much of Brunetto's output, which includes verse as well as prose, was commonplace and unremarkable; undoubtedly, the outstanding achievement of his later years was his translations of some of Cicero's speeches. Unlike most rhetoricians of his generation, Brunetto had a real appreciation of Cicero's style which he tried to convey into Italian; more remarkable still, Brunetto presented Cicero in his civic context as a statesman rather than a sage, driving home, by way of his example, the ways in which eloquence could be of service to the commune. That Cicero had been a new citizen, who had made his name through his own talents rather than through advantages of birth, were further points which appealed to the *popolano* Latini who had a hearty distrust of hereditary aristocrats. In his mature understanding of the Roman orator, Brunetto was a world away from Boncompagno and far in advance of his contemporaries and pupils; he accepted Cicero the politician in a way which was even beyond Petrarch, and which links up with the ideas of the fifteenth century humanists. This flash of insight makes Brunetto unique, yet in other ways he remained a typical representative of the school of rhetoricians which went back to the beginning of the thirteenth century. No less than Boncompagno, Brunetto was a populariser of practical knowledge, and it was as such that he was remembered by the next generation; Dante rejected many of his ideas but revered his memory and Giovanni Villani praised him as 'the beginner and master who refined the Florentines, teaching them how to speak well and rule the commonwealth according to policy'.

This may stand as the epitaph of the whole school of rhetoricians of the thirteenth century. Their aims and way of life invite comparison with those of the humanists who publicised and perhaps invented the renaissance of the fifteenth century. Indeed, both groups occupied a similar position as administrators and public relations officers, but the societies they served were very different. The humanists adorned an urban society which was already mature and relatively stable, and they, therefore, addressed themselves to a small highly educated elite which could appreciate the subtleties of their ideas and style. The rhetoricians, on the other hand, earned their livings in the highly competitive boom towns of the thirteenth century by purveying the rudiments of culture to the raw society which was experiencing the rise of the *popolo*. Like the civic politicians of the time, only more consciously, they laid the foundations of the golden age of the communes which was to follow – the age of Dante.

4. The Consolidation of the Communes, 1150–1250

From the Consulate to the *Podestà*

THE hundred years from 1150 to 1250 were in many ways the most crucial in the development of the medieval states of Europe, and the patterns of authority, law and administration hammered out during this period were destined to survive into the early modern period without fundamental change. Italy was no exception to this rule; indeed, in most respects, the Italians were the pacesetters in the art of government, and the Italian states generally developed a greater bureaucratic power to intervene in the lives of their citizens, for good or ill, than was to be found in the other states of the time. This relative efficiency was made easier by a difference in scale. While the kingdoms and principalities of northern Europe or Spain struggled to assert their control over a largely rural population scattered over areas measured in tens of thousands of square miles, in Italy, outside the kingdom of Naples and Sicily and some of the fringe areas of the north, the typical state consisted of a principal city and the surrounding region, extending to between a thousand and two thousand square miles only, sometimes considerably less. To put this in another way, while a northern king or duke might need up to a week to march from one part of his territory to another, a day's hard riding would normally suffice to travel from the average city to the furthest point of its contado, and up to a third of the population of the city-state might be living within earshot of the council-bell. Of course, the compactness of the Italian state was not an unmixed blessing, for it made it exceptionally vulnerable to invasion and sudden *coups d'état*, but in the early formative period, when the most difficult problem was to get the commands of government known and obeyed in the distant parts of the state, the communes, starting almost from scratch, were able to move forward with startling speed. By and large, by 1200 the power vacuum created by the collapse of the old regime had been filled, and the problem of lack of government was being superseded by the struggle to defend the citizen from the new leviathan and the forces of violence and corruption which might divert its powers in their own interests.

In this constructive work the governing classes of the new Italy responded to local challenges, virtually without any central control or support. The surge of social and political advances in Italy left the unwieldy and archaic Empire far behind; the noisy and expensive efforts of Frederick I Barbarossa (1152–90) and his grandson Frederick II (1198–1250) proved in the end to be no more than abortive attempts to catch up with forces which they could not control. The contribution of the emperors to the restoration of effective government was in the end so small as to be of marginal significance. Nor did the papacy provide a focal point to Italian politics at this time. Although the fear of imperial domination often drove the papacy and the communes to make common cause, and turned some popes, such as Alexander III (1159–81) and Gregory IX (1227–41), into staunch allies of the northern cities, the Holy See never sincerely embraced the political ideal of communal self-government, and remained profoundly suspicious of the social and many of the religious ideals of the urban classes, and especially of the *popolo*. The endemic struggles of the popes with the commune of Rome in this period, and the policy of restricting communal freedom in the papal states prove that the universalism of the pontiffs was, in the last resort, just as inimical to the sovereignty of the local state as were the claims of the Empire. If there was any centre to Italian politics in this period, it was provided by the small corps of dedicated administrators in the individual communes who drafted the laws and devised administrative machinery in response to local needs, drawing on such professional expertise as they might have, and on the experience of their colleagues in neighbouring and allied cities. Although very few of them were academic jurists, most of these men had some legal training or experience, and they, therefore, tended to look, directly or indirectly, towards the fountainhead of legal culture which was to be found in the schools of Bologna. So it was that at certain crucial moments, Bologna was able to play the role of capital of communal Italy, with an informal pre-eminence based not on force or wealth but on intellectual leadership and a central position, which assisted the spread of her ideas to the heartlands of the new society in Lombardy and Tuscany.

By the mid-twelfth century the major cities of Italy outside the boundaries of the Norman kingdom of Sicily, were becoming accustomed to *de facto* rule by their communes without any regular outside interference; from the death of the emperor Henry V in 1125 until Frederick Barbarossa's arrival in Italy in 1154 the Empire was much too weak to intervene seriously in their internal affairs. Yet the communes still showed traces of their informal and irregular origins. As we have seen, at Genoa in the 1150s it was still thought necessary to make special provisions safeguarding the interests of those who entered into long-term contracts with the *compagna* in case the association should cease to exist.[1] Since the communes were still, in theory, temporary, continuity could not be assumed in the offices they created. An example of this is a provision in the Pisan *Constitutum Usus* (dated 1161) which allows that any space of time during which the city of Pisa lacks consuls, rectors or *podestà* should not be reckoned to count against litigants in the time allowed for answering to pleas.[2] At Genoa, too, one can glimpse a moment in the process by which the essentially personal association of the commune came to be attached to a specific territory. For most cities the ecclesiastical diocese came to be the territorial goal for the nascent city-states from an early date; in the oath of the Genoese consuls of 1143, on the other hand, their sphere of action was defined by reference to the three terminal points of Gesta, Iugum and Rovereto, with a wider sphere of influence extending well beyond along the coast in both directions.[3] Everywhere, the idea of the commune as a permanent corporation with rights and obligations separate from those of its members took root very gradually, lagging far behind events as the communes became heirs by default of the old imperial system.

On the plane of practical politics the leaders of the communes did not begin modestly, and gradually advance their claims with the passage of time; if anything, the reverse was true, the early consuls intervening in many areas where their powers would be consolidated only after years of effort, if at all. It is true that at the core of the early communes is to be found a preoccupation with the defence of the persons of its members and their individual and corporate property. But it was impossible for the authority of the consuls to be restricted to these matters for long; inevitably they became involved in public order and local defence. Thus the maritime communes of Genoa and Pisa built and armed war-fleets apparently from their very early days, and inland communes were not slow to take on the public duties of building and maintaining walls and fortifications. Defence was impossible without taxation. The administration of common property, especially markets and sea or river ports, and the takeover of tolls or ancient taxes of imperial origin, such as the *fodrum*, all of which were generally farmed out to individuals, must have played a large part in spreading the idea of the communes as permanent and public institutions. The raising of very large loans either from members or outsiders, such as are recorded at Venice and Genoa from the 1160s, must have contributed to the same effect; in both these ways different classes of individuals acquired a vested interest in the stability and continuity of the communes. Nor was the ruling class slow to realise the importance of direct taxation; in Genoa about 1143 there were *collecta* on land and sea which could be imposed with the consent of the council of the *compagna*, and as early as 1162 the Pisan commune was attempting a detailed assessment of the resources in land and movable goods of each inhabitant of the city in a precocious plan for a graduated taxation system.[4] In this way the communes moved apparently without second thoughts from the consolidation of old powers to the creation of new ones.

The consuls of the Italian cities in the twelfth century staked out the widest claims for their communes; the constitutions of the communes themselves almost compelled them to take up a dynamic role in consolidating the powers which they had snatched. At the core of the commune was the oath which the members took to each other and the elected officials took to the whole body; as the terms of office were short, these oaths had to be repeated at frequent intervals, and this was felt to be a good thing in itself. At Pisa, for example, it was laid down that the oaths were to be read over in public every month. Such recitals constituted an open invitation to the making of additions and amendments, so that even the earliest extant *brevi* are complex and untidy documents, the result of a process of intense activity and development. The oaths provided a convenient repository, not simply for decisions affecting the rights and duties of officials but also for legislation of all kinds; as treaties with outside parties were normally sworn to, these, too, were frequently enshrined in the *brevi*. Moreover, the rapid changes in personnel encouraged the definition and writing down of matters which could have remained the subject of unwritten custom under a different form of government; in particular the communes demanded much more sophisticated methods of accounting for communal property and income than were necessary for a contemporary king or prince, who scarcely needed to distinguish between this private income and the finances of the state. It is hard to overestimate the importance of these tendencies in an age which regarded the making of written law as an exceptional rather a routine activity and where any kind of bureaucratic government was rare.

Reading the early records of the communes the prevailing impression is of vigorous and practical-minded leaders who responded to problems with immediate common sense, showing scant regard for theoretical considerations of any kind. The communes quickly became the guardians of the pre-existing body of local customary law; at Pisa the boundaries between the *Constitutum legis,* which related mainly to procedure and family law, and the *Constitutum usus,* which dealt with commercial customs, had already been marked out by the commune by 1160. The communes not only defined the law but added freely to it, not hesitating to override imperial prerogatives and Roman law if it seemed expedient to do so. For example, in 1135 the Piacentine commune passed a series of statutes relating to land tenure and dowries which were confirmed by oath in the general assembly of the inhabitants; later that year the public notaries of the city were made to take an oath relating to their professional conduct, though on this occasion the form of legality was preserved by the presence of a palatine count to whom the regulation of notaries pertained according to the letter of the law.[5] One imperial right which seems to have been fairly widely respected was that of minting, most communes going to the trouble to obtain authorisation before they began to issue their own coinage. On the other hand, every commune was compelled to take over rights of jurisdiction both within the city and in its territories in order to fulfil its self-appointed public functions, whether this was sanctioned by the emperor or an imperial agent or not. Consequently, the rights of every commune were threatened when Frederick I tried to reclaim the imperial *regalia* in 1158. Although both sides were often willing to compromise over details, the communes were not really secure until the emperor had been compelled to accept defeat in all but name. By the Peace of Constance of 1183, Barbarossa granted to the cities of the Lombard

League the *regalia* and *consuetudines* which they had enjoyed in the past both inside and outside the walls, whether the commune could show a specific grant or not. While many of the clauses of this peace were ineffective, this, the most important of all, was given the widest possible interpretation by Italian lawyers; it was used not only to justify the existing state of affairs, but was regarded as legitimising in advance almost any measures which the communes might choose to take.

While in the end the communes got virtually everything they wanted from the Empire, with the Church they had to constantly strive for a *modus vivendi*, as did all forms of medieval state. The relations between the communes and the local church have not been adequately studied in recent times; they were clearly very complex with many legal and social aspects, and they passed through many different phases. At first sight the most surprising feature is the degree of intervention by the secular power in church affairs in the early days of the communes. At Milan, for example, the consuls seem to have judged cases involving church property and tithes as a matter of course; at Pisa in 1162 the lay judges swore to uphold the laws of the commune against the clergy and judge according to the secular law, excepting only in cases of tithes and spiritualities.[6] How the post-Hildebrandine church came to tolerate these infringements of ecclesiastical liberty it is difficult to say; the social solidarity existing between the upper clergy and the leaders of the communes, and the political alliance against the Empire must have had something to do with it. Again, the communes had a financial power which the church could not afford to ignore; many of the great romanesque churches and cathedrals of the twelfth century were symbols of civic pride, largely built by means of grants voted for this purpose by the communes. The moral unity of local church and commune does not seem to have been generally broken until the rise of the *popolo* in the early thirteenth century; at Ferrara in 1173 it was so much regarded as a part of the eternal order of things that an extract from the consular laws was inscribed in stone and affixed in a band two feet high right across the length of the southern wall of the cathedral.[7] It is hard to imagine a more striking expression of the self-confidence of the early communes and their faith in the power of written law and bureaucracy to tame the disruptive forces at work in human society.

Another aspect of this faith can be seen in the rapid proliferation of offices by the communes. The earliest consuls were supposed to look after all the interests of the commune without exception; a model letter of about 1115 describes their duties as 'to advise justly and mercifully those who make legal complaint; to oppose those who injure others unjustly and mercifully help those who have been injured; to extend protection in all things to the poor who have been unjustly condemned and despoiled'.[8] Very soon, however, routine judicial business was handed over to separate panels of officials known as *consules de placitis* (consuls of pleas) or consuls of justice, leaving only appeals and the most important cases to be decided by the 'first' consuls. Chamberlains or treasurers, responsible for looking after the property and income of the communes, make their appearance before the mid-twelfth century, their activities fenced about by complicated regulations and checked by panels of auditors to discourage the embezzlement of the *res communis*. Another common provision was for a scribe or letter writer for official correspondence; in the twelfth century an individual might hold this office for life, but with the proliferation of the bureaucracy in the thirteenth it became normal for groups of notaries to be appointed to the various courts and offices in rotation. In addition to these essential functionaries who were to be found everywhere, the fertile minds of the administrators produced offices for lawyers, notaries or laymen, together with councils, panels and committees in seemingly endless variety to meet all kinds of particular needs of government, so that by the middle of the thirteenth century the list of officials of the average commune was extraordinarily long and complicated.

While administrative offices proliferated freely, as a rule political authority remained in the hands of a few, who in the twelfth century were almost always called the consuls; the most common number holding office at one time was, in normal circumstances, two. For about a century this arrangement represented the accepted compromise between the need for a strong executive and the rooted suspicion of unchecked power which is unmistakable in all the records of the early communes. Inevitably, some communes were led to experiment with a single executive official; the earliest examples seem to come from the year 1151, when we hear of a *dominus civitatis* at Siena, a *rector civitatis* at Verona, and a certain Guido de Sasso with the title of *rector* or *potestas* at Bologna.

It seems that these innovations arose quite independently from the local situation in each city. Guido de Sasso, for example, was a feudal landowner by origin who enjoyed the support of the leaders of the Bolognese law school, Irnerius' pupils, with whom he shared imperialist sympathies.[9] He remained in power long enough to be able to greet Frederick I in person outside the walls of Bologna in 1155. This meeting between the man who has a good claim to be considered among the first of the *podestà* (the word means 'power') and the new emperor on his first Italian expedition was a portent for the future. Among the rights claimed by Frederick at the diet of Roncaglia three years later was the appointment of civic magistrates; when, after he had destroyed Milan in 1162, the rebellious communes began to submit to him once more, Barbarossa tried to ensure their obedience by sending his own men to take charge with the title of imperial vicar or *podestà*. Not unnaturally these powerful outsiders aroused great hatred in the cities, and it was primarily against them that the communes rose and formed the Lombard League in 1167. Yet somehow, the idea of the *podestà* survived the ruin of the imperial regime which followed, and took on a new lease of life in the communal Italy which emerged strengthened at the peace of Constance. For a transitional period which lasted up to forty years, the communes experimented with native and outside *podestà*, sometimes more than one in number, reverting intermittently to the time-honoured consular regime. Finally, after about 1210, the *podestà* became a permanent institution throughout communal Italy; significantly, only in Rome and Venice did this unique and characteristic office fail to take root. In a way it was Barbarossa's most lasting legacy to his Italian lands.

The regime of the *podestà* commended itself to the leaders of the Italian communes because it afforded the possibility of reconciling their conflicting needs for an executive which would be strong yet impartial, detached from particular factions and interests within the commune yet responsive to the desires and opinions of the governing class. The method was to invite an outsider of ability and good reputation to serve for a fixed term of office, which was generally one year, with his powers and duties carefully defined and agreed beforehand. These might vary in detail, but the essence of the office was that the *podestà* was the head of the commune, the guardian of the law and the highest judge, master of the bureaucracy and chairman of the various councils, defender of the internal peace of the city and commander-in-chief in time of war. To assist him in these duties the incoming *podestà* was required to bring with him a household, including professional soldiers for police duties and a number of judges to preside at the benches where the most contentious cases were heard. When accepting the office the candidate was required to agree to the conditions of service in general terms; his first public act on entering the city was to take the oath in accordance with the *breve*, which was usually long and detailed. In return the members of the commune proffered their obedience in the *sacramentum sequimenti*.

Most of our information about the *podestà* comes from after 1250 when the hedges around their powers had grown high and thick. The meticulous regulations which went so far as to restrict the *podestà*'s social contacts with the citizens so as to prevent his being exposed to undue influences, and which levied penalties and deductions from his salary for infringements of the law and negligence in the performance of his duties, tend to make his position look weak and even ridiculous. The *sindicatus*, or detailed examination of his acts by a panel of citizens to which the *podestà* had to submit at the end of his term, could be a considerable ordeal, and there are stories of *podestà* denied their salaries, sacked without ceremony and forced to flee for their lives; some, indeed, were murdered. Yet the chronicles also record *podestà* who were bearers of peace and justice and who led armies to victory; some were commemorated in inscriptions on bridges or public buildings, a few had statues put up in their honour celebrating their achievements. And although local circumstances obviously varied greatly, there is not much doubt that, in general, the appointment of a *podestà* sprang from a desire to strengthen the machinery of government as well as increasing its impartiality. The *Oculus Pastoralis*, for example, includes the following passage in the model speech for an incoming *podestà*:

> I am not the kind of person to take insults to my face; I will not permit it, nor ought I to do so, for it is not good for the *podestà* to leave crimes unpunished. So lay this to heart: that I will punish the delinquent with such severity that the penalty of one will be a deterrent for many...[10] [See Plate IV]

Although it may be unwise to generalise, it seems likely that in many cities the establishment of the office of *podestà* represented a widening of the basis of city government and a victory over an oligarchy which had monopolised the consulate. Often it was factional strife which provided the occasion for the change of regime, the *podestà* being called in for the immediate purpose of mediating between factions.

Monarchy subject to the law was a widely held ideal of government in the twelfth and thirteenth centuries both north and south of the Alps, and the *podestà* regimes of the Italian cities represent an ingenious attempt to put the ideal into practice. It strengthened the government of the communes at a crucial moment in their development, and probably held off the emergence of the city-despots for up to half a century. Although this was not its main object, the new form of government also helped to modify the political self-sufficiency of the major communes at the very time that the inter-city leagues, born of united opposition to the Empire, were in the process of breaking up. The exchange of *podestà* was a way of expressing and cementing an alliance between communes; a city might honour a great nobleman by choosing him as its *podestà*. Very soon certain individuals built up a reputation as efficient magistrates and became more or less professional *podestà*; with the passage of time the occupation became traditional in certain families. The great majority of the early *podestà* came from landed families with some claim to nobility; the more professional among them, in particular, were often drawn from the ranks of the lesser feudal nobility of regions near the centre of communal Italy, such as the territories of Bologna, Parma, Piacenza and Cremona, where the outlets for men of this class were perhaps more restricted than in the more marginal areas. Boncompagno, with typical exaggeration, denounced the majority of the *podestà* of his day as illiterates skilled only in military matters; an exception was his friend Ugolino Gosia, grandson of Irnerius' pupil Martino, who was elected *podestà* of Ancona in 1201 when he had just graduated at Bologna and had begun to teach in the law school there. As the thirteenth century wore on, the number of legally-trained *podestà* gradually increased. A significant minority were doctors of law of Bologna or Padua, and some of them were men of mediocre or obscure background; if a man could acquire the necessary education and had ability, the career of judge and *podestà* could provide a unique road for personal advancement. Expert *podestà* and their staffs provided an obvious channel for the dissemination of ideas as they passed from commune to commune or from the law schools and universities to administrative posts and back again. The case of the jurist Giacomo Balduino, pupil of the great Bolognese doctor Azzo, who in 1239 went as *podestà* to Genoa, where he revised the local statutes and divided them into books, apparently an early example of codification, is unusual in being reported by a contemporary chronicler. The names of a number of the early thirteenth-century *podestà* of Milan are associated with various pieces of legislation, including the great work of recording the customary law of the commune which was completed in 1216.[11] Usually, however, the influence of professional advisers, and especially of outsiders like the *podestà* and his judges, was exerted behind the scenes and can only be inferred from the results. It was probably due in the main to their efforts that the institutions and practices of the Italian communes were far more standardised in 1250 than they had been in 1150.

The Triumph of the *Popolo*

The picture we have drawn of the communes advancing from strength to strength is a one-sided one, for it ignores the fact that at the same time the problems of government were increasing too and threatening to overwhelm the forces of order; indeed, the chronicles of this period record instances of cities torn by prolonged periods of civil war when society could revert to a state of virtual anarchy. Government under medieval conditions was always a precarious matter, and to some extent the problems of the communes were those inherent in all small-scale government, arising from the difficulty of divorcing public policy from private interests and personalities in a restricted arena where everyone knew too much about everyone else, resulting in a persistent tendency to faction and party strife. In addition the Italian cities faced special problems of their own, derived from the fact that the commune was originally no more than one kind of *societas* in a society which abounded in *societates*, so that it was an uphill task to assert any special claim to the loyalty and obedience of the citizens.

For example, the *consorterie*, which had existed before the communes, continued to spread and develop during the twelfth century; indeed, the best evidence for their internal organisation relates to the period between 1175 and 1300. Only the simplest *consorterie* consisted of the members of a single family; many were inter-family alliances or a leading family with its clients, and some were composed of fellow members of the same grade in the social hierarchy, such as imperial or ecclesiastical tenants-in-chief (*cattanei*) of a particular area. Their purpose was always the conservation of the persons, property and interests of the members; to do this, the corporation exercised what was, in effect, a kind of jurisdiction over them, regulating marriage and the inheritance of property and arbitrating in disputes. With the passage of time, the more ambitious of the *consorterie* evolved elaborate regulations which they did not hesitate to call statutes and ordinances, enforced by officials called consuls or rectors who were bound by an oath of office and who might receive a salary for their services. Where the members were the leading landowners in a particular area, the *consorterie* could easily acquire something like a territorial jurisdiction, as the *consortes* of Ribafatta, between Pisa and Lucca, seem to have done; if the members were of comital descent, the corporation would be entitled to exercise powers which were undoubtedly of public origin. In such cases the distinction between a powerful *consorterie* and a small commune might be a fine one. There is evidence that *consorterie* and communes might co-exist more or less peacefully in the same area, as in the small north-eastern town of Conegliano in 1218; in other cases it may be surmised that the *consorterie* succeeded in taking over the commune. This is what seems to have happened in a number of smaller towns of Piedmont and at Belluno, where, in the thirteenth century, all power was monopolised by the members of four noble clans; this phenomenon gave rise to a theory put forward in the early years of this century, according to which all communes originated as *consorterie*. This view, championed by Gabotto, has rightly been rejected by the majority of historians, but it does point to the fact that communes and *consorterie* arose from a common matrix of ideas and their paths often crossed.

The major communes of the episcopal cities probably embraced members of many *consorterie* from the start; as they expanded, they took in many more. In the very early stages there was a tendency to restrict duties and privileges to full members of the commune, but once the communes took on responsibility for defence and taxation within a given area, their original voluntary character was lost and they set out on the long road that led to the acquisition of the highest jurisdiction over every person and corporation within the city and its contado. In particular, the powers over the regulation of trade, and especially the import and export of foodstuffs, which the communes assumed at an early stage, made it impossible to accept that anyone should be allowed to stand aloof. Consequently, the major communes were committed to a programme of bringing in or subjugating every individual or community of any importance within their territory. The means employed ranged from persuasion, through bribery and purchase to terror and naked force; every local chronicle of the period is full of accounts of campaigns against recalcitrant nobles or market towns. By the early thirteenth century most communes had progressed a considerable way towards taming their contado.

The so-called conquest of the contado solved one set of problems for the communes but created others. The expansion not only increased the amount of territory and the number of persons with which they had to deal, it also added to the complexity of the society which they sought to govern. In general the communes filled in their powers over the contado in a piecemeal manner, striking individual bargains with the families or *consorterie*, minor communes or religious communities, which lay in their path. Normally an oath of obedience with a promise of taxes and military service was exacted; subject communes were compelled to receive a *podestà* nominated by the city and noble families or individuals were required to build a substantial house within the walls as a pledge of good behaviour. Rarely, if ever, did the victorious commune try to modify the structure of the groups which it brought under control; minor communes in market towns, *castelli* or rural areas retained most of their customs and rights, and great landowners kept most of their power over their tenants, whether serf or free, and often their fortresses and bands of armed retainers as well. For example, the Florentines spent many years in bitter conflict with the counts Alberti, yet when they capitulated in 1200 the commune specifically promised to support them against their debtors and feudal subordinates.[12] In fact the leaders of the communes belonged to much the same social and economic milieu as their adversaries and, therefore, lacked the will and probably also the means to effect a social revolution. Social changes, like the decline of serfdom, came about gradually as a result of economic rather than political pressures.

So it was that, as the communes grew, they did not build up a citizen body with uniform rights; instead the population of the rising city-states was divided into numerous legal and social categories. Each section with its resources of men and money and its own particular interests constituted a potential pressure group or faction. Of course the statutes and *brevi* of every commune came to include prohibitions of illicit *coniurationes*, especially any which might be formed to promote the election of particular persons to high offices; it may be doubted whether these were ever very effective. The history of the communes could hardly be other than tumultuous, for they were trying to practise government on conciliar principles in a society which remained intensely hierarchical. Moreover, they lacked a convincing rationale for their claim to loyalty and obedience, for there was no belief that the city-state embodied a way of life uniquely favoured by God or nature such as had been prevalent in Greece and Italy in ancient times. As we have seen, the lawyers were slow to forget that the powers of the communes were largely founded on usurpations; even the Peace of Constance contrived to give many privileges and liberties to the cities without once mentioning the commune by name. Moreover, if the communes took their stand on the situation *de facto*, it was hard to avoid the corollary that other *societates* had power *de facto*, too. For example, we have pointed out that Boncompagno was unusual in his forthright recognition of the legislative sovereignty of the communes. However, when discussing this point in the *Cedrus*, he admits that statutes are also made by the inhabitants of castles and *borghi*, the villagers in rural communes and noble *consorterie*. According to Boncompagno, there are even certain societies of young men, especially prevalent in Tuscany, which have their own *statuta* which are sworn to by the members.[13] This passage may serve as a reminder that, at least until the mid-fourteenth century, any idea of the sovereignty of the city-state is almost completely lacking; the provision in the *consuetudines* of Milan (1216) which declares that a vassal shall not forfeit his fief for failing to help his lord in a war against his city, because it is his *patria* for which he is obliged to fight by the *ius gentium*, rings out like a lone cry from another world.[14]

Despite these handicaps, communal government survived and evolved without revolutionary change into the early thirteenth century, finding a *modus vivendi* with those forces which it could

not entirely subdue. In the late twelfth century the guilds of capi-
talist merchants were associated with the government without
causing any fundamental rupture. However, early in the next
century the dominant classes found themselves under pressure
from a new quarter, from the newly well-to-do and the artisan
guildsmen, many of them recent immigrants from the contado, who
found that the modest activities of the trade-guilds and ward or
neighbourhood associations (vicinanze) no longer satisfied their
social and political aspirations. It seems that in some places the
governing class, however divided it may have been before, formed
a united front in the face of the new threat; the Piacentine
chronicles, in particular, present a picture of a more or less
straightforward conflict between the rich and powerful, or the
party of the knights, and the poorer but more numerous foot-
soldiers of the popolo.[15] At Milan too, the feudal tenants-in-chief
and the vavassors, the lesser knights and the merchants who had
maintained their separate identities and officials from the earliest
days of the commune, closed their ranks in the face of the popular
oragnisation which took its name, credenza di S. Ambrogio, from
the patron saint of the city; in 1202 each party elected its own
consuls and, according to the fourteenth-century chronicler, Galvano Fiamma, 'the city of Milan was divided into two cities and
two peoples', who then went on to quarrel about their shares in the
public revenues.[16] Both these stories are probably over-simplified;
it is unlikely that the popolo would have got far without the
leadership of deserters from the governing class with some experience of war and politics.

While something like straight conflicts between commune and
popolo were taking place in some cities, in others events were
taking a different course, with the popolo exploiting a split in the
governing class to emerge as a third force. A good account of a
development of this kind is to be found in the chronicle of Ezzelino and Alberico da Romano by Gerardo Maurisio. Maurisio
was a judge of Vicenza but he was no friend of the popolo; his
father had been a knight in the service of the Da Romano family,
and Gerardo's loyalty was firstly to the clan and its local allies, and
through them to the emperor Frederick II and the imperialists of
north-eastern Lombardy. Maurisio's 'chronicle' was written in
great haste in 1237 with the aim of ingratiating himself with the
leaders of the victorious party by praising the Da Romano to the

skies and drawing attention to his efforts and sufferings for their cause. The story he tells is subjective and highly partisan; its value is that it gives a picture of the rise of a *popolo* in its contemporary setting, written before the success of the new order was assured and a version of events favourable to the *popolo* had become an essential part of political orthodoxy.[17]

Maurisio takes up the thread of Vicentine affairs in 1194 when the body politic was already divided into two factions, headed by the Vivaresi clan on the one hand, and the counts of Vicenza on the other. The rules of the political game at this stage seem to have been that each party tried to trick the other into agreeing to the appointment of a *podestà* favourable to itself; when this failed the factions would each nominate their own *podestà* and the commune would be compelled to suffer the rule of two leaders, who would be unlikely to agree on any matter of importance. This state of affairs dragged on, accompanied by a good deal of legalised and illegal violence in the city and contado, until the *popolo* was driven to assert itself in 1207, calling in as *podestà* a Milanese named Guglielmo Pusterla who had held office during the ascendency of the *credenza di S. Ambrogio* in his native city three years before. This first attempt at rule by the *popolo* in Vicenza did not last long, for the next *podestà* provoked the nobility by attempting to take hostages for good behaviour from them, and he was deposed by the Vivaresi. Affairs returned to their former state for a few years, until about 1215, when what Maurisio calls a new commune was formed, inspired by hatred of the Da Romano who were supplanting the counts as the leaders of the party opposed to the Vivaresi. In 1217 this body successfully claimed a third share of all the offices in the city; since its nominees proceeded to act with the Vivaresi against the Da Romano party, Maurisio stigmatises it as an 'iniquitous and fraudulent commune', but no doubt others saw matters differently. Despite manful efforts by the Da Romano and the fighting bishop of the city, the 'false' commune prevailed, its noble leader Ugucio dei Rambertini driving out the Da Romano partisans 'even when they were plebians and *popolani*'. Periodically reformed, the 'new commune' remained in control for most of the decade which followed; in 1229 it was able to call on the help of a similar body in the nighbouring city of Verona, where the popular organisation was called the *communanza*, to depose a pro-Da Romano *podestà*. About this time, the spirit of revolt flared up among the unfree mounted soldiers (the equivalent of the German *ministeriales*), drawn from the small towns and rural estates around Bassano, who formed the fighting force or *masnada* of the Da Romano. Some of them, calling themselves 'the party of the free', went over to the enemies of the Da Romano or took refuge in the city. Although they were in control of Verona, the Da Romano party remained in a precarious position until they irrevocably threw in their lot with Frederick II in 1235. It was the storming of Vicenza by the emperor in person a year later which established the power of the Da Romano over the city which was to last without interruption until 1259.

A more detailed study of Maurisio's chronicle would reveal more fully the bitterness of party strife at this period, relieved only by occasional reconciliations, such as the one presided over by the famous Dominican Brother, John of Vicenza, in 1233; these events generated a great deal of emotion but the peace which they initiated was always short-lived. What is clear, even from a brief *resumé*, is the fact that party and class coincided only very roughly in this period when conflict seemed to revolve around the rivalry of the knights and *popolani*. In describing some of the ways in which he, as a member of the administrative class, was able to serve his noble patrons, Maurisio unconsciously reveals some of the reasons why this was so. By his own account, Maurisio went on a number of embassies for the Da Romano, and in the councils of the Vicentine commune he tried to further their interests and block the schemes of their enemies; his appointment as one of the revisers of the statutes in 1230 shows that his legal expertise was highly regarded, and he describes himself as a faithful trumpet of the party of the Da Romano and the emperor, preaching their cause as if he were a member of the Order of Preachers.

It is unfortunate that Maurisio does not tell us more about the character of the Vicentine *popolo*; the little that he says is, however, very significant. For him the *popolo* is always a kind of new or second commune, an idea echoed by Galvano Fiamma writing about a century later. All the evidence concerning the *popolo* indicates that it was a new *societas* which arose in each city alongside the commune. As a hostile witness, Maurisio displays no interest in the internal organisation of the *popolo* and his narrative throws virtually no light on this; from what is known of a number of other cities, however, it is clear that this could be a very complicated matter. This arose in the first place because many of the members of the *popolo* already belonged to other organisations, notably the artisan and trade guilds (*arti*) and the parish, ward or neighbourhood associations (*vicinanze*), so that it was natural for the *popolo* to take the form of a federation in which some of these bodies could retain their own identity. But political circumstances also had a profound effect on the structure of the association. Unlike the commune, which had to face little resistance from the pre-existing regime, the *popolo* had to assert itself in the face of the commune which, with all its shortcomings, could be a formidable adversary; hence, the apparent need in many cities for a split in the governing class before the new movement could come to the forefront of the political scene. To make headway the *popolo* was compelled to become militant, and for this purpose the *vicinanze* and the *arti* were often supplemented by a third type of organisation, more specifically directed towards self-defence and more easily mobilised for street-fighting. The earliest notice of these *società d'armi* seems to be one relating to the city of Lucca in 1197; it is possible that Boncompagno had these in mind when he referred in his *Cedrus* (written about 1216) to the societies of young men, chiefly in Tuscany, among the bodies which customarily made statutes. This suggests that the Bolognese *società d'armi* were not yet formed when he wrote; they first emerge into the light of day in 1230, some two years after the *coup d'état* which brought the Bolognese *popolo* to power.

Bologna seems to have been the key city for the development of the *popolo*. Compared with many Lombard cities the movement there was slow off the mark; after some obscure rumblings during the second decade of the thirteenth century, it was a disastrous campaign against Modena in 1228 which discredited the existing government and touched off the revolt. There is no proof that the *società d'armi* played any part in this event; only the leaders of the artisan guilds are mentioned by the chroniclers. Yet five years later, when the constituent oath of the *popolo* came to be renewed, the *armi* stood beside the *arti* under their own leaders. In the earliest general statutes of the *popolo*, which date from 1248, is found the formula that the *armi* and the *arti* are one and the same – that is, that they are politically equal in all respects and are bound by the same oath. The statutes of the *armi* make unexciting reading. They contain the oaths of members and officials, and the familiar mass of detailed regulations for the internal administration of any society or corporation of this period; only the obligation of the members to keep arms and rally to the standard-bearers when required gives any hint of their political functions.[18] The lists of members are more revealing, for they show that the *armi* were truly voluntary bodies whose membership frequently overlaps parish and neighbourhood boundaries. Two, or perhaps three, were composed of immigrants from other regions; one, that of the butchers, had a trade basis. It is a reasonable conjecture that this gave the *armi* an *ésprit de corps* difficult to develop in the other organisations of the *popolo*; fostered by common religious ceremonies, banners and insignia, it gave the *popolani* the morale necessary to stand up to the knightly élite with their military expertise and long fighting tradition.

The stiffening provided by the *armi* was particularly vital in the early, struggling days of the *popolo*; compared with the other regimes which emerged about this time, the Bolognese *primo popolo* showed a greater staying-power and stability. It was at Bologna too that the problem of providing permanent leadership for the great unwieldy body of the *popolo* was solved. The early movements of the *popolo* all seem to have been led by a single outstanding individual, such as the noble Ugucio dei Rambertini at Vicenza, Giuliano di Ranieri, the son of an innkeeper at Verona, or Urseppo dei Toschi, described as 'a great lord, although a merchant' at Bologna; behind them stand a shadowy group of guild and neighbourhood officials (sometimes called consuls), created with other aims in mind than the overall direction of the party. With the emergence of the *anziani* (ancients) at Bologna, first recorded in 1231, the *popolo* acquired permanent leaders of its own, for although they were elected by the various corporations, (the *armi* and the *arti* at Bologna, the *arti* and the quarters of the city in most other places), the *anziani* were officials of the *popolo* as a whole and not of the bodies which had elected them. The new office was inspired by the same ideals of corporate leadership as those which created the consulate in the early communes. The usual number of *anziani* in office together was twelve, and their term of service was very short, generally two or three months only. To offset this, great emphasis was placed on the collegiate nature of the office; all decisions had to be taken with the agreement of all, and it later became general practice for the *anziani* to be required to leave their homes and live a common life during their term of office in a public building set aside for the purpose.

The institution was adopted far and wide throughout communal Italy, for it met a vital need not just in the sphere of the *popolo* but for the communes as well, bridging the awkward gap between the foreign *podestà* and the various councils which had been opened by the disappearance of the political consuls. The *anziani* came to occupy a central position in the fully evolved constitutions of the communes of the later thirteenth century. It was their duty to advise the *podestà* and prepare the agenda for the councils; they sent and received all official correspondence, they appointed ambassadors, and so on. The most serious constitutional limitation on their powers was the obligation to consult with others, particularly the heads of the guilds and other corporations, about especially weighty matters. There can be no doubt that under normal conditions the most important political decisions were taken through them, and their office, therefore, becomes the most significant barometer of the political condition of any particular commune. As long as the *anziani* retained their power and freedom of action, the free commune survived; once a *signore* consolidated his control, the *anziani* became his puppets and eventually disappeared. The most long-lived of these offices was undoubtedly the Florentine priorate, established in 1282 but a functional descendant of the Bolognese innovation of fifty years before. The priorate weathered all the upheavals of the fourteenth century, acquiring in the process a considerable social as well as political prestige; in the fifteenth century the ascendancy of the Medici rested largely on their power to control the selection of the priors.

By the mid-thirteenth century the constitutional development of the *popolo* had practically run its course; significantly the Bolognese statutes of 1248 contain a prohibition of the formation of any further *societates*. There were by this time some twenty-four *società d'armi* and about twenty trade-guilds or groups of guilds with the right to participate in the election of *anziani*. The appointment of the first foreign captain of the *popolo* in 1255 provided the coping stone of the new structure. This office, which represented the final regularisation of the position of the numerous individuals who had led the *popolo* in most cities at one time or another under various titles, seems to have first appeared in

Florence in 1250. The essence of the innovation was the appointment of an outsider as the constitutional head of the *popolo* in
the same way as the *podestà* was the head of the commune. In principle, then, the powers of these two officials were parallel, with the
one presiding over the councils and supervising the administration
of the commune and the other doing the same for the *popolo*;
persons of the same class and similar qualifications, military or
legal, were generally selected to each. In practice, however, the captain's most essential function was to defend the *popolani* from the
violence and injustice of the more powerful citizens; for this
reason, in some cities, the office could be left in abeyance except at
times of tension. Where the *capitano del popolo* became a permanent element in the constitution, his duties tended to be concentrated on policing and public order; although it is never stated,
there was an underlying idea that the *podestà* and *capitano* and
their staffs would act as a check on the possible corruption or in-
efficiency of the other.

The relations between the commune and the *popolo* generally
passed through three stages. At first the *popolo* was a pressure
group alongside the commune, mainly concerned with the defence
of the persons and interests of its members. During the second
stage the *popolo* emerged as a public body, dividing power and
offices with the governing class of the commune. After this transitional phase, which was usually accompanied by instability and
violence, the *popolo* would succeed in securing the main centres
of power, establishing its ascendency over the commune without,
however, entirely transforming its constitution or, in practice,
eliminating the influence of the old ruling class. The position of
the *popolo* at the end of this evolution was that of a dominant
party within the state; although the rights of others were not
abolished, members of the *popolo* enjoyed greater rights than other
citizens. The constitutional machinery could vary greatly from one
city to another. In Florence, for example, in the later thirteenth
century the *podestà* and the *capitano* each had their own greater
and lesser councils, those of the *podestà* alone being open to non-
popolani; all these councils were, in fact, quite small, not exceeding
three hundred members, and their membership was frequently
revised by committees co-opted for the purpose. Overall direction
came from the six priors (seven after 1292) elected by the members of the upper and middle guilds on a territorial basis, who

acted in frequent consultation with the officials of the *arti maggiori* and *medie*. In the communes of Lombardy direction came from the college of *anziani*, eight, twelve or more in number, elected by the *popolo* partly on a guild basis and partly to represent the administrative quarters of the city. North of the Apennines it was also usual for the *popolo* to take over the greater council of the commune whose membership was increased considerably; by the later thirteenth century the Paduan *consiglio maggiore* had a nominal strength of a thousand, and the equivalent body at Bologna was called the council of four thousand. Assemblies of this size were not often re-made and in practice membership tended to become hereditary. One of their functions was to pass all statutes, with the result that the northern communes built up a single corpus of legislation, which was usually codified, to which the additional regulations of the *popolo* formed only a brief appendix. The Florentines, by contrast, retained two equally weighty bodies of law – the statutes of the *podestà* and the statutes of the *capitano* – until the codification of 1355.

The triumph of the *popolo*, despite many differences of detail, marked everywhere a revolution of the first magnitude in the life of the Italian cities – the only successful 'democratic' revolution in the history of the communes, involving far greater changes in the distribution of power than the rise of the communes themselves a century and a half before. Some say in the government, which under the old commune seems to have extended to some 200–300 persons at the most, was now shared by thousands; the *popolo* at Cremona in 1270, for example, numbered between 7000 and 8000; at Bologna in 1294 the books of the *armi* contained 7000 names and those of the *arti* 10,000, though, of course, there was an enormous overlap in the membership of the two groups of *societates*. For cities whose total population is unlikely to have exceeded 50,000 these figures are remarkably high; while most power was no doubt concentrated in the hands of a small élite, every member of a *societas* which elected an *anziano* or whose leaders were consulted by the *anziani*, might participate, in however small a way, in the public life of his city. It is only necessary to think of the slender opportunities for similar participation in most of the territorial kingdoms and principalities of the period to realise that, although they were small in geographical terms, the Italian city-states were large in terms of the active membership of the body politic. The problems faced by the city governments, in controlling the great urban populations of the thirteenth century and ensuring the economic and military survival of the community in a period of intense competition, were also without parallel in the medieval world. The advent of the *pòpolo* created a new approach to these problems, for although it only represented a proportion of the inhabitants – the mass of the poor and some less-esteemed trades which were not allowed to form autonomous guilds were strictly excluded – the numbers involved were great enough for even its most self-interested policies to acquire a certain public character, and there was a move towards defining many matters which had been left to custom or informal agreements in the days of the old communes. Outright innovations were few or none, but policies in almost every field were pushed forward with a new vigour.

The first pre-occupation of the new regimes was with the protection of their members and hence with the administration of justice and public order. In these fields there was a steady elaboration of the governmental machinery and a corresponding expansion in staff until, by the end of the thirteenth century, the average commune would have on its payroll a dozen or more judges, and up to fifty notaries, some knights and a body of armed security troops, not to mention a host of minor officials both in the city and spread over the contado. Government became, in a new sense, a major interest within the state; as employers of labour and collectors and spenders of money the communes far exceeded even the greatest of the banking houses of the period. Naturally, the *popolo* took a special interest in the distribution of public burdens. The idea of a direct tax related to actual property and income, the *estimo* or *libra*, was taken up and pursued energetically, both in respect of citizens and the inhabitants of the subject territory. The universal obligation to military service was rationalised, with the population placed in categories according to their means; the most wealthy were required to keep chargers and equipment to serve as cavalry, the less well-to-do were enrolled as infantry or archers, the rural poor served in the supply train. Another field in which advances were made was in the regulation of trade, the new regimes showing particular care to ensure a reliable and cheap supply of foodstuffs to the city markets.

All these changes increased the impact of government on the individual and placed a new premium on the territorial and jurisdictional solidarity of the state. This meant conflict with independent and privileged groups. For example, the rise of the *popolo* touched off a round of struggles with the church, which had achieved a remarkable solidarity with the old communes and their governing class. The points at issue were mainly connected with the church's liability to taxation and the treatment of criminals who were clergy, and it was suggested at the time, and has been since, that the new regimes were influenced by heretics or heretical ideas. Such charges are easily made but difficult to substantiate. Most of the *popolo* seem to have been orthodox in their beliefs but out of sympathy with the hierarchy of the church, whose upper ranks were closely allied with the nobility; on the other hand they favoured the new piety associated with the friars, with its emphasis on religious feeling and practical works of charity. This is proved by the popularity of the Third Orders for laymen organised by the friars. The same kind of zeal was tapped by the leaders of the church when they promoted the formation of confraternities, like the Great Company of the Virgin Mary founded in Florence in 1244, whose ostensible aim was co-operation with the Inquisitors in the suppression of heresy. By the mid-thirteenth century, the heretical churches were a declining influence, but constitutional battles with the clergy during which the populace often manifested a violent anti-clericalism, continued to break out from time to time. The outcome of these struggles was generally a concordat defining more exactly the boundary between the liberty of the church and the jurisdiction of the commune. Although this was eventually stabilised, the moral solidarity between the commune and the local church was rarely re-established; both the clergy and the laity became divided into rival factions, and the strong undertow of radical criticism of the clergy became a permanent feature of the urban scene.

The other category of the population with whom the *popolo* had great difficulty in finding a *modus vivendi* was composed of certain members of the old landowning nobility, and others whose property and wealth could give them a power over men which could make them a threat to the law. The *popolo* had initially been formed to curb the violence of the men of this class. After the party had attained power it was necessary to protect the government against infiltration by them or their minions; hence statutes were passed, for example, against the holding of offices by individuals tied by an oath of vassalage to a great noble or magnate. It is doubtful if any legislative measures could have been effective against all the many forms of patronage, but at least it might be kept within bounds. It was natural that these anti-magnatial policies should be extended to the contado, where the lesser landowners and *livellarii* were given legal protection against their greater neighbours who might try to overawe them and secure their land. Such smaller landowners might be members of the *popolo* or their kinsmen, and many of the *livellarii* held their leases from men of the same class. From this it was a short step for the *popolo* to attack the feudal jurisdictions of the nobility on which their power over great tracts of country and their inhabitants seemed to depend. On the other hand the governments of the communes were less interested in furthering the cause of the serfs, who in the more economically advanced regions, were a dying class anyway; the Bolognese statute of 1256 which abolished serfdom in the name of the natural freedom of man was somewhat exceptional. Such measures did not, of course, destroy the power of the magnates – only a revolutionary re-distribution of property could have done that – but they sometimes kept it within tolerable limits. Thus there persisted great families who could not sincerely accept the new state of affairs, and whom the *popolo* could not trust. Some of them were the descendants of nobles who had given trouble to the communes before the rise of the *popolo*, and the steps which the new regimes took against them, such as the taking of hostages or of caution money as a surety for good behaviour, were probably not new. Gradually the line against the magnates hardened; the early *matricule* of the *armi* at Bologna show, for example, that noble members were not admitted after 1274. The creation of a legal class of magnates, subject to special legal disabilities and excluded from the greater part of political life, was a striking feaure of the life of the communes in the last two decades of the thirteenth century, but it was only the completion of a process which had been set in motion by the rise of the *popolo* many years before.

Frederick II and the First Despots

CUTTING across the internal development of the communes, the second quarter of the thirteenth century saw the most determined attempt to restore imperial power in north and central Italy so as to create an Italian state comparable to the other monarchies of western Europe. The driving force sprang from the unique personality of Frederick II who, being descended from Barbarossa on his father's side and the Norman Roger II on his mother's, had managed by 1215 to make good his claim to the kingdoms of Germany and Sicily, and in 1220 was crowned emperor in Rome by Pope Honorius III.

In his self-appointed task of restoring imperial rights, Frederick II enjoyed considerable advantages over his grandfather Barbarossa, and even over his father Henry VI. While his predecessors had all been German in upbringing and outlook, Frederick was the first of the Hohenstaufen to be at home in the south. His character was formed by the Norman kingdom of Sicily where he passed his first years. This was the only part of Italy where the centralised, autocratic state of Justinian's *Corpus Iuris Civilis* had any real counterpart in contemporary reality; Frederick's high view of the imperial office – and it could scarcely have been higher – was much more deeply influenced by Roman law than his grandfather's had been. At its zenith Norman Sicily had possessed the most highly developed bureaucracy of any western kingdom, and the young Frederick, having seized on the importance of this, did not rest until he had restored the governmental machine and raised it to a new peak of efficiency. By so doing, Frederick acquired for his ambitious schemes two things which his grandfather had notably lacked, money and trained bureaucrats. By all accounts, the fiscal system of the southern kingdom under Frederick became frighteningly powerful, while the foundation of the university of Naples in 1224 provided a training centre for civil servants for the whole of Frederick's Italian territories. Germany, on the other hand, was exploited for what it could most abundantly supply, fighting men for the subjugation of communal Italy. Frederick's earlier interventions in the 1220s were tentative and quickly dropped when they encountered opposition, but his plan for the government of the north and centre of the peninsula, as it emerged after 1235, was far more sophisticated than his predecessors had been. He instituted a series of imperial vicars or captains general with very wide powers over large regions as a new administrative unit intermediate between the central government and the individual *civitates*. This attempt to create a kind of provincial government was undoubtedly a prime necessity if Italy was to be welded into a real state, and in acting as he did, Frederick showed that he had grasped the principles of practical administration.

If the Empire was much more formidable than it had been, the forces which it had to overcome were stronger too. The opposition of the communes, especially north of the Apennines, was much more radical than anything Frederick I had had to face. The papacy under Gregory IX (1227–41) and Innocent IV (1243–54) was far more intransigent and unscrupulous in promoting the anti-imperial cause than it had been under Alexander III. It could deploy wealth obtained from the taxation of the whole Catholic church and it began the struggle with its prestige riding high after the successful pontificates of Innocent III and Honorius III. Moreover, its stake in the secular government of Italy had been vastly increased by the acquisition of extensive territory in central Italy. It was Innocent III who in 1198 had taken advantage of the sudden death of Henry VI and established papal hegemony over the duchy of Spoleto and the March of Ancona, thus putting into practice, after some four and a half centuries, much of the dream embodied in the Donations of Pepin and Charlemagne. The Papal State at this period had little military significance, and Frederick was able to overrun most of it at will, but it was a sign of the papacy's commitment to preventing the domination of Italy by any power and a pledge to its allies that they would be supported to the end.

In fact the communes had enormous weaknesses which the emperor could exploit. Rivalries between cities had flourished from time immemorial and were, if anything, more bitter than ever; in addition the communes were more deeply divided internally than ever before. In countless cities and regions of Italy the first years of the thirteenth century were a time when the factions within the aristocracy hardened into parties which were to polarise their internal politics for a century and more. For example, a split within the Florentine governing class can be traced back to 1177–9 when it probably centred on the ambitions of the Uberti clan for a greater share in political power within the commune. This, however, was

largely forgotten by later generations who remembered instead
the trivial insults and follies which led Buondelmonte dei Buon-
delmonti to jilt his Amidei bride, in revenge for which he was
murdered by her kin at the head of the Ponte Vecchio on the morning of Easter Sunday 1216. A similar tale, only this time involving
the jilted suitor of a rich heiress, was told to explain the enmity
between the Camposanpiero and their allies, the Este and the Da
Romano clan, which dominated political alignments in eastern
Lombardy during the first half of the thirteenth century. By the
time of Frederick's intervention the feuds among the nobility of
the communes were deeply rooted. They had, moreover, been
further complicated by the emergence of the *popolo* as a political
force in the Lombard cities which, as it impinged on the existing
factions, gave rise to conflicts which were long drawn out and complex. The overall effect was that civic patriotism was diluted by the
spirit of party, as one *popolo* called on its neighbour for armed
help against the knightly class of its own city; even alliances between the knights of one city and the *popolo* of another are not
unknown.

Frederick's attitude to these divisions seems at first to have been
entirely opportunist; he befriended those who showed themselves
most willing to serve him. These were generally the weaker parties.
Smaller cities like Cremona, which was afraid of the expanding
power of Milan, and the nobility threatened by the rising force of
the *popolo*. The significance of the *popolo* seems to have escaped
Frederick altogether, which is remarkable considering his undoubted intelligence. His legislation for the Sicilian kingdom
shows that he saw the protection of the weaker classes, such as
peasants and women, as a part of his role; in the *Regno* too he
made great use both of the lesser nobility and the educated bourgeoisie in his administration. But in Lombardy and central Italy,
although he sometimes worked with popular parties as a matter of
expediency, Frederick shows no sign of appreciating the importance of the *popolo* or of the increasing economic resources of its
leading elements. His civil servants were drafted in from the South
and his elite troops were Germans; his centralised state, which
might have offered great opportunities both to the administrative
and commercial classes of the northern communes, instead closed
the doors of advancement to them.

By failing to build up support among the *popolani*, Frederick was left in the end at the mercy of his only real allies in northern Italy, the aristocracy. However, this class was deeply riven by long-standing private feuds, and although most noble families had a traditional loyalty to the crown, it required exceptional diplomatic skill to keep them working together for the imperial cause. In eastern Lombardy, for example, in the late 1230s Frederick managed to persuade the two rival faction leaders Azzo d'Este and Ezzelino da Romano to join his army though, far from implying a reconciliation between them, the motive of each party seems to have been to use the emperor to secure advantages over the other. Feelings ran so high that a chance encounter between troops on the road to the imperial camp threatened to become a battle until one of the leaders agreed to direct his men into the fields so as to allow the others to pass. Fears and suspicions ran rife in the imperial entourage and were hardly allayed by Frederick's practice of taking hostages from his leading supporters. According to the Paduan chronicler Rolandino, it was a gesture towards his head and neck by one of Frederick's servants which convinced Azzo d'Este that his life was in danger and induced him finally to throw in his lot with the enemies of the Hohenstaufen.[19] Frederick was forced in effect to become a party leader working through and with a network of local allies. As the emperor's indispensable lieutenant in the Venetian hinterland, Ezzelino da Romano was able in a few years to establish despotic control over Verona, Vicenza and Padua, while his brother Alberico was installed in Treviso. At Frederick's death in 1250 the Da Romano were one of the pillars of the imperialist party in Lombardy, Oberto Palavicino, whose head-quarters was at Cremona, being the other. By this time, however, these two powerful *signori* were so well established that their position was more like that of independent despots than imperial officials. How little they depended on the emperor in fact was proved by the way they both continued to prosper after Frederick's death. Though he lost Padua in 1256, Ezzelino seemed about to recoup himself by occupying Milan when he was unexpectedly defeated and captured in 1259; Oberto's state passed through many vicissitudes but was not finally broken until 1266.

The only lasting effect of Frederick's policies on communal Italy was an increase in party strife and the spread of the first wave of city despots. The latter was in part the result of deliberate policy; the Sicilian autocrat preferred to act through a handful of his own nominees rather than deal with the corporate leadership of the communes. Palavicino became the imperial vicar-general for Lombardy below the river Lambro, and generally held the office of *podestà* in the cities he controlled, though he also took the title of 'perpetual lord'; Ezzelino frequently held no office at all but his word was law. He enforced his will by sheer terror, particularly on the recalcitrant Paduans. However, this kind of uncontrolled power which was so contrary to the ideology of the communes was, in fact, born of the necessities of bitter party strife and would have come to the fore anyway, without the help of imperial legitimisation. This is shown by the success of Ezzelino's rival Azzo d'Este, who in 1240 seized Ferrara and established a lordship (*signoria*) there very similar in style to those of Palavicino; Azzo not only succeeded in holding the city for his lifetime, but alone among these early *signori* he was able to build up a party strong enough to make it possible for his dominion to pass to his heirs.

Thus city despotisms did not die out after Frederick's time; indeed, they were destined to increase until they superseded the free commune almost everywhere. The nature of the *signorie* will be discussed more fully in the next chapter. Here it remains only to underline that Frederick's death, despite appearances to the contrary, brought no major change in the Italian political scene. His grandiose plan for an Italian state had been broken into fragments by the persistent opposition of the communes and the Holy See; the imperialist *signori* and party could continue without him. Yet the dream or nightmare that the Hohenstaufen might extend their power from its base in the Regno, so as to take in at least the Papal States and Tuscany, persisted throughout the lifetime of Frederick's sons and only faded when the kingdom of Sicily passed by conquest into other hands in 1266. The arrival of Charles of Anjou in the south and his victories over Manfred and Conradin in 1266 and 1268 opened a new stage in the political history of Italy, whose main characteristics are the subject of the next chapter.

5. Politics in the Age of Dante

The Papacy and the Eclipse of the Empire

DANTE ALIGHIERI was born in Florence in 1265 and died at Ravenna in 1321. The greatest poet not only of communal Italy but of the whole of the Middle Ages, his lifetime is generally considered to have coincided with the golden age of the Italian medieval city. Because of this, and because the historian's source materials for this time are usually near the golden mean between the scarcity of the earlier and the daunting fullness of the later periods, the age of Dante has been much studied. There exists a fair number of up-to-date books on particular cities or regions in English as well as in Italian and other languages, so that it is comparatively easy to find information about the internal developments within the various states. It is much more difficult to form an accurate idea of the general political atmosphere and the currents which affected the policies of the cities in their relations with their neighbours and the outside world. The period of the eclipse of the Empire beginning in 1250, or more accurately in 1266–8, is usually regarded as one of extreme political decentralisation in Italy, and indeed, the wealth and freedom of the communes after the elimination of the Hohenstaufen threat allowed them to express their cultural and political individuality to the full. Yet the very lack of external pressure brought the communes into direct and closer contact with each other and permitted the maturing of purely Italian notions of the theory and practice of political life. The aim of this chapter will be to sketch in the political setting and explain the terms in which contemporaries framed their political actions, before going on to look more briefly at the internal changes within the individual communes.

Dante aptly described the Italy of his day as 'a ship without a pilot in the great tempest'. Insofar as there was any hand on the helm, it was that of the papacy. Papal influence on Italian politics no longer rested to any great extent on moral leadership or spiritual powers. Interdict and excommunication, their force already much weakened by over-use against the Emperor Frederick and his followers, came to be regarded very largely as routine diplomatic weapons not only by their actual or potential victims but even by some of the popes themselves. The power to preach the crusade was a rapidly wasting asset both inside Italy and outside. Innocent IV's crusades against Frederick and the tyrannical Ezzelino da Romano had some moral justification and brought some response, but Martin IV's crusade against Aragon (1283) or Boniface VIII's against the Colonna family (1297) were all too obviously dictated by purely political considerations, so that such crusading idealism as still existed became increasingly estranged from the papacy. On the other hand the papacy was not yet the considerable military power which it became in the fourteenth and fifteenth centuries; papal armies were still too indisciplined and badly led to be effective in more than local campaigns, and the popes could do little without secular champions whose interests coincided with their own. Again, although it was in this period that the popes began to claim and exercise imperial prerogatives, such as the appointment of imperial vicars while the empire was vacant or contested, these acts only gave a justification in law to powers which already rested on another basis. The real foundation of papal political influence was financial – the power to channel the ecclesiastical taxation of the whole of Christendom and to raise funds on the security of its unparalleled assets in land, taxation and treasure. Supplementary to this was the patronage exercised through the greatly increased use of papal provisions, through which friends could be made or services rewarded by the gift of offices in the church throughout the Catholic world. In addition, at a time when the Italian states were small and powerless to protect their citizens' interests far from home, the papacy's unique European standing and its contacts throughout the Christian world were invaluable to the Italian merchants and financiers whose affairs extended far beyond the boundaries of their own communes. In the first half of the thirteenth century papal patronage had helped Italian merchants to penetrate into nearly every region of Christendom; during the second half the papacy systematically exacted a political price for its continued custom and support, and those who enjoyed the privileges of papal bankers were expected to do all they could to further the current policies of the Holy See. Finally, this period saw a considerable increase in the size and importance of the Papal States, and although they remained throughout a ramshackle confederation of independent communes rather than a state, their central position within Italy meant that the effects of papal policies were more readily felt in all parts of the country than would otherwise have been the case. The Papal States were beginning to assume the role of political barometer of Italy which they held in the later fourteenth and fifteenth centuries.

Taken together, the assets which the papacy could convert into political influence were very considerable, though if they were exploited too openly they were liable to produce an adverse reaction, particularly among the larger states outside Italy. Other circumstances, moreover, militated against the papacy following a single clear-cut policy in temporal affairs. The later thirteenth century was a period of short pontificates and some extraordinarily long conclaves; between 1254 and 1294 the average reign was less than three and a half years, and the vacancy on the death of Clement IV dragged on for nearly as long. This situation naturally strengthened the position of the College of Cardinals, and some of the cardinals were long-lived men with strong political views who were powerful enough to pursue their own policies, whether these coincided with those of the reigning pope or not. The political aims of the papacy remained the same as ever: namely, to preserve its freedom of action by maintaining a balance of power, especially in central Italy, while building up the Papal States as a safety zone in which the Pope could live secure from the dangers of sudden attack. But in the fluid conditions of the later thirteenth century it was no easy matter to determine where the greatest danger to papal freedom lay, whether it was the vast but distant power of France, the largely theoretical threat of an imperial claimant, or the immediate menace nearer home raised by the Tuscan imperialists or a great family of the Roman contado, like the Colonna. In these circumstances papal policies tended to oscillate and their contradictory impulses helped to keep the Italian political scene in a characteristic state of ferment. A rapid succession of papal helmsmen struggled with a broken rudder to bring the ship, by a series of tacks, into a haven of tranquillity which was further away at the end of the century than at the death of the imperial anti-christ Frederick of Hohenstaufen in 1250.

It is commonly stated that after Frederick's death, the papacy worked consistently for the utter extirpation of the vipers' blood of the Hohenstaufen which was finally achieved eighteen years later, but this attractive legend is a rationalisation after the event. In fact, the papal aim was not to destroy the Hohenstaufen but to ensure the separation of the kingdom of Sicily and the Empire, and the disappearance of the distrusted Frederick opened the possibility of negotiation along these lines with his heirs. Both Innocent IV (1243–54) and his successor Alexander IV (1254–61) were reluctant to break with the Hohenstaufen, and even the papal grant of Sicily to the English king, Henry III, for his son Edmund in 1254 was regarded by both sides as no more than a working agreement which might be cancelled or amended subject to suitable compensation. While it is hard to believe that the legitimate heir, Conrad IV, would ever have sincerely agreed to the division of his inheritance, his premature death in 1254 created the possibility that Frederick's illegitimate son Manfred would be content to rule in Sicily with papal blessing, leaving Conrad's infant son in far-away Germany. Both Alexander IV and Manfred shrank from making irrevocable decisions and waited on events, and in the end it was Manfred's Tuscan allies who upset the balance by winning an unexpectedly crushing victory over the Florentines at Montaperti in September 1260, which delivered the whole of Tuscany except Lucca into Manfred's hands. Rome and the greater part of the Papal States dropped into his lap, and Manfred found himself, almost unawares, stepping into the role left vacant by his father ten years before.

The Conclave which met in the summer of 1261 reacted to this crisis by electing a Frenchman, Jacques Pantaleon, Patriarch of Jerusalem, who was uncommitted to any of the Italian parties. Regarded by a contemporary as the most authoritarian pope since Alexander III, who had sustained the Lombard communes against Barbarossa nearly a century before, Urban IV made the decisions which his predecessor had postponed for years. It was natural that he should take a firm stand against Manfred's encroachments in the Papal States and that he should link up with Manfred's enemies in Tuscany, but Urban also developed a new weapon to bring the Tuscan bankers to his side. By threatening to forbid their creditors to pay Urban presented first the Siennese and then the Florentine bankers with a stark choice between their cities and their financial interests; many chose to go into exile and those who were reconciled to the Holy See were taken under the special protection of the pope. At the same time Urban broke off the fruitless negotiations with Henry III of England, whose troubles with his barons made it clear that he would never be able to give his son's claim to Sicily adequate backing, and transferred the grant of the kingdom to Louis IX of France's younger brother, Charles of Anjou. Charles was an ambitious and experienced soldier and administrator who already held Maine and Provence as well as Anjou; he belonged to the greatest royal house in Europe and enjoyed the qualified support of his brother Louis IX, who was willing to allow the French church to be taxed to finance his brother's enterprise. Charles' expedition was as much a financial as a military operation. Only a part of his army marched from the north; the rest was hired in Italy on funds collected in France or by loans provided by Tuscan bankers on the surety of church property. By these means the papacy became entirely committed to his cause. On the army which Charles led out of Rome in January 1266 depended the fortunes not only of the Holy See but also of the greatest Tuscan banking houses. His early and decisive victory at Benevento, where Manfred was killed, ensured that they had made a sound investment.

Pope Urban did not live to see the fruition of his policies at Benevento, but the decisions of his short pontificate left their mark for well over a century. Charles' conquest of the Regno was sealed in 1268 with his second great victory at Tagliacozzo, which led to the capture and death of the young Conradin and the extinction of the male line of the Hohenstaufen. The South passed into the hands of another foreign dynasty and its supporting aristocracy, but the Angevins were followed by a wave of Tuscan merchants and financiers who were their creditors, and who quickly established a dominant position in the trade and banking affairs of the kingdom. Venice and the great cities of Tuscany were the obvious markets for southern agricultural produce, and the export trade now passed almost entirely into foreign hands; the economic subjection of the South to central and northern Italy was firmly established. The Neapolitan Angevins took on the Mediterranean policies which the Norman and German dynasties had followed before them. Charles came near to realising his ambition to recover the Latin Empire of Constantinople and to dominate the eastern Mediterranean. But he did not turn his back on France and drew from his possessions there, particularly Provence, money and men to administer his newly conquered kingdom. The main line of communication was by sea, but northern and central Italy had a certain importance for Charles, especially the sea power of Genoa, and Piedmont in the north west, where he had accepted the lordship of a number of towns before his conquest of Naples. During the scare created by Conradin's intervention, Charles was given the nominal lordship of a large number of Lombard and Tuscan cities, and was appointed Imperial Vicar of Tuscany by the frightened pope, but after Tagliacozzo the Lombard cities drifted away, and although Charles retained the senatorship and effective control of Rome, his position in Tuscany was essentially defensive. The central link in what it is convenient to call the Guelph axis was held in place by the financial interests in the Regno and France of the Tuscan merchants, among whom the Florentines came to occupy the leading place. The banners of the Guelph alliance were loyalty to the Church and the house of St Louis, but it was its underpinning of solid financial interest which made it the most stable feature of the Italian political scene in the turbulent years which followed.

The most uneasy member of the Guelph alliance was, in fact, the papacy. After Tagliacozzo, it looked as if the popes had destroyed the Hohenstaufen only to put the Capetians in their place. True, Charles' renunciation of any claim to the Western Empire was apparently sincere, and while St Louis lived there was nothing to fear from France, but the enormous power held by a single family constituted a potential danger. The first pope to react to this situation was Gregory X, elected in 1271, who laid down the lines of an alternative, moderately anti-French policy, which was followed and developed by a number of his successors. Its main feature was to promote the election of a German Emperor, who would provide a centre of resistance to France in northern Europe and imperial Italy. At the same time, Angevin power was to be eased out of Tuscany and Rome and contained within the frontiers of the Regno. The central space, thus cleared of outside influences, was to be held in tranquillity partly within a strengthened and enlarged papal state, and partly through an equitable division of power between the parties in each commune, initiated by papal mediation and enforced by papal sanctions. In pursuance of this plan Gregory X secured the election of Rudolph of Habsburg in 1273, from whom he obtained the promise of the cession of the Romagna. This was finally carried through in 1278 by Nicholas III, who may also have planned to create some kind of

north Italian kingdom in favour of his kinsmen at the expense of
the Empire, though nothing came of this. The reconciliations
between parties sponsored by these two popes, though they rarely
achieved lasting success, had some effect on the central Italian
communes, particularly Florence and Bologna. The most difficult
part of the programme proved to be the internal strengthening of
the Papal States, for it seemed that this could only be achieved by
reliance on members of the pope's own family, so that under
Nicholas III the Orsini, under Nicholas IV the Colonna, and
under Boniface VIII the Caetani were raised to positions of
authority in the Romagna and elsewhere in the Papal States. This
policy was not only largely self-defeating, as each successive pope
struggled to uproot the relatives of his predecessors and replace
them with his own, but it also produced a hostile reaction among
contemporaries, to whom this seemed to involve the papacy in
simony and nepotism on a new scale. It was not the existence of the
Papal State but the methods used to govern it which gave scandal;
thus Dante chose Nicholas III as the spokesman of the simoniacs
in the eighth circle of the *Inferno*.

The popes of the last decades of the thirteenth century were
thus by no means all the staunchest supporters of the Guelph alliance, and some seemed to contemporaries to be neutral or even to
favour the imperialists. But notwithstanding the stories which
circulated after the event, the papacy almost certainly had nothing
to do with the blow which effectively clipped the wings of the
Angevins. In March 1282 a spontaneous popular uprising against
the French in Palermo set off a long-prepared revolt led by the
native Sicilian aristocracy which enjoyed the support of Charles
of Anjou's Mediterranean rivals, the Emperor Michael Palaeolo-
gus of Constantinople and King Peter of Aragon. Within a short
time the whole island of Sicily was lost to the Angevins, and Peter,
who had assembled his forces under the pretence of a crusading
expedition, entered into possession. For the next twenty years the
Angevins were tied down by fruitless efforts to drive the Aragonese
out of Sicily, and their interest and influence in north and central
Italy declined accordingly. This really saved the papal alliance, for
the papacy had now nothing to fear from the house of Anjou. The
Aragonese were unacceptable to the popes, for they had seized a
papal fief, and besides, Peter's wife Constance, who claimed to be
queen of Sicily by hereditary right, was a daughter of Manfred.

So the popes expended much time and money, and sacrificed much
of their credibility as the impartial arbitrators of Christendom, in
backing a series of unsuccessful attempts to restore the integrity of
the Regno.

The pontificate of Boniface VIII (1294–1303) marks the culmination of this phase of papal history. A very able lawyer, with
the highest possible view of the dignity of his office, Boniface,
where his immediate interests were not involved, could seek to
play a balancing and mediatory role, as between Edward I of England and Philip IV of France. But nearer home, his policies were
often ruthlessly partisan. Here his main political concern was to
place as much power as possible in the hands of his own family, a
task made more difficult by the fact that the Caetani did not belong to the first rank among the clans of the Roman Campagna. To
further his family Boniface used and abused the powers of his
office to an extent unsurpassed even by the most worldly popes of
the Renaissance. Boniface never seems to have questioned the
obligation to recover Sicily, and when a negotiated settlement
broke down, he backed a new French intervention led by Philip
IV's brother, Charles of Valois, whom he sent in vain not only to
conquer Sicily but also to 'pacify' Tuscany. Boniface's policies in
Tuscany were menacing because he had approached the weak imperial claimant, Albert of Habsburg, with a view to securing the
cession of the province to the direct rule of the Church; it seemed
possible that before long, Tuscany would join the Romagna among
the provinces of the Papal States. In the end, it was not his more
dubious ambitions, but a dispute with the king of France over
clerical privileges, which precipitated the pope's downfall; Boniface had made so many enemies that there were many ready to help
Philip IV's minister Nogaret seize the person of the pope at Anagni
on 7 September 1303. The scandal of Anagni did not prove that
the papal position in Italy had become untenable, but it did show
that, after more than a century of effort, the temporal power could
not ensure the safety of even an indigenous pope in his own native
city. The conclusion that the Church might be governed more
safely from elsewhere was drawn by the Gascon Clement V, who
remained in southern France; his successor John XXII fixed the
papal residence at Avignon, where it was to remain, with only one
brief return to Rome, until 1377.

The Age of the Guelphs and the Ghibellines

There is no great mystery about the Guelphs and the Ghibellines. Anyone with any knowledge of political parties will know that they are rarely monolithic structures whose members are united behind their declared ideals; more commonly they resemble makeshift alliances of heterogeneous groups, and their slogans and actual policies are often very different. As we shall see, the Guelphs and Ghibellines differed in many respects from modern political parties, the most important being that they operated not within a single sovereign state but in and among a multitude of semi-autonomous city-states and signorie, so that in some ways they resembled an international alliance like NATO more than the modern Conservative and Labour or Republican and Democratic parties. As is well known, in their early days the Guelphs and the Ghibellines were regarded as the supporters of the papacy and the empire respectively, and these associations lingered in their ideology until the end; they become significant precisely at the moment when they cease to be synonymous with the church and imperialist parties and take on a life of their own, creating institutions and inspiring loyalties which permeate the political life of late thirteenth- and early fourteenth-century Italy.

As we have already seen, the factions which divided the governing classes of every Italian city in the thirteenth century were traced by contemporaries to disputes between leading families which had crystallised within a decade or so of 1200. Originating among the ruling aristocracy, these factions had entangled the *popolo* as this class grasped its share of political rights. The names Guelph and Ghibelline must have first gained currency between 1198 and 1218, during the rivalry between Otto of Brunswick, whose family name was Welf, and Philip and Frederick of Hohenstaufen, the name of whose castle of Waiblingen appears to have been used as a battle-cry. At first they seem to have taken root only in Florence, but during the sharp conflicts between the papacy and Frederick II in the last decade or so of his reign, the terms spread slowly outwards from Tuscany, and it was during this period that they became identified with the papal and imperial parties respectively. After the death of Frederick and the extermination of the Hohenstaufen, the names, at least, held their ground; they were well-known in Bologna in the 1270s and to Salimbene of Parma in the 1280s, but their currency did not yet extend to Milan, where the battle of Desio in 1277 was described by contemporaries as a defeat of the party of the Della Torre by the party of the nobles, led by Visconti.[1] This survival is remarkable in view of the break-up of Frederick's party in Lombardy after his death, and the creation of a number of cross-party alliances seeking to promote Manfred's reconciliation to the Church; the appeal of the Tuscan Guelphs to Conradin after Montaperti, to the legitimate Hohenstaufen against the illegitimate, is even harder to reconcile with the official ideology of the parties. After 1273 theory and fact were forced even further apart by the existence of a line of imperial claimants who, so far from being the enemies of the papacy, were actually the creatures and allies of the pope, and in this period the first ambassadors of a king of the Romans, with papal support, came to embarrass the ruling Guelphs of Italy, who saw no reason to surrender any real power to a figure so distant and powerless. Clearly the Guelph and Ghibelline parties now had a life of their own quite independent of papal and imperial leadership, and their identity was firmly enough established to be unshaken by an increasingly obvious divergence between their supposed foundations and their actual practice. Contemporaries sensed that Guelph and Ghibelline were no longer simply descriptive terms but had a force of their own; the southern chronicler, Saba Malispina, imagined them as demons and the poet Geri d'Arezzo berated his fellow citizens, calling them worse than pagans in their idolatry of these names.[2]

The terms Guelph and Ghibelline flourished on account of their function in defining inter-city relations; everywhere except Florence the local parties had their own local names. They were spread almost certainly in the first place by groups of exiles in search of hospitality and support; the Florentine Ghibellines between 1250 and 1260, and the Guelphs after Montaperti, were homeless and disinherited wanderers seeking to work with other parties with whom they had little or nothing in common except hostility to the government of Florence. The Guelphs, for example, were driven from their first refuge at Lucca and settled in Bologna, where they helped the commune to install a friendly government at Modena; many of them took service with Charles of Anjou's armies before Benevento. With their return to Florence in 1267, the Tuscan political scene settled down to a fairly stable balance between Guelph Florence, with her ally Lucca and the Ghibellines of Pisa, Siena and Arezzo. Both opposing leagues were bound together by treaties which defined exactly the forces to be provided for the service of the alliance by each member; the *tallia*, as each came to be known from the tally of knights which was their characteristic provision, became the prime embodiment of the parties in Tuscany. Charles of Anjou was naturally the nominal head of the Guelph *tallia*, which tended to supplement local forces with French mercenaries; the Ghibellines, on the other hand, enlisted Germans and later Catalans. Both sides, of course, gave employment to the exiles of the other and fostered dissidents within their rivals' territories; the Florentine Ghibelline Ubaldini clan, for example, had close links across the Apennines with the enemies of papal authority in the Romagna.

Outside Tuscany and the Romagna the system was not generally so well-defined, but most local factions went under the banner of one party or the other so far as their external relations went. The terms defined where exiles could expect to find refuge and even a second citizenship; they also regulated the movements of the small but influential band of itinerant officials, podestà, captains and judges and their staffs, for, generally, foreign officers were chosen only from cities and families belonging to the party in favour. One aspect of the Tuscan parties seems to have spread much less widely than the names. This was their corporate aspect, which seems to have been present in Tuscany from an early stage. There are references to the captains of the Florentine *parte Guelfa* going back to the 1240s, and this implies the existence of councils and possibly of common funds and treasurers, for which there is certain evidence at a later date. In fact, the Tuscan *parti* were yet another instance of the medieval Italian *societas* formed in the same mould as the commune and the *popolo*. Like the early communes, the *parti* could be mobile, retaining their officials, councils and corporate identity as they migrated from place to place. In exile they operated as mercenary bands and political pressure groups, making war and signing treaties, but when they gained the upper hand in their native city, it was easy and natural for them to take over effective control of the commune in much the same way as the *popolo* had done before them. Thus, from 1267 to 1280, the Florentine commune was in the grip of the *Parte Guelfa*, whose captain and council formed an integral part of the government. At Parma from 1266 to 1303 the commune was controlled by the Society of the Cross, which had emerged during the coup in which pro-Angevin forces had expelled Oberto Palavicino; this became a mass movement and enlistment in the books of the society became necessary for the enjoyment of full political rights.[3] Guelph societies of this kind seem to have proliferated, especially in central Lombardy, under papal and Angevin patronage around the time of Benevento; Bologna had both a *parte Guelfa* and a more extremist Society of the Cross which had to be curbed by Nicholas III's legate Cardinal Latino in 1280. Further north the parties were generally less formally organised, though they were not necessarily any less influential on this account. When the Veronese statutes of 1276 laid down that the General Council of the commune was to be composed of five hundred citizens 'of this party ruling Verona', they gave no further definition, but contemporaries must have understood well enough what was meant.[4]

If more of the internal records of these political societies had survived, it would be possible to speak more generally of their character and methods, and how these changed when they passed from being voluntary pressure-groups to mass organisations to which all citizens were expected to belong. In Florence it is possible to observe part of the reverse process by which the *Parte Guelfa*, having dominated the commune up to 1280, thereafter continued as a private corporation to exert great influence in the city. To a large extent this was done through the financial power of the *Parte*, into whose hands the property of the exiled Ghibellines had passed in 1266–7. When the *Parte Guelfa* ceased to form a part of the constitution of the commune in 1280 it was allowed to retain its property. The records of the *Parte* show that loans to the commune, which had been considerable before 1280, continued to be made, presumably on condition that the policies pursued by the priors met the approval of the captains of the *Parte*. A memorandum, which states that in March 1288 the commune and *popolo* were in debt to the *Parte* for the sum of 13,000 gold florins, for which the *gabelles* on wine and other commodities had been pledged, suggests that the party was promoting war against the Tuscan Ghibellines which brought the victory of Campaldino in the following year.[5] The leadership of the *parte* was predominantly aristocratic, so that it is not surprising to find the radical reformer

Giano della Bella including the nationalisation of the party's property in his programme when he came to power in 1293. However, Giano fell before this measure could be put into effect, and the *Parte* went on into the fourteenth century to become the censor and guardian of political orthodoxy in Florence, striving, with a considerable degree of success, to keep the commune faithful to the Holy Church and to the house of France, the touchstones of the traditional Guelph creed.

For a time, the Guelph–Ghibelline terminology enabled Italians to conceptualise realistically enough the chequer-board pattern of political alignments among the cities, which, with the disappearance of other forces, now dominated the scene in northern and central Italy. But in the last years of the thirteenth century there were signs that the terms had outlived their usefulness. In southern and eastern Lombardy, for example, a bloc of cities including Parma, Bologna, Modena, Ferrara and Padua, had come into existence, whose governments all professed the Guelph allegiance; the inevitable inter-city rivalries in this area could only take the form of conflict between Guelphs. In 1289 the lord of Ferrara Obizzo II d'Este, the head of a family considered to be the pillar of the church party in the area, formed an open alliance with the Ghibelline Alberto della Scala of Verona against his Guelph neighbours, and thereafter the traditional parties had little or no relevance to inter-city relations in this region. In 1308 a further blow was dealt to traditional ideas when Clement V took advantage of a dispute among Obizzo's heirs and asserted the dormant papal claim to direct rule in Ferrara. This began a struggle between the papacy and the Estensi over Ferrara which divided the Guelphs of the whole region and was not finally settled until 1332. In the Romagna, on the other hand, Guelph continued to serve well enough to denote those who supported the papal government of the region or had found a *modus vivendi* with it; the opponents of the papal rectors continued to be known as Ghibellines.

In Tuscany, where papal temporal power was near enough to be felt, but was not as directly active as in the Romagna, there was a split within the Guelph party of some ideological significance. The names of the Blacks and the Whites may have originated in Pistoia, but they became attached to factions in Florence which were defined through a series of family feuds between 1295 and 1300. The rivalry between the leaders, Corso Donati of the Blacks and Vieri dei Cerchi of the Whites, was largely personal, but among their followers there were significant differences of opinion and interests. The Blacks adhered to the uncompromising Guelphism represented by the house of Anjou and such popes as Urban IV and Martin IV, and the party included a strong group of merchants and bankers with financial interests in the Regno and France. The Whites, on the other hand, attracted new men no longer dominated by memories of Montaperti and Benevento, and some of them had significant interests outside the territories of the Guelph axis, at Pisa or in Ghibelline Romagna, through which lay the shortest route to Venice.

The party conflict for control of the Florentine commune came to a head during the pontificate of Boniface VIII, who was prepared to support the Blacks by all the considerable means at his disposal. The fear that a Florence ruled by the Whites might harbour his arch-enemies, the Colonna, was probably uppermost in his mind, but Boniface must also have been thinking of probable White reactions to his project to incorporate Tuscany within the Papal States. His first move was to summon Vieri dei Cerchi to an interview, in the belief that no banker with international business on a large scale would risk the displeasure of the pope. When this failed, Boniface sent a legate as mediator to Florence in the summer of 1301, but the Whites who controlled the commune refused to accept his mediation. Boniface then played his final card and sent Charles of Valois, younger brother of Philip IV of France, to 'pacify' the city. This new Capetian was no king but a knave, but in Florence he proved to be the knave of trumps and this was sufficient to take the trick for Boniface. The White government, despite well-justified misgivings, could not bring itself to break with the Guelph tradition to the point of shutting the gates in the face of a representative of the house of France; once in the city, Charles' presence rendered the authorities powerless while the Blacks took up arms and drove out the leaders of the opposing party. They followed up their initial victories with the proscription of large numbers of their enemies.

In exile the Whites soon made common cause with the Ghibellines and were gradually assimilated to them, obscuring the fact that White policies were originally a valid form of moderate Guelphism, broadly consistent with the aims of popes like Gregory X and Nicholas III. Dante, from being an unimportant member

of the party when it was in power, might have become the spokesman of the exiled Whites; but he never made this point clearly,
probably because he was becoming absorbed in his own highly intellectual brand of imperialism. However, the extraordinary personal animus which he bore against Boniface VIII shows that he
was aware that his party had been unusually unfortunate in the
pope with whom they had had to deal. Boniface's successor, the
short-lived Benedict XI, was, by contrast, sympathetic to the
Whites, and sent Cardinal Nicholas of Prato to Tuscany to do what
he could to help them and secure peace. The refusal of the Blacks
at this stage to consider any compromise, or to raise the siege of the
White stronghold of Pistoia at Nicholas' request, proves that when
their vital interests were concerned, the Blacks felt no higher sense
of obligation to obey the particular commands of the Holy See
than any other party of the time.

In the autumn of 1310 the rulers of Italy were faced with the
necessity of defining their attitude to the king of the Romans,
Henry of Luxemburg, who had annouced his intention of coming into Italy to be crowned emperor by the pope's representatives
in Rome. Henry was the fourth of the line of imperial claimants
with papal support which had begun with Rudolph of Habsburg,
but the first to make a personal appearance in Italy; he came with
papal blessing and insisted that he would not favour any party, but
would promote justice impartially and institute a reign of harmony and peace. It was obvious that he would be welcomed by
avowed Ghibellines, especially the exiles, but his arrival presented
a difficult choice to the Guelphs and many, like the commonwealth
of Padua and Riccardo da Camino, lord of Treviso, resolved to
recognise him and co-operate, provided he did not make too
severe demands upon them. But there were many, particularly in
central Lombardy, who were uncertain where they stood: lords
from families with Ghibelline traditions ruling over cities whose
political alignment was regarded as Guelph, like Filippo Langosco of Pavia; or Guelph nobles who had seized power at the
expense of the Church party and were ruling with the support of
neutrals or Ghibellines, like Ghiberto da Correggio of Parma. The
greatest lord of northern Italy, Guido della Torre of Milan, was
quite unable to decide whether Henry should be welcomed or resisted, and the Emperor-Elect was swept forward on a tide of accept-
ance which, in fact, concealed many insincere and ambivalent

attitudes. Even Charles of Anjou's grandson, King Robert of Naples, played for time, but after some debate the government of Florence, which was firmly in the hands of the Blacks, decided that no emperor could be good for the Guelph cause, and refused to send representatives to Henry's coronation as King of Lombardy in Milan in January 1311. The Luxemburger's action in repatriating exiles, who were mostly Ghibellines, to the cities which accepted him, aroused the Florentine's worst suspicions, which were confirmed when Henry's troops became involved in a battle with the Della Torre party in Milan in February 1311. From this moment the Florentine *signoria* opposed the King of the Romans with all its power, not hesitating to teach the Pope his duty to protect the Guelphs and prodding Robert into the role of party leader which was his by tradition. Gradually all those who were dissatisfied with what Henry had done or failed to do, fell into line behind the Florentines and raised a sporadic opposition which delayed the imperial coronation until August 1312. The new Emperor's fund of money, men and goodwill was now almost exhausted; after wasting the autumn in a desultory siege of Florence, Henry scraped together new forces and was leading them against Robert of Naples, whose opposition had finally been unmasked, when he died of fever near Siena in the summer of 1313.

By his premature death Henry of Luxemburg just avoided an open breach with the Pope, but Clement V condemned his political acts afterwards, for he was under irresistible French and Angevin pressure and had come to realise that even as just a man as Henry would be a danger to the papacy in Italy if he was too successful. This experience did not, however, bring the idea of an imperial champion for the papal cause into disrepute, and the role was handed on in the Luxemburg family for the duration of the fourteenth century. Ironically Henry VII's intervention in Italy served to revive the Guelph and Ghibelline parties which he detested and sought to eradicate for ever; the conflicts stirred up by his death gave the well-worn names an emotional content which carried them forward a century and more, long after any relationship to their original meaning had been completely overlaid.

It should now be clear that, even in their heyday, the Guelphs and the Ghibellines were far from being organised parties solidly under the control of their nominal leaders, the Pope and the Emperor; they were, rather, a loose chain of local factions, co-operat-

ing up to a point under a convenient banner. Guelphs frequently
defied the Pope, and Ghibellines often were entirely out of contact with the nominal imperial claimant. Until the time of Lewis
of Bavaria and John XXII, the connection between Ghibellinism
and doctrinal heresy was minimal and many Ghibelline rulers
followed Frederick II in persecuting religious dissent; just as Ghibellines accepted the Church, so Guelphs normally did not reject
the Empire in theory, though they might reduce its practical claims
to a minimum. Above all, Guelph governments often ran into
violent disputes with the local church which frequently involved
them in papal interdicts and excommunication; prelates were
often drawn from aristocratic families with Ghibelline traditions
so that cardinals, and even popes, could be accused of Ghibelline
sympathies. Yet with all these limitations, the terms did stand for
something, and it is impossible to give a true picture of the politics
of Dante's lifetime without some attempt to elucidate their meaning.

Until the end of the last century it was common for historians
to draw a social contrast between the Guelphs and the Ghibellines.
The typical Ghibelline was seen as a member of the feudal nobility, addicted to war, while the Guelphs were imagined as peaceful *popolani*, artisans and traders given to the arts of peace. This
view was already current in Guelph circles in the later fourteenth
century. Its origins may, perhaps, be seen in a remark of the Florentine Dominican Remigio Girolami (d. 1319), who likened the
Ghibelline to a lion and the Guelph to a calf, because it was a
sacrificial animal.[6] This characterisation of the parties went out of
fashion after the socialist historian Salvemini had described it as
mistaken from top to bottom, but perhaps the time has now come
to look at it again. That there was some social difference between
the parties is suggested by the difference in the sources which express the point of view of each. For the Guelph outlook the historian can turn to a large number of typical city chronicles,
written by worthy *popolani* of simple or moderate culture. Ghibelline chronicles of this type are relatively rare, and the chief
presenters of the Ghibelline case are a few men of considerable intellectual ability and culture. As always academic lawyers tended
to uphold the office of the successor of Justinian, but these were
now joined by a small group with a more than superficial knowledge of Roman history. These men were not heretics; they were

sophisticated enough to distinguish between the Pope as Christ's Vicar and his role as temporal ruler and governor of the Church in the world. All this points towards the conclusion that, while Guelphism attracted the solid *popolani* of the average trading town, Ghibellinism was upheld in the main by inarticulate traditionalists and a handful of sophisticated intellectuals. The reasons for this tendency are clear. The links between the papacy, Naples and France would attract businessmen with interests in these areas towards the Guelph alliance, and once Guelphism had become the official allegiance of the majority, there would be advantages for even a small town with local interests only in linking up with it. A significant exception is provided by Verona, whose position on the Brenner road to Austria and Germany drew her trading class into the Ghibelline camp for exactly the same reasons as led those elsewhere to favour the Guelphs. In other places opposition to the dominant majority was an important determinant of Ghibellinism, both in cities and in individuals. Pisa's opposition to Florence and Pavia's jealousy of Milan both took the form of a persistent Ghibelline tradition, while the noble clans, who sought to hold their own in the interstices between the territories of Guelph communes, naturally tended to prefer submission to a normally distant emperor to the daily subjection to their neighbours. Moreover, the holding of an imperial fief was an important part of the tradition of such families and constituted a vital element in their claim to noble status. That feudal loyalty to the emperor was far from a dead letter in Henry VII's time is proved by the reported speech of Filippo de Langosco, that he was unwilling to be a traitor to the lord from whom his ancestors had received so many benefits, and by Nicholas of Butrinto's account of the favourable reception he found as an imperial ambassador among the noble families of the Florentine contado, even among those who were traditionally Guelphs.[7] The rather different connection between the Empire and those who sought to rule their cities as *signori* will be explored in the next section.

The *Signoria*

The transfer of power to a single individual or family in all the major communes except Venice and a handful in Tuscany, was undoubtedly the most important political development of the period 1250 to 1350, and it was one over which the empire and the papacy exercised little influence. The new kind of political regime, which in vital respects marked a radical departure from the ways and ideals which had been followed by the communes from the beginning, was generated by forces arising within the individual cities or from the relationships between them, and spread most rapidly during the time when the papal–imperial struggle had least significance and the communes were most free from imperial intervention. During his brief reign Henry VII did little more than set the seal of legitimacy on governments already established *de facto*, and the papacy gradually followed suit by recognising local *signori* as papal vicars in the outlying parts of the Papal States, especially in the Romagna.

As we have seen, in Frederick II's time some individuals had seized power over a city or group of cities but, with the exception of the Estensi, all these were eliminated in the twenty years or so following the emperor's death. Many of the new despotisms which arose after 1250 were, by contrast, very long lasting, the medieval *signoria* evolving imperceptibly into the renaissance *principate*; the Visconti of Milan ruled continuously from 1311 until 1447, after which their state passed to the Sforza, while the Gonzaga of Mantua lasted until the mid-seventeenth century. Again, the *signorie* of the second wave were accompanied by changes in the constitutions of the communes which, if they do not tell the whole story of the revolution involved, do form a clear contrast to Frederick's lieutenants like Palavicino and Ezzelino da Romano, who seem to have been content with purely *de facto* power.

It is the legal and constitutional aspects of the *signorie* which have been most intensively studied by historians up to the present time. Over half a century ago it had been clearly established that a *signoria* might be formally established through extending and prolonging the powers of almost any one of the major offices which had been developed by the commune. The lordship of the Estensi, for example, evolved from the office of perpetual *podestà*; many others grew up linked in a similar way to the captaincy of the *popolo*. Napoleone della Torre took the title of perpetual *anziano* in Milan, and Alberto Scotto of Piacenza was captain of the *popolo* and rector of the merchant guild; headship of the *mercadenza* was also one of the stays of the Della Scala of Verona during the period when they were closing their grip on the commune. The formal transfer of power might take place through statutes duly passed by the city councils, or through acclamation at a mass *parlamentum* assembled in the city square; often both were combined with the swearing of oaths, the reading of notarial documents and the ceremonial reception and giving out of banners. The powers thus formally conferred varied widely; the essential feature was some degree of freedom or *arbitrium*, as it was termed, to vary the strict application of the statutes which bound all other officials. In some cases the documents give the impression that these powers are being created temporarily to meet some crisis, or for a fixed term of years, and provision may be made for an annual salary to be paid by the commune; others use phrases like 'captain general of the commune and *popolo*', or perpetual *signore*, with freedom to make, amend or suppress statutes, which all but spell out a dictatorship without any legal limits whatsoever. Wherever the *signoria* took root control over taxation was soon established, if it had not been secured by the original act of election, and while the various councils might continue to meet, their composition and the business they were permitted to discuss were closely controlled by the *signore*. With the passage of time some of the offices of the commune might be allowed to lapse, especially those with executive powers, like the *anziani*, but the process was a slow one which lagged far behind the effective take-over of government. The final step, formally making the office of *signore* hereditary, was often delayed, sometimes by as much as a couple of generations; the custom of election and acclamation of each successive lord kept alive the fiction that the commune was still a living political force long after it had become a carcass retained only for administrative convenience.

So much for the official records of the early *signorie*, which even more than most such sources reveal only a fraction of the true nature of the situation; the statutes and acts of election of *signori* are no more than ripples on the surface of the deep tide which was sweeping all the communes towards personal government which carried many along against their will. The sources which throw light on these deeper levels are scarce and difficult to handle, and the roots of many of the *signorie* will probably remain buried for ever; in the case of the Este *signoria* of Ferrara, however, a chronicle has survived which gives, as it were, the obverse of the official account. By way of background, it should be understood that from about the year 1200, control of Ferrara had been contested by two factions, led by the Este and Torelli families respectively. In 1240 Azzo d'Este, and his allies under the Guelph banner, had driven out Salinguerra Torelli, a supporter of Frederick II, and thereafter Azzo had ruled Ferrara, sometimes holding the office of *podestà* and sometimes, from behind the scenes, without holding any office at all. On his death in February 1264 his heir was his grandson Obizzo, a youth of seventeen. On the day of Azzo's funeral the official account describes how, at an assembly of all the inhabitants of Ferrara held in the principal piazza, the *podestà* enacted that Obizzo was to be Governor, Rector, and Perpetual Lord of Ferrara and its district with the widest powers, whereupon a notary swore obedience to the new law in the name of the whole commune and *universitas* of the city.[8]

The unofficial account explains these curious events in the following way. According to the chronicle, on Azzo's death a secret meeting of his party's supporters, both in Ferrara and outside, was held, at which it was decided that Obizzo should be given the *dominium* of the city for the good of the party. As a precautionary measure troops loyal to the party leaders and other supporters were moved into the city, while certain suspect citizens were temporarily banished. The troops and other outsiders were well in evidence at the meeting in the piazza, at which Aldigherio de Fontana, 'the architect of this sacred edifice', harangued the crowd as follows:

> Let the friends of our party not fear, nor our enemies rejoice or take hope on account of the burial of the late Marchese Azzo. For he has left to us this talented young man here present, of whom we may hope much. And indeed, if we lacked an offspring of the house of Este who was worthy to govern, we would make ourselves a lord out of straw.

At this the multitude all cried 'So be it', and the formal election took place by which, the chronicler comments, Obizzo was empowered to do anything, just or unjust, according to his own will. Thus, more power was given to him than to the Eternal God, who cannot be unjust.[9]

The chronicler, who was probably Riccobaldo da Ferrara, was writing over thirty years after the event and was strongly prejudiced against the Estensi, but he claims to have been present at the assembly in the piazza and the general lines of his story ring true; in particular, the importance of the party and key role played by the noble family which provided its nucleus is well-attested enough with regard to other *signorie* to stand, even if doubts are cast on the truth of this particular account. In short it is not in the constitutional niceties but in the nature of parties and faction, and the relationship of the *signore* to these that the key to the true nature of the various *signorie* is to be found.

As we have seen, from one aspect the Italian parties of the thirteenth centuries were chains of alliances linking the rulers of some cities with the exiles of others, fluctuating in membership and extent according to circumstances. Some *signorie* stemmed directly from this; for example, Charles of Anjou and later his grandson, Robert, became the nominal *signori* of a large number of Guelph communes frightened by the threat of Conradin or Henry of Luxemburg, while on the Ghibelline side *signorie* fell into the hands of regional leaders like Guido da Montefeltro in the Romagna or Guglielmo da Montferrat in Piedmont. *Signorie* of this kind were created, expanded and disappeared with astonishing rapidity, the classic case being the Italian state of Henry VII's son, John of Bohemia, which grew in a matter of months and was entirely liquidated within three years. The reason for this is that the powers enjoyed by this kind of *signore* were and remained strictly limited. Normally he appointed the *podestà* and *capitano* and, perhaps, a military commander, but the communes remained entirely independent in their internal affairs and were, therefore, free to terminate the arrangement when it suited them. The real strength of such *signorie* was that of the threat they were created to meet; when this was no longer pressing these nominal or limited *signorie* usually faded away.

For the consolidation of a real and lasting *signoria* it was necessary to have power deeply rooted in the local setting, which, in effect, meant control of the local parties, or at least a large measure of support from them. As we have seen, local parties in the earlier thirteenth century were built up either around a nucleus of noble clans or around *societates* with some kind of class basis; however, soon after 1250, the struggles of *milites* and *popolo* had been resolved in favour of the latter and the *societates militum* survived as pressure groups only, if at all. Communal legislation, however, suggests that class conflict remained alive and became acute once more in the 1280s and 90s, when a new wave of statutes against magnates and *potentiores* spread outwards to the major communes from Bologna. The main feature of these laws was that they applied only to named persons and families who were classified as magnates; these men were not only debarred from most public offices but were required to deposit a sum of money with the commune as surety for good behaviour. They were also placed under certain legal disabilities *vis à vis* the *popolani*, with heavier penalties for violence and intimidation, and they could be convicted of such crimes by the testimony of only two or three *popolani* attesting that their guilt was notorious. For acts of public disorder, the penalty was immediate destruction of property by an armed force of the *popolo* led by a special official (called the standard-bearer of justice at Florence), who was obliged, under heavy penalties, to act whenever a complaint was made according to the form prescribed.

The anti-magnatial legislation of the late thirteenth century raises a difficult problem of interpretation. Taken at its face value, it should have meant the political extinction of the magnates and have made even their private lives extremely insecure. In fact, however, apart from a few periods of crisis, the magnates as a whole do not seem to have suffered much, and in most places they can be seen from time to time still exerting influence as ambassadors and military commanders on behalf of their communes. Moreover, by 1330 *signorie* had been set up in nearly all the major communes which rested firmly on the support of members of the magnatial class. This apparent contradiction can be resolved only if the anti-magnatial laws are seen as an ineffective reaction against a deep-seated movement which was increasing the powers of the great families, who eventually reasserted their position under the *signorie*. Despite the prosperity of the *popolani* and the political activism of the guilds, the natural locus of power was still with the relatively few families with overwhelming landed or commercial wealth, who could be prevented from dominating the communes only by effort and vigilance which were not sustained.

In fact, as the thirteenth century progressed, the class-based party steadily declined in importance, and the co-operation of classes in politics became more intense. By mid-century the increasing complexity of the economic life and administration of the major communes was already making them unmanageable by a noble faction without substantial middle class support, as is proved by the problems of the Florentine Ghibellines between 1260 and 1266. The victories of the *popolo* confirmed this tendency; from this point onwards the nobles were compelled to build up a following among the *popolani* through whom they could exert pressure on the organs of the commune. Inevitably, the leadership of the parties devolved upon the great families and the anti-magnatial measures were the reaction of *popolani* who sensed that they could not compete with the magnates on equal terms. Significantly, the periods of class conflict, during which the anti-magnatial legislation was strictly or even aggressively applied, were relatively brief compared with the ruthless party struggles whose stakes were exile and total ruin, which often dragged on for decades. For example, the regime led by Giano della Bella, which passed the Ordnances of Justice in Florence, lasted only fifteen months, while the Blacks and Whites were contesting control of the commune from 1295 to the end of 1301, and the Whites remained a threat in the contado until the fall of Pistoia in April 1306.

The detailed composition of parties within the Italian communes has as yet been little studied, and in many cases the evidence is lacking. However, it is reasonably clear that the role of the magnates was hardly diminished; tendencies of the earlier part of the century continued and great landed families provided a territorial base and numerous retainers whose dependence on their lords was no less, though it was now more financial than feudal in nature. The great families often provided leaders with skill in war and diplomacy to add to the social prestige which was their birthright. For the carrying through of their policies, however, they were dependent on the trained service of men of the administrative classes – judges, notaries and minor officials of various kinds. In the economically developed cities, the support of merchants and bankers with their liquid wealth was invaluable, particularly during the difficult stages before the administration of the state was taken over, and the party could be nourished on the public revenues and rewarded with the property of exiles. Finally, the support of the city mob was worth having, as an expendable destructive force to be directed against one's enemies; no one was better able to obtain this than a certain type of traditional nobleman of the kind typified by Corso Donati, who was greeted with cries of 'Long live the baron' as he rode along the Florentine streets.

To return to the *signori*: in a few cases they were appointed as mediators between the parties to hold the government impartially between them. If this was their sole mandate, they were rather like men trying to drive two untamed horses at the same time, and their rule was generally short. The vast majority of the *signori* were, in fact, the leaders of victorious parties, and it was the strength of their parties rather than the form or terms of their election, which ensured the permanence or otherwise of their rule. The Della Torre and Visconti, who disputed the control of Milan for nearly half a century, were typically family-based parties, and though the Della Torre rose as leaders of the *popolo*, while the Visconti were originally more aristocratic, the social composition of their supporters was probably much the same by the fourteenth century. Elsewhere class distinctions between the parties are increasingly difficult to trace; often it was an issue of external policy, peace or war or a particular alliance which served to polarise opinion and define the factions. In a few cases the process by which an outstanding leader created his own party can be glimpsed, as at Parma where Ghiberto da Correggio overcame his rivals, the Rossi, with the help of members of the Imperialist party who had just been allowed to return from long years of exile in 1303. Within a few years the Guelph party which had ruled the commune of Parma since 1266 had become known as the old party (*pars antiqua*) and was led by the Rossi, in distinction to Ghiberto's supporters, made up of elements of both parties, who were called the new party (*pars nova*). The struggle between these two rapidly choked the freedom of the commune and it is hard to believe that the anti-magnatial laws were put into effect any more. The commune enjoyed a brief revival in 1316, with the guilds and the *società d'armi* forming a front against the magnates, but by 1322 the city was seriously divided again and the administration was corrupt and in difficulties; finally, after years of increasing instability, the Rossi were elected lords of the city in 1328.[10]

The fact that the great majority of the *signori* belonged to landed magnatial families has led some historians to see in their triumph some kind of takeover of the cities by the country or a reversal of the 'conquest of the contado', and have even spoken of a revival of feudalism. In some economically less developed areas

like the Romagna or the north-west, this view may have some
justification, for in these regions wealth had remained almost
solely dependent upon land, and the attempt of the communes to
keep power in the hands of guildsmen and artisans was obviously
unrealistic. But as a general description of the *signoria*, this
generalisation ignores the special nature of Italian society as it
had evolved through two centuries or so of civic life. The magnates
of the thirteenth century were a class of mixed origins who, except
in the fringe areas, had long been mixed up in the life of cities,
where they had served as *podestà* and *capitani*, war leaders and the
heads of parties. Although they undoubtedly originated in the
contado, it is meaningless to describe the sophisticated Visconti
lords as in any way rural; on the other hand, the Della Scala had
risen from obscurity in the city of Verona, yet by the fourteenth
century their outlook was typical of the landed, feudal and warlike *signori*. As a cultural phenomenon feudalism was not confined to any one class. The *signoria* was an authentic expression
of the mixed Italian *vita civile*.

The direct role of the empire and the papacy in the establishment of the new political order was very small – a matter not of
power but of the legitimisation of power. The *signori* knew that,
by their personal rule, they were violating the ideals on which the
communes had been built and it was clear that the power which
they exercised through their parties was illegitimate. A mandate
of a sort could always be obtained by going through the forms of
election and popular acclamation, but the disadvantage was that
powers conferred in this way could always be revoked by the same
means. Imperial recognition sanctioned power from above and
usually from afar, and so was not easily called in question. It gave
a unique prestige which gratified both the populace and the intellectuals, and especially the lawyers without whom no government could be carried on. While the Emperor and the Pope were
in alliance, the quest for imperial titles did not necessarily mark a
man as a Ghibelline. The first of the new *signori* to become an
imperial vicar was the Guelph Napoleone della Torre of Milan,
who obtained the office from Rudolph of Habsburg in 1273. Henry
VII, who at first pursued the policy of appointing men without
local power as imperial vicars, was compelled to give way and
legitimise *de facto signori* in return for money and troops when
he was reduced to desperate straits during the siege of Brescia.

Characteristically Henry tried to maintain his impartiality by appointing Guelphs as well as Ghibellines, but this was not a success; before a year had gone by Ghiberto da Correggio had rebelled against the empire, and within eighteen months the Da Camino had been expelled from Treviso. Ironically, therefore, a crop of Ghibelline *signori* with imperial titles became Henry's most lasting political legacy to Italy; after his time *signori* continued to look towards the empire as the ultimate source of their authority. The considerable services and sums of money, which the *signori* were willing to advance to emperors whose military power was much inferior to their own, are a measure of how precarious and irregular they felt their position to be throughout the fourteenth century.

At a deeper level both the empire and the *signoria* appealed to the desire for a more hierarchical and authoritarian political and social structure which had never been entirely overlaid by the ideals of the communes. One cannot but be struck by the lack of an ideological opposition to the spread of despotism. The situation at Padua, where the humanist poet, Albertino Mussato, wrote a Senecan tragedy warning the citizens of the dangers of tyranny in 1311, was exceptional and is explained by the memories of the brutal domination of Ezzelino da Romano half a century before.[11] More typical are the brief and unconvincing denunciations of tyranny as incompatible with the Milanese temperament which may be found in Bonvesin della Riva's description of Milan, written in 1288, a decade after the Visconti party had taken over the state as a result of the battle of Desio.[12] The social roots of the general acquiescence in the personal rule of the *signori* may be illustrated from the well documented attitudes of the poet Dante. Considering that, until he was thirty-six years of age, Dante lived as a full citizen of the Florentine commune for which he held the highest office open to a native – that of prior – the lack of any defence of the commune's ideals of shared and temporary authority is altogether remarkable; while he remained passionately devoted to Florentine *civilitas*, the poet showed no real appreciation of the political regime under which it had flourished. As a wandering exile from 1302 it was probably inevitable that Dante should seek the protection of *signori*, who had more patronage to offer a talented outsider than the private citizens of a republic. What is significant is Dante's wholehearted praise for the city despots whom he came to know. For example, in the *Convivio* the contemporary singled out as the epitome of nobility is Gherardo da Camino, the captain general of Treviso; Cangrande della Scala [see plate V], the aggressive *signore* of Verona, whose court was a renowned centre of warlike chivalry and display, received the unique honour of having part of the *Divine Comedy* dedicated to him. If such attitudes were at all prevalent among the governing classes of the communes, it is easy to understand how the statutes against the transfer of power to any individual proved so ineffective when it came to the point.

However, the real driving force towards the *signorie* was not idealism but expediency. Contemporaries realised well enough that tyranny was the consequence of disunity within and discord between cities. In the recurrent crises of party and inter-city conflict, only one man or a tightly knit family group could possess the singleness of purpose and make the quick decisions which were essential to survival. It was in the cramped political arena of Lombardy, where the *signorie* were first to appear and where they spread more widely; in Tuscany, where the greater distances made the competition rather less intense, a few of the free communes survived. Among the greatest cities, Venice had the unique privilege of security given by the sea; otherwise, only Florence could afford the lumbering administration, inefficient and expensive armies, and the periodic outbreaks of civil disorder which were the price of the communal regime. Up to a point the *signorie* favoured the creation of larger states since they provided a strong executive, and common subjection to a lord was possibly more acceptable to a city than domination by a neighbour's oligarchy. But in the event, little permanent progress in this direction was achieved until the last quarter of the fourteenth century. Certain shortcomings of the new personal states were chiefly to blame for this; the lack of fixed rules of succession made signorial families particularly prone to feuds and assassination, but did not prevent divisions of the state among co-heirs, or the passing of power into the hands of incompetents.

Since it was the *signoria* which generally prevailed, there has been a tendency among historians to assume that it must have represented some kind of political advance over the communes. But what this may have been is by no means clear, while certain disadvantages of the *signorie* need to be taken into consideration.

While one would not wish to press the moral distinction between a selfish oligarchy and a selfish lord, the fact remains that, so long as they functioned at all, the communes, with their principle that officials acted under the law and were answerable to some form of council, were more complex political organisms than the *signorie*, where the fount of law and the executive were virtually one and the same. Whatever their practical shortcomings – and these could certainly be very great – the communes were based on a distinction between public and private affairs, the implications of which had been elaborated with great finesse over the centuries. In the *signorie* the two tended to become confused again as the state came to be regarded almost as the personal property of the ruling family. For this reason if no other the *signorie* brought with them a certain political impoverishment.

6. The Flowering of the *Vita Civile*

The Heyday of the Cities

WHATEVER obscurities may surround other aspects of the medieval Italian economy, there can be no doubt that the second half of the thirteenth century and the first years of the fourteenth saw the heyday of the Italian cities. The new circuits of walls laid out at this time, of which the Florentine third circle is the most famous, were generally not outgrown until a hundred years ago. The process of economic and demographic growth, which had begun so mysteriously in the tenth century, reached its climax in these years, with the whole of Italy supporting a population which has been credibly guessed at between seven and nine millions, or perhaps about twice that of the British Isles at the same period. True, the area within the frontiers of modern France probably contained twice as many again; it was the number and size of the cities which really marked Italy off from the rest of Europe. About 1300 the four super-cities of Venice, Milan, Florence and Genoa were probably approaching the 100,000 mark; Paris alone in northern Europe came anywhere near this figure. In the second rank there were some twenty-two Italian cities with a population of between 50,000 and 20,000 inhabitants, while across the Alps only London, Cologne, Bruges and Ghent belonged to this class; cities like Bologna and Verona were comparable with contemporary London. (See Map 5.)

The distribution of urban population within Italy was extremely uneven, reflecting the economic development of the various regions. South of Rome there were only three cities of any magnitude, Messina, Naples and Palermo, and the latter two prospered mainly as the capitals of foreign dynasties and the largely alien merchants and administrators who served them. The thriving urban society was essentially restricted to communal Italy; Rome itself, after brave attempts to keep up with developments further north in the mid-thirteenth century, had begun to slip back even before the removal of the papacy to southern France brought in years of depression and despair. Even within the area of communal Italy the cities were by no means evenly spread. In central Italy there was a stark contrast between the east with its cloud of miniscule cities under the uneasy suzerainty of the Church, and the west which contained some of the finest examples of urban civilisation. The Arno valley boasted the three major cities of Pisa, Florence and Arezzo, with a fourth, Lucca, not far away; when smaller centres like Pistoia and Prato are taken into consideration, it is clear that this area had a high degree of urbanisation. Over the Appenines in the Po valley there were at least twelve major cities of over 20,000 inhabitants and many more minor ones. In the fringe areas of the north-east and the north-west they were well spaced out, but in the centre they were very closely packed indeed. For example, Parma, Reggio, Modena and Bologna, whose aggregate urban population must have been well over 100,000, were strung along the Via Emilia with an average interval of only fifteen miles between each. The differences between these two areas of dense urbanisation in north and central Italy and the rest of Europe were not simply quantitative but were qualitative; it was primarily in these regions that the distinctive Italian *vita civile*, which had been growing painfully for some three centuries, came to maturity.

Without doubt, the vast majority of the inhabitants of these teeming cities were very poor; whether they were any less poor than in the past, we have no means of knowing. Those who recorded their thoughts and feelings were all at least well-to-do, or were religious men writing for the well-to-do, and the writers of this period reflect unmistakably the feeling that the middle and upper classes were riding a high tide of prosperity. The fact that some said so in as many words is itself a sign of a self-consciousness and self-confidence which was new. Take, for example, the description of Milan written in 1288 by the minor poet and rhetorician Bonvesin della Riva.

What can be said of the huge number of the multitude living in Milan and its contado? Silence! whoever can grasp it, let him grasp it. This however will be forgiven me: that I am by no means silent. For, as I roughly estimate, and many definitely assert the same, more than 700,000 mouths of the two sexes, including all infants as well as adults, obtain their sustenance from the surface of the Ambrosian earth. Every day – and it is wonderful in what manner – they receive from the hand of God

Ambrosian food. Why should their number not be so great, since in the city alone, with its dense population, there are undoubtedly 115 parishes, among which there are certainly some in which more than five hundred families live, while in a few about one thousand live? . . . Whoever wishes to know how many warriors there are in time of war should know that more than forty thousand live in this city who are able to fight the enemy with sword or lance or other weapon . . . In it and its contado, more than ten thousand could easily maintain war horses if ordered by the commune . . . There are in this city alone 120 doctors of both laws . . . the notaries are more than 1500. The experts in medicine, who are properly called physicians, are twenty-eight. The surgeons of different specialities are indeed more than 150 . . . There are three hundred bakeries in the city (as one learns from the books of the commune) which bake bread for the use of the citizens . . . The shopkeepers who sell at retail an amazing amount of goods of all kinds are undoubtedly more than a thousand. The butchers number more than 440, and excellent meat of quadrupeds of all kinds, as suits our customs, is sold in great quantity in their shops . . . The hostelries giving hospitality to strangers for profit number about 150. The smiths who equip quadrupeds with iron shoes, number about eighty, and this indicates the multitude of horsemen and horses. How many saddlers, how many smiths of bridles, spurs and stirrups, I pass over in silence.[1]

Bonvesin was a member of the Third Order of the Umiliati, but here his enthusiasm carried him far from the ideals of that ascetic confraternity; while earlier Milanese writers emphasise the local saints and the magnificence of the Ambrosian church, Bonvesin seems to put his faith in material things, and his pride in sheer size and statistics is quintessentially bourgeois. The atmosphere of a great city could sweep a nominal ascetic of much greater learning than Bonvesin into almost unqualified approval of civic wealth, as can be seen from a sermon by the Florentine Dominican Remigio Girolami. In it the learned friar enumerates the seven principal blessings which have been bestowed on Florence: these are great wealth and population, a noble currency, a civilised way of life, the textile and armament industries, and noble buildings.[2] Perhaps without realising it Remigio had here morally justified

the material wealth of the citizen body; provided the citizens were
not themselves possessed by it, he accepted the Aristotelian view
that such wealth was useful and good. It was in this period that
the battle for absolute poverty was being gradually lost within the
Franciscan order; the early thirteenth century reaction against
affluence, represented by the mendicants, was losing its general
appeal, though it was still vigorously upheld by the spiritual wing
of the Franciscans.

Nearly all the contemporary writers who have anything to say
about economic matters saw wealth primarily in terms of an
abundance of goods available for purchase – the consumers' point
of view. Bonvesin has a chapter entitled 'In praise of Milan's
fertility and abundance of goods', in which he boasts that

> . . . in our territories fertile, fortunate and fruitful, all kinds
> of cereals are produced: wheat, rye, millet, panic from which
> bread is made, and all kinds of vegetables which can be cooked
> and are excellent to eat . . . in such amazing quantity that after
> being distributed in different places they not only make good
> the deficiency of foodstuffs in the city of Como but are also
> transported and distributed to feed peoples beyond the Alps.
> And why not, since . . . more than thirty thousand oxen cultivate
> our territory? . . . Sour and sweet cherries of all kinds, both cul-
> tivated and wild, grow in such great quantity that sometimes it
> happens that more than sixty cartloads of them are brought
> through the gates of the city in a single day . . .[3]

In a description of Padua written about 1318 the judge Giovanni da Nono dwells particularly on the city markets and the
plentiful supply of meats, cereals, vegetables and fruit to be obtained there. The popular poet Antonio Pucci described the
Florentine market in the mid-fourteenth century; he sums up his
praises by likening the Mercato Vecchio to a noble garden in its
abundant fruitfulness.[4] No doubt this emphasis on locally produced victuals rather than industry or high commerce is a reflection of the interests of the writers and their readers, most of whom
must have been *rentiers* or professional men not directly concerned
with production. Yet it may be that their view was nearer the truth
than that of some modern historians who have written as if long-
distance trade and the textile industry were the sole *raisons d'être*
of the medieval town. Although the detailed local studies which

could prove the point are lacking, it seems likely that the great majority of Italian cities remained, even at the peak of their economic development, primarily centres for the distribution and consumption of the produce of the contado which they administered.

It is significant that the only city description of this period which projects a markedly different point of view should be the work of a merchant and a Florentine. Giovanni Villani's famous account of the wealth of his native city in 1338 is the work of a man who was a partner in one of the great Florentine merchant banks and who had travelled on business as far as Flanders and Naples. This was during the first two decades of the fourteenth century when the Florentine companies were supreme, having beaten their rivals from Siena, Pistoia, Lucca and Piacenza into second place. The gold florin was the standard of international exchange for the greater part of Europe, and the houses of the Bardi and Peruzzi had grown into the biggest business organisations the medieval world was to see. Fittingly enough, Villani's picture of Florence grows out of his account of the enormous sums which the commune was able to spend on the war with Verona; throughout he shows the same fascination with statistics which we have seen in Bonvesin, but he is far more interested in commerce and industry, and he tries to give a dynamic dimension to his description by comparing the figures for different years when these were known to him. For example, he places the peak of the woollen textile production by the *arte della lana* around 1308, when more than 100,000 pieces were made in some three hundred shops; by 1338 the total had dropped to 70–80,000 pieces, but improved quality had doubled their value to 1,200,000 gold florins, and he estimates that 30,000 persons lived by this industry. The once dominant Calimala guild of finishers of imported cloth was in relative decline, with only twenty workshops and an annual import of 10,000 pieces; however, the annual strike of gold florins from the Florentine mint had risen from 350,000 to 400,000.[5] These figures have often been questioned but have not yet been discredited. Still, if the testimony of a Florentine in praise of his birthplace is suspect, it must be pointed out that other Italians regarded the city as unique. Thus Benzo d'Alessandria, a Lombard living in Milan with no reason to flatter the Florentines, wrote in his encyclopaedia: 'Indeed this magnificent city flourishes to such an extent that it may be called the most opulent, populous and rich of the cities of the world.'[6] It is unlikely that Florence was any more populous than Milan at this period, so it must have been Florentine affluence which so impressed Benzo; the common reputation for wealth is reflected in a story that when Charles of Valois asked the pope for more funds on his return from Florence, Boniface VIII replied, 'I have already sent you to the source of gold.'[7]

It cannot be too much emphasised that the Florentine economy in this period was not typical but altogether exceptional. Her industrial development was almost unique in Italy, for the Lombard textile manufacture did not really get under way until the middle of the fourteenth century. Participation in long-distance trade by cities varied greatly according to local circumstances, and the distinction between centres with far-flung rather than primarily local interests had little to do with size. Milan was very large, but it has not yet been shown that she had merchant bankers to compare with those of Piacenza, who almost alone among the Lombards disputed the Tuscan near monopoly of finance on the premier trade routes to northern France, Flanders and the British Isles. Padua, a city of much the same size as Piacenza, had its ill-famed moneylenders, but their activities were relatively local and their organisation was primitive compared with a third-rate Tuscan city like Pistoia, whose bankers were well-known in France and England. Even a little Tuscan town like San Gimignano was swept to prosperity in the wake of the Florentine miracle; its famous towers which attract the tourists today were built on the profits of saffron, an important dyestuff which was grown locally and marketed first in Florence and then in the world at large. In any picture of the period the great merchant bankers, whose operations stretched from the shores of Asia and Africa to the North Sea, must be given their due, for they were the pioneers of a new way of living; but it must always be remembered that, even in the governing classes of the Italian cities, they were no more than a small élite, heavily outnumbered by men whose way of life, though much more circumscribed, had behind it a long tradition yielding much honour and prestige.

International Merchants

About 1340 Francesco di Balduccio Pegolotti finished compiling the book which has become known as *La Pratica della Mercatura*

(The Practice of Commerce), a working manual of useful information for the long-distance Italian merchant of the day.[8] Pegolotti was exceptionally well qualified to write on this subject, for he had been an employee of the great Bardi company for at least thirty years, serving as their representative in Antwerp, London and Cyprus, where in 1336, he negotiated a trade agreement with the King of Armenia on behalf of the company. He could, therefore, draw on a lifetime of personal experience, as well as on the records of the largest company of the time; it is clear that he also used official documents on such matters as tolls and customs. Pegolotti was not the first to compile a book of this kind; indeed, all large companies must have kept records and memoranda as a guide to the conduct of their business, but, in addition to being one of the earliest to survive, Pegolotti's book was exceptionally comprehensive, including even such matters as a calendar and Easter tables, and instructions on how to refine and test the purity of gold and silver. It is unequalled as a guide to the far-flung multifarious activities of Italian merchants in the days when their hegemony over European and Mediterranean trade was at its peak. (See Map 6.)

Pegolotti's own title for his work was 'The Book of Descriptions of Countries and of Measures of Merchandise', indicating that the contents fall roughly into two parts. In the first information concerning weights and measures, currencies and their rates of exchange, costs of transport and customs payable on the more common types of merchandise, is arranged under the headings of the chief trading centres of the world, thus giving a clear picture of the extent of Florentine trading connections at the time. Beginning in the East Pegolotti deals with the Italian trading stations in the Crimea and the Sea of Azov, then Tabriz in Persia, Trebizond, Constantinople, two centres in Turkish Asia Minor, then Armenia, Acre and Alexandria, Famagusta, Rhodes and Candia in Crete. The most striking entry is an itinerary for reaching Peking from Tana on the Sea of Azov in some 270 days of travel by horse and ox cart, ass, camel and river boat. The land routes across central Asia had been made practicable for westerners by the Mongol conquests of the mid-thirteenth century, one of the first to pass that way being the Franciscan Giovanni da Piano Carpini, sent to the Grand Khan by Pope Innocent IV in 1245. Pegolotti attests to the effectiveness of the Mongol peace when he notes 'this route from Tana to Cathay is very safe both by day and night', and, in fact, we know that in the first half of the fourteenth century a handful of Italian merchants, missionaries and diplomats were to be found scattered along the main lines of communication in central Asia, China and India. These tenuous contacts with the Far East, knowledge of which was spread by Marco Polo's famous book, were gradually cut off by worsening political conditions after 1350.

Pegolotti next turns his attention nearer home to the central Mediterranean, dealing in detail with both the mainland of Italy and the islands. An interesting and unique feature is a meticulous account of the cost of minting coins in Florence. Finally Pegolotti turns West to complete the first part of his book with descriptions of the trade of such centres as Bruges, Antwerp, London, La Rochelle, Seville and Morocco. In England, his main concern is naturally with the sources of wool which was the chief export. He gives the price of the three main qualities of wool both for the 'collected' wools of the various regions and for nearly two hundred religious houses in England, Wales and Scotland with the same care as a wine merchant today might list blended and vintage wines. His renderings of English names have made his list a challenge to editors to display their skill in unmasking such places as Cilesi in Condisgualdo (Hayles in the Cotswolds) and Rovincestri in costa al Pecche as Rocester near the Peak.

The second part of *La Pratica della Mercatura* deals mainly with different kinds of merchandise and is chiefly valuable for showing the wide range of goods handled by the great Italian firms which are usually thought of as having been primarily commercial banks. Naturally, the majority of the items listed are spices, dyestuffs and precious stones, all with a high value in proportion to their weight and bulk; these had been the staple goods of long-distance trade from the earliest times, and Pegolotti describes many of them in detail with hints as to how to judge their quality for, as he says, it is necessary for the merchant to be able to recognise all kinds of merchandise so as to avoid being swindled. He also mentions merchandise of greater bulk, such as skins, silk, cloth and metals, and there is a section on the selling of grain to *signori*, communes and individuals, which is a reminder that the bulk shipping of corn had become a normal feature of Mediterranean trade. The governments of the Italian cities took direct responsibility for the import of grain in times of shortage, and in dealing with them Pegolotti advises the merchant to be sure that he has a firm contract for a fixed term which he should endeavour to meet, in case a change of regime should lead to difficulties – sound advice in view of the political instability of the time.

The trading world which Pegolotti described had taken on its present form during the last quarter of the thirteenth century, when a series of developments in the organisation of business had brought about some important modifications to the pattern of trade. Up to this point the merchant had been essentially a man who travelled, either with his goods or in advance of them, and the main centres of exchange between northern and southern Europe had been the fairs of Champagne, temporary meeting places remote from the large towns of both north and south. However, in the later thirteenth century the Italians began to settle in the chief trading cities of the north like Paris, London and Bruges, on a semi-permanent basis, where they inevitably established associations, usually called 'nations', for their mutual protection and benefit. Some of these settlers were independent merchants, but many were agents or factors employed by the large Italian firms, whose business was now carried on mainly by correspondence. At the same time changes came about in the nature of the companies themselves. In the earlier days associations between merchants had either been short-term, for the duration of a single voyage or venture, or they had been a matter of lifelong partnerships patterned on the common property of the family. Now the terminal partnership became common, in which the members contributed shares of the capital in an association which lasted for a fixed number of years, after which profits were distributed. Family groups remained at the core of these companies, which were renewed again and again with little change in membership; investments by outsiders were classified as *fuori del corpo*, outside the main body of the company's capital, and drew a fixed rate of interest. The number of investors increased greatly in this period and they were almost all Italians. Accounting methods had to be improved, and although full double-entry bookkeeping was not introduced until the mid-fourteenth century, those company books which have survived from before this time have been found to be generally accurate and adequate for their purpose, which was the equitable distribution of profits; when business was bad, the standard of accounting tended to fall off, as there was no incentive to find out exactly how the company's affairs stood.

The lifeblood of the new system was the ability to transfer credit freely and rapidly to any of the main trading centres such as those listed by Pegolotti; the great companies maintained permanent branches in many of them and where these were lacking agents were employed. The chief instrument was the contract of exchange, by which money advanced in one place in one currency was repaid at a later date somewhere else in another currency. In this way the prohibition of usury, which forbade the taking of interest for a simple loan, was circumvented, and speculation on rates of exchange between the various currencies was encouraged. That some of the factors which affected these were well understood, is proved by a letter sent from the fair at Troyes to the partners of the Tolomei bank in Siena in November 1265 on the eve of Charles of Anjou's conquest of southern Italy.

> Lord Simon the Cardinal [Simon de Brie, later Pope Martin IV] is trying as hard as he can to have the tithe collected which is to be paid for the enterprise of King Charles. And I believe they will collect a large sum between now and the coming Candlemas, and I believe the said king will have a good deal of that money sold in order to have money in Rome and in Lombardy. And it seems that if this is done, deniers of Provins ought to fall in price. And on the other hand, I believe that people from this country who are going to assist the said king are now in Lombardy, and they have with them a huge stock of money and letters of exchange. And I believe they will spend a good proportion of it there, so that deniers of Tours and letters of exchange ought to be a great bargain there ... and if you can see a way to draw profit from this, do try to do it at once.[9]

These men clearly saw money as a commodity, and its handling was their special expertise. The transport of goods was a simpler matter, often left to specialised carriers; the only innovation of importance in this field was the opening of direct sea communications between the Mediterranean and Southampton and Sluys, the port of Bruges, by the Genoese in 1274, followed by the Venetians in 1314. Goods passing through the fairs of Champagne declined, but they remained a convenient occasion for the clearing of money and credit transactions between north and south.

By the early fourteenth century, their superior commercial techniques had enabled the Italians to dominate the trade of Europe in a way they never equalled either before or after. They were active in southern Germany and the Rhineland, in Hungary (where descendants of Charles of Anjou ruled from 1308) and in Bohemia rich in silver, and they reached out towards the Baltic. But their main field of operations remained the Mediterranean and its outlets to Asia and Africa, and the great axis of trade running north-west to Paris, Bruges and London. Here were to be found scores of individuals and small partnerships, engaged not only in trade and banking but also in pawnbroking, money-changing and the administration of mints. As Pegolotti's book shows, this was also the sphere of operation of the great companies, which were mostly Tuscan, and which had become enormous and highly complex organisations by medieval standards. For example, the Peruzzi Company was re-formed six times between 1300 and 1331 with between fourteen and twenty-one partners, between five and eight of these being members of the Peruzzi family who held a majority of the capital until 1331. The capital reached a peak of £149,000 *a fiorino* in the company formed in 1310, equivalent to over 600 pounds of gold, and the recorded profits were between 14 and 20 per cent per annum. In its heyday the Peruzzi company employed some ninety factors and maintained some fifteen branches outside Florence, ranging from London, Paris and Bruges, through the Italian ports and central Mediterranean islands to Tunis, Cyprus and Rhodes. The records of Pegolotti's company, the Bardi, are less complete, but it appears to have been larger still; in the number of factors employed and branches maintained, the Bardi and Peruzzi were each almost twice the size of the Medici bank at the time of its greatest expansion in the fifteenth century, and the geographical range of their activities was also somewhat greater. It is very doubtful if the capital of the Peruzzi company of 1310 was ever equalled by the Medici; it was only in the sixteenth century that it was exceeded by the Fuggers of Augsburg. From nearly every point of view the great Florentine companies appear to be far ahead of their time; if the combination of banking with unspecialised commerce seems to be a primitive feature, it should be remembered that this remained a common feature in European companies until the eighteenth century.

One side of the companies' business with which Pegolotti does not deal is loans in which commerce was not involved. Over large areas of northern Europe Italian moneylenders and pawnbrokers, known locally as Lombards, were familiar figures. The great companies, too, advanced loans to meet the expenses of their clients, who were chiefly prelates, nobles and, above all, kings, who desperately needed liquid capital for many purposes, but mainly, of course, for war. Although the risks were great, investment in successful wars of conquest could be highly profitable, as the expedition of Charles of Anjou in 1265–6 had proved, so the position of banker to kings and great princes was much prized. The dependence of Philip the Fair of France on the Franzesi of Florence was well known; Musciatto Franzesi accompanied the king's brother, Charles of Valois, on his journey to Italy in 1301, no doubt in the hope that he would repeat the triumphs of his famous namesake. In England the line of Italian bankers to the crown goes back to Edward I, who had probably learnt to appreciate their services while on crusade. The English king favoured Lucchese and Pistoian companies as well as Florentine, but by far the most important of his bankers were the Frescobaldi Bianchi of Florence, who between 1290 and 1310 lent the crown at least £122,000 sterling or about 732,000 gold florins. They were made receivers of the English customs in 1304, and in 1309 Edward II granted them the wool customs of Scotland and Ireland; closely identified with the king and his unpopular favourites, they fell foul of the Lords Ordainers in 1311 and forfeited their position. Their place was taken by the Bardi, who had been financing the export of English wool since at least 1277; they became the king's merchants in 1313, and four years later, with the Peruzzi, they were appointed papal agents for England. Both companies steered a skilful course through the troubles surrounding the deposition of Edward II, switching their support to Edward III in good time. The new king's desire for military glory regardless of cost boded ill for the future, but the Italians were in no position to refuse his requests. At home in their own city, they might be great and respected, but abroad they were suspected aliens whose governments could do little or nothing to protect them. They were unpopular and regarded as social inferiors by many of their clients, for whom they were upstarts tainted with usury; they could flourish only under the patronage of the great and powerful.

The Ruling Class

The economic 'bonanza' of the late thirteenth century produced a situation in which the upper classes of the cities of communal Italy were not only more rich and prosperous than their forebears but knew themselves to be so. The realisation produced mixed reactions; alongside the enthusiasm of Bonvesin and Remigio there were many who took a pessimistic attitude. Dante was never more conventional than when he attacked the Florentines for abandoning the virtuous austerity of their ancestors in the pursuit of gain and usury. Riccobaldo da Ferrara considered that a moral decline had taken place since the time of Frederick II.

In those times [he wrote in about 1300], customs and habits in Italy were rude. For men wore fillets of metal plates on their heads, sewed into caps which they called *maiatas*. At meals a man and his wife ate from one dish; wooden trenchers were not yet used for dining. There were one or two drinking vessels for a family. By night the supper table was lighted by torches, held by a boy or servant; it was not yet customary to have tallow or wax candles. Men wore mantles of skin without linings, or of wool without skins, and hoods of linen; women were married in tunics of linen. The style of living of men and women was primitive; they wore little or no gold and silver on their garments and their diet was without refinement ... The glory of men was to be rich in arms and horses; that of nobles was to have lofty towers. Many dissolute habits have now stifled these early customs, many indeed which lead to the destruction of the soul. Parsimony has been changed into extravagance. One sees garments of rich material which are decorated with exquisite and excessive artifice, with marvellously fashioned silver, gold and pearls, with wide embroidery and linings of silk, and trimmed with exotic and precious skins. Incitements to greed are not lacking. Foreign wine is drunk and almost everyone is a public tippler, feasts are sumptuous, and their masters, the cooks, are highly paid. Whoever incites to gluttony and ambition is sought for, and avarice labours that it may be supplied with these things. Thence come usury, frauds, rapine, pillaging, contentions in the state, unjust exactions, oppression of the innocent, destruction of citizens, banishment of the rich ...[10]

That there had been great changes in customs and dress during the second half of the thirteenth century is confirmed by the Paduan Giovanni da Nono; what he disliked most about his own times was the way in which social distinctions had been broken down by the arrival of the new rich, most of whom he denounced as usurers. These men and their sons aped the ways of the aristocracy by attending knightly festivities; in the good old days, Da Nono relates with relish, no *popolano* could have shown his face on such an occassion without being set upon by the young nobles.

It is not difficult to detect that what contemporaries disliked was, not so much wealth in itself – their attitude to corporate wealth and civic magnificence was, as we have seen, very different – but what Dante called the 'sudden gains' which, by bringing new men to the fore, seemed to threaten the time-honoured social hierarchy. A recurring theme in the *Divine Comedy* is the contrast between the small, poor but stable and peaceful Florence of the past, the 'sweet dwelling-place' and the 'sheepfold of St John' of Dante's imagination, and the bustling city full of immigrants, money making, ostentation and violence which the poet knew. Although this viewpoint is found in other writers, it would be unwise to take it at its face value. In fact, social mobility had probably been a feature of Italian communal society from its very beginnings. Dante puts his most moving eulogy of the old order into the mouth of his great-great-grandfather Cacciaguida, whom he believed to have been knighted by the emperor Conrad III, yet one of the things which most impressed Conrad's brother, the historian Otto of Freising, about Italian society was the way in which men of humble origins could rise to knighthood.[11] It is likely that the time of the greatest social change had been the first half of the thirteenth century which saw the rise not only of certain individuals and families but of a whole class which constituted the leading elements in the *popolo*, yet there is little evidence of contemporary reactions in that period.

By comparison with what had gone before the later thirteenth century was, in general, a time of social evolution rather than revolution; even those features which seem to be new were, in fact, the working out of developments which had begun a long time before. For example, one characteristic of the period was the enormous increase in the number of professionally trained men, masters of grammar, surgeons, physicians and, above all, lawyers,

the products of a veritable explosion in higher education. Some
idea of the change involved can be gained from a look at the number of judges in some of the Lombard cities during the thirteenth
century. Up to 1260 or 1270 these appear to have been quite modest
and stable; a roll of Bolognese councillors from 1219 names about
a dozen; and a very long list of Paduan citizens in 1254 contains
only fourteen. Yet by 1285 the active judges in Padua had risen to
something like 120 and Bonvesin, as we have seen, put the number
of doctors of laws in Milan at the same level. An influx on this
scale means that the judiciary must have attracted many new men
seeking to better their fortunes and social status, for judges had
long been regarded as the social equals of knights. Yet the long
and expensive training required made it necessary for an aspiring
judge to have the backing of at least a moderate fortune; moreover,
the fact that qualified men multiplied even faster than the judicial and administrative posts available must have meant that, for
the majority, their profession was no more than a part-time activity,
yielding influence, prestige and supplementary income to men
who were already substantial *rentiers*. The structure of communal
administration, with its numerous posts held for terms as short as
three or four months, must have created difficulties for career
lawyers who, unless they excelled as advocates, would probably
need to travel in the staff of *podestà* or *capitani* to obtain continuous employment. Permanent salaried posts were very few and
far between; the well-paid chancellorships which nourished the
fifteenth century intelligentsia had not yet been created, though
the appointment of Riccardo Malombra, who had made his reputation as a professor of law at Padua University, to the position of
resident legal adviser to the Venetian government in about 1311, is
a sign of the increasing value placed on the lawyer's skills at this
time.

The case of the notaries was somewhat different. They were far
more numerous than the judges; in the later thirteenth century
there were about 600 in Padua, 1,500 in Milan, and in Bologna,
the fountainhead of the *ars notaria*, there may have been as many
as 2,000. Although their services were indispensable for any kind of
business, and every institution carried its staff of notaries, some of
the communes employing as many as sixty or seventy at a time,
there must still have been flocks of notaries looking to other kinds
of employment for a major part of their subsistence. This was the

source of their strength as a group of literate men with adminstra-
tive experience which they could deploy in any kind of business, or
in politics; moreover, unlike the judges, they were not restricted
to the major cities, but were to be found even in small towns and
villages. Socially inferior to the judges, because their professional
training was cheaper and more widely available, they constituted
something like a strategic centre of the *popolo*, below the wealthy
rentiers, merchants and bankers, but above most of the retailers
and artisans. They probably formed the backbone of most communal councils and seem to be particularly associated with certain
radical movements in the later thirteenth century, characterised
by stringent measures against magnates and attempts to shift the
centre of power from the upper ranks of the *popolani* to the artisans and tradesmen. The classic example is the regime which held
power in Bologna in the early 1280s, whose moving spirit seems
to have been Rolandino Passaggieri, famous for twenty-five years
as the author of the standard textbook of the *ars notaria* and now
the leader both of the notaries' guild and the ultra-Guelph political Society of the Cross.

Although far fewer in number and much less evenly spread than
the lawyers, the increased influx of merchants and mercantile
families into the governing classes of many cities was another
marked feature of the later thirteenth century. The new business
methods, which made it possible to engage in the most far-flung
commercial and banking activities by correspondence with agents
without leaving home, must obviously have made participation in
public life much easier and probably raised the social standing of
the merchant as well. At all events, the merchant-statesman, up to
now a rather rare figure outside the great ports, now began to
appear more frequently in the leading inland cities also. Yet here
again, those best placed to take advantage of the new conditions
were those who already had capital, commercial expertise and
business connections at their disposal. So, although 'new men'
were not unknown, the general tendency was to strengthen the
position of those who were already at least on the road to wealth.
The best-known example of a city whose governing class was
largely composed of merchants and mercantile families is, of
course, Florence, and here research has shown that the families in
power changed very little from the restoration of the Guelphs in
1266 up to 1343. The high offices of the commune rotated among

the members of a restricted circle of families associated with the
Arti Maggiori, especially the three textile guilds of the Calimala,
Lana and Por S. Maria, together with some bankers and judges;
many were the descendants of men who had been already rich and
powerful at the time of the *Primo Popolo* between 1250 and 1260.
By contrast, not only were the offices held by members of the lesser
guilds relatively few, but there was a rapid turnover of office-
holders of this class, so that it was difficult for any individual to
acquire the experience necessary for him to make his weight felt.
Moreover, the curious arrangement whereby the judges and notaries were members of a single guild which was classified as one of the
Maggiori, seems to have robbed the middle guilds of their natural
leaders, the notaries. The governing class at Siena was even more
circumscribed. From 1287 to 1355 the city was ruled by a council
called the Nine, whose members were recruited among the
middling landowners, bankers, textile manufacturers and some
merchants from the more highly capitalised trades, dealers in
spices, dyestuffs and the like. Excluded from office were not only
the great landowning magnates but also the judges and notaries.
Regimes like these could hardly have survived in a period of drastic
social change, and although some of the Lombard communes, with
their large legislative councils, appear on the face of it to have
been more democratic, it is noticeable that radical movements
such as those associated with Rolandino Passaggieri in Bologna or
Giano della Bella in Florence, held control only for brief periods
both north and south of the Apennines.

Not only did some contemporaries exaggerate the numbers and
importance of new men in this period, they also put about the
myth of the catastrophic decline of the old nobility. Dante's list of
ancient Florentine families now extinct or reduced to obscurity is
paralleled in the writings of Da Nono about Padua and of Riccobaldo about Ferrara. There is no need to doubt the examples
which these sources give, for in this period as in any other, there
were plenty of families which were ruined for one reason or
another. However, this does not prove that there was a general
decline of the nobility as a class, and there is a good deal of evidence to suggest that, far from declining, many of the aristocracy
found ways of at least holding their own amid the rising prosperity.
Some succeeded in doing much more than this, as can be seen from
the fact that we have already noted, that among those who gained

lordships over the major cities, the great majority were men of ancient lineage, many of them with impeccable claims to nobility. What enabled them to do this was not the prestige attached to a great name, although this could be an asset, but great resources in men and money which were indispensable to a party leader at least until such time as he could control the public revenues. The social changes which accompanied the establishment of the *signorie* are still obscure, but some generalisations may be ventured. The magnate families who found themselves on the losing side might be ruined, but those who were lucky enough to back a successful *signore* stood to better themselves in every way. *Signori* who, whether they were nobles or not, tended to adopt the outlook of the upper class, had no reason to be prejudiced against the magnates in the way that governments controlled by militant elements among the *popolo* were liable to be. One important consequence of the establishment of the *signorie* seems to have been that the anti-magnatial laws, which had handicapped the greater families during the regime of the *popolo*, were allowed to fall into abeyance.

It would be a capital mistake, however, to attach too much value to social distinctions within the governing classes of communal Italy, which in this period shared a common culture and aimed at a common style of life more self-consciously than ever before. Marked off from the rest of society by inherited wealth which could be supplemented by honourable business or a respected profession, the communal elite consolidated a way of life which was neither purely feudal, mercantile nor professional, neither urban nor rural in outlook, but a blend of all these which was unique and distinctive; it was quite unlike the life of the ruling classes in France, Germany or England at this time. For example, when the Italian friar Salimbene visited France he was surprised to find that the nobility had their homes only in the country; in the most advanced parts of Italy, which he knew well, the landed aristocracy had their town houses and the enriched townsmen had their lands, farms and, if their means allowed, their castles in which they and their families could pass the hot summer months. Giovanni Villani considered that the majority of the nobles and the wealthy citizens of Florence spent at least four months of the year in the contado: some spent more. The result of this long-standing custom was that the social division between town and country had been practically obliterated in large parts of Tuscany and Lombardy at the level of the ruling class. An idealised picture of this way of life is to be found in a series of sonnets by the Tuscan poet Folgore da San Gimignano. Dedicated to a certain Nicolò, who is described as the flower of Siennese society, each poem enlarges on the pleasures of a month of the year. Nicolò and his friends are represented as moving from city to the country and back again according to the seasons, enjoying the best sport and victuals. November is spent in great comfort at the baths of Petriolo, but the programme for August is perhaps the most revealing. The poet conjures up a high mountain valley with thirty castles which have no need of the sea breeze to keep them fresh and clear as the stars, and the nobleman is invited to take for his pleasure short rides from one to another in the morning and the afternoon, his saddle bag open to receive the best country delicacies of Tuscany. The poems portray a class equally at home in town and country; the poet and his audience know the countryside intimately but are entirely free from the anxieties of country life.[12]

If the dominant colours of this pattern of life were aristocratic and chivalric rather than civic, this was because there was no alternative set of ideals to which laymen could turn except the religious asceticism typified by the Third Orders, which was conscientiously followed only by a devout minority. The belief that the merchant followed a distinct style of life which was modest, industrious, calculating and peaceful, in contrast to the ostentation and violence of the nobility, seems to be largely a myth; the modest demeanour expected of a man in the middle ranks of society was soon shed when he believed that he had reached the top. The vendetta is commonly regarded as the hallmark of the anarchic rural nobility, yet it seems that it was practised by all classes of Italian society according to their means, but was rarely thought worth recording except when it concerned the upper classes. The feud seems to have been a part of the *mores* of the great merchant families as far back as records survive. The Velluti, for example, were typical merchant *popolani* with their own warehouses in Florence from at least 1244; writing in 1367, Donato Velluti was able to trace the family vendetta with the magnate Manelli back for a hundred years. Indeed, the merchants contributed something of their own to the feud by sometimes recording debts of honour in their books of personal memoranda; the same term, *quietanza*, could be used for the conclusion of a debt paid in blood or in cash.

Some of the advice given to merchants in the vernacular literature of the period on how they should behave repays careful examination, for it is extremely revealing. While honesty, diligence and caution are given their due weight, there are signs that the successful merchant was expected to cut a figure in society by a suitable display of his wealth. Thus, Giovanni Frescobaldi's *Advice for Those Who Cross to England* which begins, 'Wear modest colours, be humble, be dull in appearance but in fact be subtle' goes on immediately to urge the merchant to 'spend bravely and do not show yourself mean'. Another Florentine, Dino Compagni, stresses that the merchant who wishes to achieve renown should cultivate an appearance consistent with his honourable profession.[13] Compagni shows just what this could mean in practice when he describes the leader of the Florentine White party and the events leading up to the coup of 1301. Vieri dei Cerchi was a rich banker whose family had emerged from obscurity in the time of Oliverio dei Cerchi, who had died in the time of the *Primo Popolo* about 1254. This made the Cerchi new men by Florentine standards, 'risen in a short time from small beginnings', so that when they bought the city *palazzo* of the counts Guidi and began to live in great style, surrounded by a numerous household of retainers, horses and dogs, Compagni thought it natural that they should arouse the envy of their neighbour Corso Donati, a nobleman of an ancient lineage which was no longer as rich as it had been.[14] Yet the struggle which ensued did not see the new families ranged against the old, for it was the Cerchi who enlisted the support of the most ancient and aristocratic clans, many of them with Ghibelline traditions, while Corso became the leader of the solid centre of the rich *popolani* of the greater guilds of Florence. A careful reading of Compagni's account reveals that it was not class divisions but the intense competition brought about by the breakdown of traditional barriers which exacerbated the conflict; it was presumably the atmosphere generated by this phenomenon which led Dante, Da Nono and Riccobaldo da Ferrara to exaggerate the social flux in the way they did.

In theory, the most vital asset in the struggle for power, leadership in war, formed no part of the merchant's equipment; hence Compagni could attribute the failure of the Cerchi to the fact that they remained merchants at heart and therefore cowardly. He chose to forget that he himself had described the courage of the Cerchi in the front line against the Ghibellines at the battle of Campaldino, and that his chronicle provides a number of instances of military ineptitude and fatal indecision shown by leaders of noble blood, whose ancestors were supposed to have cultivated the art of war for generations. He seems to criticise the Cerchi for failing to establish a family *signoria* in Florence, yet it is doubtful if this was practicable, for when the magnate-bankers, the Bardi, made the attempt a generation later in 1340, it failed miserably. For the few instances of merchant families which succeeded in winning the lordship of a major city, it is necessary to look outside Florence; in most cases the evidence for business activity ceases as the family reaches the apex of political power. The Della Scala of Verona, for example, seem to have been urban in their origins and the real founder of the *signoria*, Mastino I (d. 1277), seems to have drawn his strength, at least in part, from his control of the Veronese merchant guild. But after his death his successors went out of their way to create a court which would be a beacon of chivalry to the whole of north-eastern Italy; in Cangrande (d. 1328) the family produced one of the most admired and successful miltary leaders of the period.

For a combination of business and politics at the highest level it is necessary to turn to the Scotti family of Piacenza. As we have seen, this medium-sized Lombard city had been an important centre of commerce and banking from the early days of the communes. During the thirteenth century the Piacentines managed to hold on to a share of the banking activities in north-western Europe; fifty-seven of them have been identified in business in France between 1238 and 1267, including several members of the Scotti family. The election of Tebaldo Visconti of Piacenza as Pope Gregory X in 1271 came as a heaven-sent windfall to his compatriots; it comes as no surprise to find the Scotti advancing money for the projected crusade, or being entrusted with others with the collection of a papal tithe imposed on England for the same purpose. Bernardo Scotto was the head of the main banking firm at this time, while Renaldo was regarded as the family's leader in politics. However, the distinction between business and politics was not always preserved. In 1271, for example, Renaldo was allowed to buy the castle of Gravagni for £3000 from the com-

mune which had just bought out the previous owners for the sum of
£7000; in 1290, his son Alberto was only prevented from carrying
through a similar transaction in respect of Zavatarello by the
intervention of the Genoese, near whose borders the fortress in
question lay. The role played by money in Alberto Scotto's election
to the office of perpetual lord of Piacenza in 1290 does not seem to
have been recorded, but a chronicler accuses him of rifling the
communal treasury in 1302 for £6000 with which to buy property
for a private exchange with the bishop; the pattern of territorial
power built up with money from trade, political influence or
simple robbery is clear enough. Apart from an eye for such transactions, there is nothing to distinguish Alberto Scotto's career
from that of any other unscrupulous and insecure tyrant. He
seized power in Piacenza three times and was three times expelled;
he changed his allies both outside and inside the city frequently
and with no trace of principle or sentiment; he was a renowned
war leader in his day and his intransigence led finally to his deser-
tion by his followers and his surrender at Castell 'Arquato, a mountain fortress-town where he had held out like any lawless feudal
baron for more than four years after his last expulsion from the
city in 1313.[15]

To the Cerchi, the Della Scala and the Scotti there could be
added numerous examples of business families who adopted the
mores of the nobility; such cases are relatively easy to trace, but it
must not be assumed that the cultural influences moved in one
direction only. Although it is much more difficult to prove, it seems
that the spirit of the Italian nobility was profoundly modified by
accommodation to civic life, and that in the process of transmission to new families its essence was diluted and transformed. While,
at home, the Italian aristocracy was widely admired and imitated,
to outsiders their chivalry appeared tainted with bourgeois traits.
In a French poem,[16] Lombard knights are criticised as followers of
Roman law and the decretals and as excessively influenced by
rhetoric – for being, in fact, the kind of men which the *podestà*
literature presented as the ideal; and indeed, the knight who was
also a doctor of law is a far from rare figure from the later thirteenth century. Chivalric literature was very popular in communal
Italy and the *chansons* were not only read at home but commonly
recited in the market places; yet, like detective novels in Italy
today, they remained an essentially imported product, and the

Italian essays in the *genre* remained closely dependent on their French models and generally of poor quality. Significantly, the only region where the French epic struck deep roots was in the non-communal South.

The characteristic expression of the ideals of communal Italy is to be found in the school of poetry known as the *Dolce stil nuovo*, whose ideas can be regarded as an adaptation of courtly love to the conditions of Italian civic life. The central theme to which the poets return again and again is the ennobling effects which Love, through the Lady, produces on the gentle heart. The mood is generally lyrical, stiffened with arguments drawn from contemporary science or school ethics, and the background is either vaguely pastoral or quite unspecific. While in other literatures the Lover needs to prove himself in war, the quest, or some other kind of ordeal, in the Italian school he hardly needs to leave his house, let alone the suburbs, to realise his transformation, which is envisaged as essentially interior and qualitative.

The most elaborate exposition of social ideas by a member of the *Dolce stil nuovo* school is to be found in Dante's *Convivio*, the major work of his middle years, the fourth book of which is given over to a lengthy inquiry into the nature of nobility. In the poem *Le dolci rime d'amor* and the commentary which makes up the rest of the book, Dante refutes vehemently, and even with derision, the idea that nobility is in any way hereditary. For him, it is the noble man who ennobles the family and not the other way round; indeed, to speak of a noble family is inaccurate, since nobility is a quality belonging only to individuals and not to the group. Nobility or *gentilezza* is a virtue planted in the soul by God and, it is implied, is as likely to be found in the son of a peasant as in the son of a king. Stated in isolation, this doctrine appears to be extremely radical, and, indeed, the poets of the *Dolce stil nuovo* were of mixed origins; some were aristocrats but others, including Dante himself, though respected citizens, would have had difficulty in proving their nobility according to the traditional criteria. However, another large part of Dante's argument is taken up with an equally fierce attack on the notion that riches confer nobility. Dante maintains that riches are in themselves ignoble. To acquire them through inheritance or by chance is unbecoming since it shows an undue dependence on *fortuna*; to acquire them through hard work creates a degrading interest in unworthy things. Far

from advocating any kind of open society, Dante finds the time to
repeat the traditional clerical arguments proving the superiority
of the contemplative over the practical life. In short, the doctrine
put forward in the *Convivio* offers little comfort to anyone except
a *rentier* of moderate but sufficient means, with intellectual interests and a romantic experience which assured him that he had
indeed a gentle heart – someone, in fact, very like Dante himself.

To find a real defence of the mixed Italian society as it existed
in its most advanced form where the fusion of the landed, professional and business elements was most complete, we must look to a
lesser poet than Dante. We have already met Dino Compagni in a
number of contexts. Of an old Florentine *popolano* family and a
lifelong member of the respected guild of the Por S. Maria, Compagni was an active politician from 1282 until he was debarred
from further office by the victorious Blacks in 1301. His chronicle
shows him to have been one of the earliest masters of Italian prose;
he was also a poet in a small way on the fringes of the *Dolce stil
nuovo* circle. One poem attributed to him is addressed to Dante's
friend and fellow poet, Guido Cavalcante. The Cavalcanti were
among the oldest mercantile families in Florence, so old that they
had been entirely assimilated to the nobility. A Cavalcante had
been consul of the commune in 1176 and another consul of the
societas militum as early as 1208. According to all accounts Guido
was every inch an aristocrat; in his chronicle, Compagni describes
him as a noble knight, 'courteous and ardent, but scornful and
solitary and intent on study', and a story about him in Boccaccio's
Decameron shows he left a reputation as one who did not suffer
fools gladly.

The first half of Dino's poem presents a conventional picture;
the poet explains that he has always defended Guido's reputation
even when he has been negligent – presumably in the minor
courtesies of life. Guido is praised as a perfect knight in the Italian
manner, learned as well as graceful, brave and skilled in all
knightly exercises. But this conventional mould is shattered by
the closing lines:

> You are a man of great good fortune;
> Would that you had been a merchant!
> If God gave every man his true deserts
> Righting all that's wrong,

To whoever has a trade he would give courtesy,
And you he would make a worker,
Great in your earning and in your giving away.[17]

It is hard to imagine how this poem would have been received by Cavalcante, if it was ever sent, for the ideal it put forward probably had few devotees even among Compagni's own class, most of whom seem to have been content to ape the nobility as far as they were able. However, that such a poem could be written at all indicates how far Italian society had moved towards the recognition of the ideal of the merchant prince before its impetus was damped and its line of development changed by the troubles and disasters of the fourteenth century.

7. The End of an Era

The Disasters of the Mid-fourteenth Century

A FURTHER dimension is added to our understanding of the *vita civile* of the early fourteenth century by the knowledge that it was not destined to last. Although contemporaries had no real premonition of the fact, Italian society, which had been gradually climbing since the dark days of the tenth century, had now reached a plateau of prosperity and in front of it loomed an abyss. The catastrophes of the mid-fourteenth century, of which the Black Death was the most spectacular, affected the whole of Europe and other parts of the world besides, but nowhere were their results more marked than in communal Italy. As the most complex economy in the medieval world, Italy had most to lose from the disruption caused by famine, plague and warfare; the contraction of markets hit hardest the Italian merchants who handled such a high proportion of the long-distance trade. The ravages of mercenary armies which inflicted so much damage to France during the Hundred Years' War were at least as severe in parts of Italy, where, around 1350, free companies of soldiers and camp-followers numbering tens of thousands lived off the country uncontrolled by any political authority, in a way reminiscent of the wandering barbarian invaders at the time of the breakdown of the Roman Empire. Outside the few surviving republics, these troubles were accompanied by an obvious decline in public spirit. *Signori* treated their states as if they were private property, eroding the distinction between public and private law in a manner scarcely equalled in the Dark Ages. Cities were bequeathed by will and even bought and sold. An extreme example is Lucca, once one of the great free communes of Tuscany, which in 1329 was sold to Gherardo Spinola of Genoa by Lewis of Bavaria's German troops. During the next thirteen years the city changed hands five times – once by cession, twice by purchase and twice by conquest.

The most important casualty of these chaotic years was not the economic or political structures, although these were severely strained, but the self-confidence of the governing classes and their faith in the way of life which had been built up laboriously over the centuries. The belief in human dignity and the value of the individual, in the unique significance of the transient moment, which found its highest expression in the paintings of Giotto, received a severe setback; the popular painters after 1350 emphasise the gulf between man and the supernatural and human powerlessness before the inscrutable will of God. The critical study of classical Latin literature, which had made a promising start in the hands of a small intellectual elite in Padua, Verona, Milan and some neighbouring cities, changed in character in the 1340s. The pre-humanist scholars, as they are usually called, had tried to apply their knowledge to contemporary moral and political problems and were deeply rooted in the society of the communes in which they lived. By contrast, Petrarch, the torchbearer of humanist studies from the 1340s until his death in 1375, was a rootless voluntary exile, whose views on public affairs, though elegantly expressed, were little more than thinly disguised opportunism. Just as Giotto's realism was taken up again by Masaccio and Donatello in the early fifteenth century, so the civic humanism of Padua reappears only with Bruni and his circle in Florence round about 1400.

The explanation for the deflection of Italian society from its obvious line of development during approximately the half century beginning in 1340 must be largely sought in economic terms. It seems that there was at least a partial breakdown in the process of economic growth which had prevailed since the tenth and eleventh centuries. Despite the much more ample sources available for the fourteenth century, the nature of the breakdown is almost as obscure as the origins of the economic recovery some four hundred years before; in particular, the historian is faced with a similar gap between most of the evidence which is very local, and the general nature of the phenomenon he is trying to explain. Any suggestions in this field must, in the present state of knowledge, be extremely tentative.

It is generally accepted that, although the Black Death was itself an entirely unpredictable biological disaster, it was preceded in Europe by a series of lesser misfortunes of various kinds which suggest that something was seriously wrong with the economy. In Italy these signs of strain first appear not in the cities but in the countryside. The tax records of a number of central Italian communes show that they were having unusual difficulty in collecting the *estimo*, the direct tax on property and wealth, from their territories; by the early fourteenth century the actual assessment of the various rural communities was beginning to fall. At a time when the major communes were under great pressure to spread the tax burden as much as possible, this fact is very significant. The reason given by some of the hard-pressed rural communities at the time was that the richer rural taxpayers were moving into the towns and cities and paying (or evading) their taxes there; the few cases where the records relating to a locality have been preserved and examined suggest that this diagnosis of the trouble is perfectly correct. However, we know that this kind of migration was nothing new; for a century at least the *popoli* of the major cities had grown through the influx of immigrants from the rural 'middle class'. The complaints suggest that the latest wave of migrants were not being replaced as their predecessors had been, and this is borne out by some local tax assessments which show an increasing polarity in rural society between a handful of rich proprietors (below the ranks of the nobles and magnates, who were taxed separately) and the mass of the poor. Whether, as has been suggested, this was due to a falling off in the rate of growth of the population as a whole, or whether it was on account of some particular difficulties affecting the free *livellarii* (lease-holders) and small proprietors, which prevented them from amassing the modest fortune necessary to finance their ascent into urban society, it seems clear that the social ladder had lost a vital rung.[1]

It is notoriously difficult to form an accurate idea of the condition of the free peasantry through the surviving records, but it is possible to see some of the forces which were working against them at this time. No class, for example, was likely to suffer more from taxation and the unforeseeable hazards of war and harvest failures; the early fourteenth century had more than its fair share of all these. In addition, the more progressive large landlords, such as religious corporations or noble or magnate families, were striving to consolidate their holdings into a series of compact holdings (*poderi*); no study has yet shown exactly how this was done, but it seems most likely that if anyone suffered, it would be the rural smallholder. Finally, the replacement of the long lease (*livello*) by a short-term contract, which had been proceeding sporadically throughout the thirteenth century, may have reached a critical stage in some of the more advanced areas in the decades leading up to the outbreak of the Black Death. Both the compact holding and the short lease brought economic benefits, the former by making the land easier to work and the latter by involving the landlord more closely in its management. The short leases represent the extension of commercial attitudes to the land. They created a *societas* in which the tenant supplied the labour while the landlord provided not only the land and fixed equipment, but often the tools, livestock, seed corn and the like as well. Naturally the lord took a very close interest in how the land was worked, and this was laid down in detail in the contract. In return he took a high rent or a proportion of the crop. In the *mezzadria*, which became the commonest form in central Italy, landlord and tenant took equal shares. These developments brought the investment of new capital in the land and better productivity. The peasant may have benefited from this to some extent, for it would be unwise to assume that the later abuses of the *mezzadria* were necessarily present from the start. It seems unlikely, however, that the holders of short leases had the same opportunities for eventual economic and social advancement as *livellarii* had. The new-style tenant may have made a reasonable living, but he was more socially isolated. In short, it seems as though the web of the mixed Italian society was broken at a most sensitive point.

In the cities the signs of impending crisis before the Black Death are of a different kind from those to be found in the Italian countryside. There is nothing to suggest that the growth of population, fed by immigration from the contado, was falling off before 1348; the Genoese enclosed a new suburb south of the city in 1320 and another to the north in 1346, and at Siena there were extensions to the walled area in 1323 and 1346. It was not a fall in tax yields, as in the country, but a dramatic rise in taxation which constituted the real danger signal in the cities. By the late thirteenth century the Italian communes had evolved a formidable armoury of taxes of all kinds and a remarkably efficient administrative machine for exacting them, and during the wave of intense inter-city warfare which followed Henry of Luxemburg's expedition, governments could not resist the temptation to use their tax weapons to the full. The budget of the Florentine commune, to cite the best known example, already stood at the high figure of £395,000 in 1317 but by 1336–8 it had more than doubled to about £930,000. Moreover, the bulk of this greatly increased burden was met by indirect taxes placed on foodstuffs brought into the city – wine, salt and much else besides. By 1338 the gabelles accounted for about 80 per cent of the commune's income. In Florence the *estimo* or direct tax on property and income was not applied to the city after 1315; this flight from direct taxation did not take place to the same degree everywhere, but the rise in indirect taxes seems to have been very widespread.

There can be no doubt that these changes placed a very severe burden on the poor of the cities, who were hardest hit by the rise in the prices of necessities, caused by the gabelles. Where the *estimo* had fallen into disuse, almost the only way in which the communes could directly tap the resources of the rich was by loans. Venice led the way in this method of financing public expenditure, which was specially favoured by cities with a strong commercial class. Mainly voluntary at first, compulsion was increasingly used to exact public loans, which were particularly suitable for meeting sudden demands caused by war or famine. Although attempts were made to repay in times of prosperity, generally speaking each financial crisis left the communes with a larger debt, the best known case being again that of Florence, where the communal debt rose from 47,275 gold florins in 1303 to 450,000 gold florins in 1338. Indebtedness on this scale meant that a good deal of the commune's normal income was tied down for the payment of interest. While it is doubtful if forced loans were ever actually welcomed by the rich, there are good reasons to suppose that they were looked on as the most acceptable form of public contribution. The very rich could easily bear the loss of capital involved, and if the rates of interest were low, which was not always the case, shares in the public debt were at least a secure investment, a useful alternative to investment in land. It was the lesser contributors to the forced loans, as well as those who paid the taxes from which the interest was found, who suffered disproportionately.[2]

Together with taxes of unparalleled severity, communal Italy continued to suffer from the age-old scourge of war, which was part of the price paid for city-state independence. Here again, the crisis of the fourteenth century was the culmination of processes which went back a very long way. War in Italy had always been very destructive, for with the walled cities virtually impossible to storm except by surprise or with the help of treason, the systematic ravaging of territories was often the only way of putting pressure on an enemy. By the fourteenth century, war had also become cripplingly expensive. In a sense, the communes were the victims of their own administrative efficiency. As early as 1266 it has been calculated that the Florentines were able to mobilise an army of some 16,000 men from the city and its territory alone, and since, contrary to common belief, communal militias were paid while on service, this force would have cost something like £35,000 a month in pay to keep in the field. With the passage of time not only did rates of pay rise but the campaigning season tended to get longer. Native forces were increasingly reinforced by professional mercenaries, many of them foreigners. During the war against the Della Scala of Verona in 1338 the Florentine commune assumed the role of paymaster for many allied troops beside its own, but even so, Giovanni Villani's estimate that war expenditure amounted to 600,000 gold florins (£1,860,000) in a period of eighteen months is a staggering figure; as the chronicler was proudly aware, it is unlikely that any other city could have shouldered a burden of this weight. The effect of expenditure of this order on communities lacking the wealth of Florence can only be imagined.

There would have been a military problem in Italy even without the foreign mercenaries; with them, to the problem of cost was added that of political control. The employment of professional soldiers, both Italian and foreign, was a deep-rooted practice. It did not arise suddenly at the time of the *signorie*, but went back at least as far as the most vigorous period of the free communes in the late twelfth and early thirteenth centuries. Every foreign prince who intervened in Italy, from Barbarossa onwards, brought warriors in his train, some of whom joined the ranks of soldiers of fortune who never lacked employment somewhere in the peninsula. Mercenaries were not used to supersede the communal militias, but made up part of the elite cavalry forces necessary to any balanced army of the time. The standing army of the Guelph league in Tuscany in the last quarter of the thirteenth century was a typically mixed force, including natives of the Guelph cities serving with Italian and foreign mercenaries, the latter being mainly southern Frenchmen drawn in initially through the connection with the Angevins of Naples. In 1305 there was established for the first time in Florence a permanent force of foreign troops consisting of Catalans, who had arrived with the Duke of Calabria (later King Robert of Naples) when he came as the commune's war captain in the campaign against the Whites in Pistoia. Florentine relations with the Catalan commander, Diego de Rat, were remarkably good, but the ever-increasing size of the individual contingents owing their loyalty to a single commander boded ill for the future. Fresh waves of northerners were brought into Italy by Henry of Luxemburg in 1310 and Lewis of Bavaria in 1327. When the German garrison, which Lewis had placed in Lucca, first elected Marco Visconti as their *signore* and then put the city up for sale, the political menace latent in the foreign companies emerged into the open. Some sixteen years later in 1345, when the Pisans dismissed a large foreign army which they had enlisted against the Florentines, Werner von Urslingen, a German commander, kept his force together and withdrew into the Romagna, where it formed the nucleus of the Grand Company which was to terrorise central Italy in the 1350s, a power unto itself independent of any regular political control.

Common sense would suggest that it was the expensive armies both foreign and native which caused high taxation, but it may be more true to say that it was the efficient taxation system which made the large armies possible and attracted soldiers of fortune from most of Europe. At all events, the combination of grinding taxation and the dangers of war bore hard on the weaker sections of the community, and by the late 1330s it seems that it needed only a bad harvest to create a desperate situation for the poor. Villani tells us that in 1339 food prices in Florence shot up and disaster was only averted by the commune importing large quantities of grain; the next year, the cost of corn rose still higher and there was a serious outbreak of plague which killed 15,000 in the city alone. In 1345 an exceptionally wet summer in most of Italy and southern France ruined the crops, and in 1346 the harvest failed again, and there seems to have been little relief in 1347. It was a weakened population which faced the outbreak of the Black Death at the beginning of 1348; before the plague had spent its force between a third and a half of the entire population had died, and in some of the great cities the mortality rate was well over 50 per cent.

Before the appearance of the plague the economic difficulties so far mentioned were ones which affected the poor most severely and left the governing classes relatively untouched. To complete the picture of the mid-fourteenth century disasters, which so deeply disturbed the development of Italian society, it is necessary to add one more which struck directly at some of the leaders of the most economically advanced society of the time. The position of the great medieval business houses had always been precarious. At home they ran the constant risks of disturbance by war or sudden political changes; abroad their power over money made them obvious targets for envy and extortion, and, unless they enjoyed the favour of the government in the countries where they did business, there was little their own communes could do to protect them from arbitrary confiscations or even outright robbery. When the most powerful crown in Europe was involved, as when Philip the Fair of France imprisoned the Italian merchants in his kingdom for a time in 1291, there was nothing the communes could do but protest; nor could there be any question of redress when Philip transferred his financial affairs to French instead of Italian bankers after 1303. In such conditions the only prudent course seemed to lie in being as obliging as possible to the king and members of the ruling circle of those northern kingdoms which formed a vital part of the international business world. Events were to prove, however, that the friendship of kings could be as damaging in the long run as their hostility.

As we have seen, the Bardi and Peruzzi companies of Florence became the leading bankers of the English crown soon after 1310, and from the time of his troubled accession, they were in close relations with the young Edward III. They seem to have realised quite soon the dangers into which the new king's warlike ambitions might lead them; in 1333 the Bardi were already trying to secure repayment of their loans so that they could withdraw, but Edward was determined and both the Bardi and Peruzzi were drawn into advancing large sums for the wars in Scotland and France. The Peruzzi at least had reason to know that wars of conquest could still be profitable undertakings for they had participated in the exploitation of the French conquest of Flanders after 1305; to be financially successful, however, it was necessary to occupy a lot of rich territory quickly and to hold it without dispute. Edward's early campaigns did not meet these conditions, and in 1342 he repudiated his debts to the unfortunate Florentines. At home the Florentine commune was in the middle of its abortive attempts to buy Lucca, and money was so short that the gabelle could not be sold in November 1341, and those who bought the tax in January 1342 were unable to raise the cash. Lesser merchants and small workshops began to fail about this time through lack of credit from the banks, and, as the English news spread, confidence began to fail. By a series of extraordinary efforts the Peruzzi managed to stagger on until 1343 when, with a number of other important companies, they went bankrupt; the final blow had been the refusal of either the pope or King Robert of Naples to come to their assistance. The biggest house of all, the Bardi, crashed early in 1346.

Giovanni Villani described the fall of the Bardi as 'the greatest loss and defeat that our commune has ever had' – as well he might, for he himself was among the merchants who went bankrupt in the wake of the great companies. Francesco Pegolotti was more fortunate, being appointed one of the liquidators of the Bardi in 1374; nevertheless, the business world described in the *Practica della Mercatura* was shaken to its foundations. The largest business organisations in the medieval world had been swept away. True, the disaster was largely restricted to Florence; Venetian and Genoese activities in the Mediterranean were unaffected, and even in Florence a host of smaller firms survived and new lines of business were opened up. Yet in England, at least, the situation was never restored, and Edward III had to turn to English financiers for his later campaigns. The financial hegemony of the Florentines, over the trade routes from the Mediterranean to north-west Europe, was not really restored until the fifteenth century, when the Medici bank achieved something resembling the size and scope of business which the Peruzzi and the Bardi had had. It was only in the fifteenth century, too, that the intangible but nevertheless very real loss of confidence caused by the disasters of the 1340s was made good, and the values of the *vita civile* were reaffirmed in an unmistakable manner by the writers and artists of the early Renaissance.

Marsiglio of Padua's Plan for Peace

WELL before the economic disasters of the mid-fourteenth century struck them, all but a few of the Italian communes had settled down under the rule of *signori*. The search for an equitable and stable form of conciliar government regulated by law, with as little as possible left to the individual whim of officials, had been abandoned in favour of the efficiency and unity which it was thought would be found in the personal and family regimes of the despots. The rich legacy which the *signori* received from the communes in terms of law, administrative machinery and concepts of the state and of citizenship, should not be allowed to obscure the significance of the change; from the time when the leading citizens formed themselves into a commune and elected their first officials during the anarchy of the Investiture Contest, the prevailing objective had been to ensure that authority should be shared among the members of the governing class and avoid the monopoly of power by any individual or family – the very principle on which the *signoria* was built. So, in the political sphere too, the early decades of the fourteenth century can be regarded as the end of an era.

The ideals of the dying communes were commemorated in a remarkable book which distilled the fruits of their experience, analysed their problems and made penetrating and practical suggestions for the better ordering of civil society in the future. Marsiglio of Padua's *Defensor Pacis* (*The Defender of the Peace*) was, so far as we know, the first venture into authorship by a middle-aged cleric of between forty-five and fifty who, though he still had eighteen years to live when he completed it in 1324, never reached anything like the same heights again. Born into the Paduan administrative class around 1275–80, the son of a notary called Bonmatteo Mainardini, Marsiglio's political memories must have run back to the 1290s, when the Paduan commune had been at the height of its power. Reasonably free from factions within, Padua had been secure from external attacks and had played a leading and respected role in the politics of eastern Lombardy until the coming of Henry of Luxemburg had upset the *status quo*. The revolt of the subject city of Vicenza in 1311 was followed by war with Verona, whose Della Scala *signori*, and especially the young and warlike Cangrande, made their objective the conquest of the whole region up to the borders of Venetian territory and the destruction of Padua's independence. The defeats experienced in the Veronese war and the party strife which this created in Padua changed the course of Marsiglio's life; for reasons which are unknown, his loyalties oscillated between his native city and her enemies, and in about 1319 he left Padua for ever, though his friends there continued to correspond with him. Although the Paduans inflicted a notable defeat on the Veronese in 1320, it was probably clear to Marsiglio that the days of the free commune were numbered.

Experiences such as these must have given food for reflection to any sensitive and intelligent man; where Marsiglio was unusual was in the mental equipment which his training allowed him to bring to bear on what he had seen. Early in his education, Marsiglio had deserted the family profession of the law in favour of medicine; later, and probably under the influence of his fellow Paduan, Pietro d'Abano, the outstanding Italian scientist of his day, he expanded his studies into the field of natural science and went to the university of Paris, where he was rector, a post usually held by talented young men, in 1312. The intellectual atmosphere of Paris was very different from that of Italy. From the early twelfth century the northern schools had concentrated on dialectic and theology, while the Italians specialised in law, rhetoric and medicine; during the thirteenth century the newly translated works of Aristotle had become the foundation of all inquiry in Paris. The fully evolved scholastic method, which taught the student to look for a hierarchy of causes to explain anything from the nature of the angels to that of plants or minerals, was still a northern speciality which had only begun to impinge on Italian lay and civic culture in the later thirteenth century. Scholasticism came to the Italian cities late, and in the law schools its introduction was warmly resisted by the devotees of the native tradition. Mendicants who had been trained in Paris were important disseminators of northern ways of thought. Dante, for example, acquired his scholasticism without ever leaving Italy, so far as we know; his teachers were the Franciscans of S. Croce and the Dominicans of S. Maria Novella, among them Remigio Girolami. Thus, there was some intermingling of northern and Italian intellectual currents, which made Italian culture more rich than it had been in the time of Boncompagno or even Brunetto Latini; even so, Marsiglio must be regarded as privileged in his generation in having experienced Parisian thought at first hand.

Paris did not turn Marsiglio into a professional theologian, nor did he ever master academic jurisprudence; fundamentally he remained a physician, who came in as an outsider to propose cures for the ills of church and state. In this he had a real affinity of mind with Aristotle, which enabled him to absorb the Greek's political ideas and build on them in a unique way. It might seem that Aristotle's examination of the problems of the Greek city-states, threatened by despotism and the territorial power of the Macedonian kingdom, would have had an immediate appeal to the citizens of communal Italy faced by the challenges of the *signoria* and the Empire. In fact, although the text of the *Politics* had been available in Latin since about 1260, the first real attempt to apply its approach to the conditions of the Italian communes was not made until Ptolemy of Lucca wrote his completion of Aquinas' unfinished *De Regimine Principum* about 1306. But while Ptolemy had done little more than borrow from the *Politics*, Marsiglio acquired, above all, Aristotle's method of looking at the state as a natural phenomenon. The way he saw the state as a living organism is nowhere more clear than in his account of the origins of a city or kingdom, where he draws on the analogy of the genesis of an individual animal as it was understood by contemporary embryology. Marsiglio saw the state as arising from the 'soul' of the whole citizen body or of its more weighty part, which created first the directive element in the state, or *principans*, which is likened to the heart. As the heart was believed to form the other organs of the embryo through the natural virtue or heat imparted to it, so the *principans* should institute the other parts of the state in accordance with the mandate of the citizens. This happens to be a very plausible reconstruction of how the communes may have been formed at the time of the election of their first officials; Marsiglio cannot have known this, but rather had in mind the fully developed communal governments of his own day. He saw in their complex constitutions and numerous councils and officials the essential distinction between those with the power to make the law and those who merely carried it into effect. In Padua, the former function was largely the monopoly of the Greater Council of the commune, and this was clearly the prototype of Marsiglio's Legislator, which in other cities might be shared between various councils of the commune and the *popolo*. The definition of the *principans*, with its emphasis on the subjection of the executive to the law, brings the *podestà* and the *capitano del popolo* immediately to mind; yet Marsiglio's term embraced much more than the foreign officials of the communes, and must be taken to include the native *anziani* or priors, the guild officials, the judiciary and, indeed, functionaries of any kind insofar as they were responsible for carrying out the provisions of the Legislator.

Even when Marsiglio appears to be following his authorities most closely he has the trick of introducing significant modifications or changing the context and applications of accepted ideas, so that starting from the commonplace he imperceptibly reaches a position which is all his own. For example, his view of the priesthood as a part of the state subject to the temporal control of the Legislator came from Aristotle and was quite natural to a pagan writer; its application to the Christian church by Marsiglio was original and revolutionary. Again, both elements of Marsiglia's dual definition of law – in its content a universal doctrine concerning the common good or its opposite, and in its form a coercive command – can be found in other writers like Aquinas, but no one else used these uncontroversial criteria to draw the conclusion that the articles of the Christian faith and the moral doctrines of the church did not qualify as law unless a temporal penalty was attached to their non-observance by the Legislator. Similarly, Marsiglio repeats Aristotle's quasi-historical account of the development of human associations from the nuclear family by way of the village to their culmination in the city-state, only for him each stage is characterised not by the ends which it subserves but by the different kinds of authority and law appropriate to it. This quiet shift of emphasis away from the discussion of ends and towards the practical means by which human society can be maintained in peace gives its distinctive stamp to Marsiglio's treatment of the state. By playing down the teleology which intoxicated so many of his contemporaries, he sought an escape from the dominance of the ecclesiastical power which it claimed by virtue of its more immediate relationship to the highest end of human life.

Marsiglio puts forward three rules for the health of the secular state: that the Legislator shall be composed of the *universitas* of the citizens, or of the weightier part which adequately represents it; that the Legislator must be one and undivided; and that the *principans* must be subject to the Legislator. Each of these propositions was based on an acute understanding of the internal political problems of the communes, and, taken together, they imply a programme for the consolidation of the communal regimes.

Because of his insistence on the sovereignty of the whole body of citizens, Marsiglio has sometimes been taken for an advocate of democracy in something like its modern sense. This is certainly a misconception, for Marsiglio had never seen anything remotely resembling the participation of the entire population in politics. What he did know was the Paduan *consiglio maggiore* with its thousand members, which amounted to about one in ten of the adult male population – a very high degree of democracy for the period. Moreover, it should be noted that he talks about the *universitas* of the citizens, not of the inhabitants, which is a very different thing. In fact, when Marsiglio talked in this way, he was not vindicating a theoretical right but trying to solve a problem which was recognised as serious and even fundamental by his contemporaries. It was a political commonplace of the time that civil discord had its root in pride, from which arose greed, jealousy and competition for honours, and virtually all the ills that afflicted human society. The cure most commonly proposed was a change of heart; Remigio Girolami, for example, wrote treatises and preached sermons exalting the common good which every citizen must place before his own self-interest in the cause of peace. Dante, although he, too, preaches a good deal, saw that something more than exhortation was called for. One of his reasons for advocating a world monarch was that such a ruler would possess everything and would, therefore, be free from cupidity; his personal interests would coincide exactly with those of the state. While Dante tried to solve the problem of self-interest by recourse to the rule of one, Marsiglio looked to the many. He argues that not only will a law, made with the assent of the citizens be more readily obeyed, but that it will *ipso facto* be in the best interests of the community, since the multitude can perceive where its interests lie, and no one willingly injures himself or deliberately inflicts injustice on himself. Thus, the altruism called for by the preachers is both impossible and unnecessary.

The concept of the *pars valentior*, the weightier part of the citizen-body, is a further refinement on these ideas. Marsiglio explains that *valentior* must be understood 'according to the quantity and quality of persons in the community over which the law is made', but does not elaborate further. In trying to guess his meaning we must remember that the constitutions he knew made great use of property qualifications; also, the word *pars* was the normal Latin word for party, and there were well-known examples of party government in the communes of Marsiglio's day. His words are open to the interpretation that the *pars valentior* might consist of merchants and bankers in Florence and lawyers and landowners in Padua; the only essential is that the *pars* must adequately represent the whole community. Marsiglio's doctrine left room for many variations but not for tyranny, for, unlike many contemporaries, he insisted that the consent of the governed was necessary for a legitimate government. Indeed, when he included Aristotle's classification of constitutions in the *Defensor*, he added to the criterion of the common interest that of the consent of the subjects to distinguish well-tempered from perverted forms of government.

Marsiglio's second stipulation, that the Legislator in each city or kingdom should be one and undivided, though it was mainly developed as an attack on the jurisdiction of the church, was one of great relevance to the secular government of the cities also. After more than two centuries of continuous development the communes had still not entirely shaken off the handicap of their irregular beginnings. Starting as a particular kind of *societas* in a society teeming with *societates*, they still lacked the absolute and exclusive claim on the loyalty of their subjects implied in the modern concept of sovereignty. So, although communal statutes might claim to override the regulations of lesser associations, in practice the Legislator had to contend with the semi-autonomy of the *popolo*, trade guilds, family associations and political parties, which meant that the communes were often unable to act with one mind. A celebrated example is the role of the wealthy and prestigious *Parte Guelfa* of Florence, which held on to its power to contest the policies of the commune from 1266 until the end of the fourteenth century. Marsiglio had an unusually clear perception of this problem, and condemned a divided Legislator as a pathological condition in the body politic.

The third point in the Marsilian programme was far from original. From the very start, so far as we can judge, the communes had insisted that officials be answerable to the whole body, and, by the fourteenth century, this principle was enshrined in the elaborate regulations of the communal statutes. Yet, in insisting on the subjection of the *principans* to the citizen-body through the law, Marsiglio was not simply repeating the obvious. His remarks had a special relevance to the *signorie*. By distinguishing so clearly between the Legislator and the *principans*, Marsiglio was able to explore the various forms the latter might take with an appearance of impartiality. The longest chapter in the first discourse of the *Defensor* is taken up with a discussion of whether a *signore* should be elected for a fixed term or for life, or whether the office should be vested in a man and his heirs in perpetuity. This had, no doubt, been a burning issue in Padua where there were strong feelings against personal rule. In July 1318 the Paduans had elected their first *signore*, but Giacomo da Carrara was a lord of the constitutional type who ruled in close consultation with the leading citizens, and voluntarily resigned his office after eighteen months when the policies of the commune demanded a new alliance. Clearly this is the only kind of *signoria* that could be accommodated within the Marsilian structure; a real despotism on the model of the Della Scala of Verona or the Este of Ferrara, destroyed one of his chief tenets by making the Legislator and the *principans* one and the same person. So, although it is not explicitly stated, Marsiglio's position with regard to the *signoria* is quite unequivocal. So far as the principles of secular government were concerned, Marsiglio remained indelibly marked with the creed of the Paduan commune in which he had been brought up; he was one of the last as well as the most able defender of the living ideals of the free Lombard communes before they were submerged by the ideology of the *signorie*.

Although it contains so much about communal government, the *Defensor Pacis* is not primarily concerned with the reform of the cities but with the right relationship between the church and the temporal ruler. The first discourse which seeks the basis for the state according to reason is followed by the second which proceeds from the documents of the Christian faith and their interpreters. Like Dante's Virgil, Marsiglio's pagan guide, Aristotle, can lead him only a part of the way; the second discourse is nearly five times as long as the first. While the programme for the communes has to be winkled out of the text, the plan for the church is spelt out in detail. Marsiglio must have known what this would mean for him; as soon as his authorship was known, he was excommunicated and was dependent for the rest of his life on the protection of an anti-papal ruler, Lewis of Bavaria. It is possible that he had written something about the state earlier which has been lost; the book that we have arose from Marsiglio's feelings about the church, and since he risked death and endured exile for his views, we must assume he held them very strongly indeed.

The problems posed by the government of the church and the division of responsibility between the priesthood and the temporal ruler within Christian society affected the whole of Catholic Europe in some measure. In Marsiglio's time, however, the centre of the most violent controversy had been France and the most extreme anti-papal polemics had been written by supporters of King Philip the Fair. The *Defensor* was completed in Paris, and, as one who had been present in France during at least some of the conflict, it would have been extraordinary if Marsiglio had not been influenced by some of the views expressed. Like the propagandists of the French king, he wished to make the church subject to temporal rulers, but his reasons were much more coherent than theirs. Then, while official French policy was directed against the personality and policies of Boniface VIII, Marsiglio attacked the whole idea of the Roman primacy with the claim that it had no foundation in the New Testament or the practice of the early church. He wished to dismantle the whole centralised structure of the papacy and make the priesthood, free from the trappings of wealth and power, into pure physicians of souls, exhorting and administering the sacraments. Marsiglio placed the boundary between the domain of the church and that of the state at the point where human beliefs and desires manifest themselves in overt actions; these may be regulated by the state alone, and no ecclesiastic should, by reason of his office, wield any kind of coercive power or jurisdiction.

All these arguments were aimed at the universal church and seem to have no special reference to Italy; yet, in the first chapter of the *Defensor*, the author declares that his main concern is with the peace of the Italian kingdom, and the dedication to Lewis of Bavaria, an imperial claimant of doubtful quality, can only be explained on the assumption that he seemed the only person likely to attempt to bring peace to communal Italy. And indeed, consideration of the events leading up to the Italian expedition of the most radically anti-papal emperor of the Middle Ages do suggest that the challenge presented by the papacy was different in many respects in Italy from what it was in other parts of Christendom. In the northern kingdoms, for example, the appointment and disciplining of prelates was an important issue, whereas in the

Italian cities it generally had much less political significance. Rights to tax the clergy and the role of church courts were potential bones of contention everywhere, but the direct temporal power of the papacy was something which the Italians alone had to face, and the political influence which the papacy could bring to bear by, for example, financial or family interests, was far greater in Italy than in the rest of the world. Indeed, after the fall of the Hohenstaufen, it can be argued that the papacy had often been the determining factor in Italian politics. From their virtual beginnings under Innocent III, the Papal States had gradually expanded, with the claim to the Romagna driven home with much bloodshed in the 1280s and Ferrara seized and held at the cost of a three-year war with the Venetians in 1308. As the *Defensor Pacis* was being written, the papal legate, Bertrand du Poujet, was in central Lombardy waging war on the excommunicated Visconti of Milan. However, the actual additions to papal territory, which were often insecure, were only a partial index of the total effect of papal policies on the condition of communal Italy. Running ahead of each territorial gain were the waves of further claims to land or rights which rocked the city states throughout the country. For half a century rumours had been rife concerning kingdoms to be carved out in central Italy for papal kinsmen or clients; Boniface VIII's claim to Tuscany was dormant for the time being, but no one could tell when it might be revived. The ruling Pope John XXII had threatened the position of the leading *signori* by claiming the right to appoint and confirm imperial vicars during those times when the imperial throne was vacant; the Visconti of Milan and the Della Scala of Verona, among others, based their claim to rule on their appointment by the last emperor, Henry of Luxemburg. Finally, it was Italy which had seen the use of the spiritual power for political ends on an unprecedented scale when, in 1320–2, some 14,000 persons had been cited to appear before the Inquisition on charges of adherence to the Ghibelline heresy.

Marsiglio of Padua was not alone among Italians in reacting violently against the worldly preoccupations of the papacy. Dante's disillusionment with the Holy See must have gone back to his experience as a member of the ruling White party in Florence when it came up against the ambitions of Boniface VIII. When he wrote the *De Monarchia*, probably between 1308 and 1312, Dante attacked the canon lawyers but still regarded Clement V as sincerely misguided; by the time he wrote the *Comedy* he had concluded that the Pope's conduct towards Henry VII constituted a deliberate betrayal. The election of John XXII must have confirmed the poet's worst fears, for the condemnations of the contemporary papacy, whose political involvement brought with it all kinds of corruption – excessive wealth, the abuse of spiritual power and the levying of war against Christians – grow in severity in the later parts of the *Divine Comedy*. The vision of the papacy as the harlot upon the scarlet-coloured beast breaks into the Terrestial Paradise like an ugly dream, and St Peter's denunciation of those who have usurped his seat causes all the spirits of the Eighth Heaven to blush with indignation. Dante's detestation of the way in which papal authority was being misused never led him to doubt the God-given nature of the office itself, but he manifests the same emotions which drove Marsiglio to his much more radical conclusions.

While he still had political hopes, Dante pinned them to an ideal emperor who would reconcile parties and bring harmony to rival states. More realistically, Marsiglio avoided discussing the universal monarchy, probably because he had little belief in it; he speculated that war between states might be nature's way of preventing overpopulation. Not only in this, but in other respects, Marsiglio was a prophet of the age of the sovereign state which was to come. In Florence, the one major commune (except Venice) to survive him, the *valentior pars* managed gradually during the fourteenth century to build up the power of the state and curb the freedom of the *societates*. Although Marsaglio's attempt to reform the church during Lewis of Bavaria's Italian expedition of 1327–8 was a total failure, the ideas sowed in the *Defensor* went on to swell the growing body of critical thinking about the church. Translated into the Tuscan vernacular in about 1362, it may have helped the Florentines to see through the contradictions of their traditional Guelphism and prepare the ground for the confrontation between the republic and the papacy in the war of the Eight Saints (1376), which was one of the traumas through which the Florentine renaissance of the fifteenth century was born.

★

From another point of view, Dante and Marsiglio can be regarded not as anticipating the future, but as exceptional representatives of their own age, which should be appreciated in its own right. They were the bearers of a highly evolved and complex culture which was predominantly civic yet still close to the land, partly mercantile yet fascinated by the values of chivalry, intensely pious yet intermittently kicking against an over-political church, subscribing half-heartedly to the oligarchical ideals of the commune and yet increasingly tolerant of despotism in practice. This culture was not a sudden efflorescence, but was the outcome of a long evolution which can be traced back to the dark days of the tenth and eleventh century, when the cities of the *Regnum Italiae* began to compete with their Byzantine neighbours and the long impoverished and depopulated soil of Italy became able once again to support the *vita civile*. There was no consciousness that there had been any sudden breaks; the city-state had replaced the empire with hardly anyone being fully aware of what had happened and the civil life enjoyed by a few had gradually extended to the relatively numerous governing class of communal Italy. During the process Italian culture had emerged as something distinctive and clearly marked off from that of other parts of the world, yet it is doubtful if the Italians who visited the England of Edward I or the France of Philip the Fair fully appreciated the difference; Marsiglio seems to have assumed that his uniquely Italian insights would be immediately understood in the circle of Lewis of Bavaria.

It is this sense of continuity both with the past and with other parts of the Catholic world – assumed rather than consciously formulated – which distinguishes the Italians of the age of Dante from the spokesman of the Florentine enlightenment of the early fifteenth century. The humanists stood against continuity, using the metaphor of rebirth to express their desire to draw selectively from the past. Rejecting 'intellectual cathedrals', they concentrated on what was close at hand, digging deep rather than spreading wide, so that their world revolved around central Italy, and only gradually was their new outlook exported to other parts of Europe. If this attitude is labelled 'renaissance', it can cause nothing but confusion to use the same term for the civic life which evolved in Italy in the three or four centuries up to 1340. Instead of back-dating the Renaissance, we should rather enlarge our picture of the Middle Ages so that, beside the kings, nobles and prelates of the rest of Europe, we find room for the representatives of the Italian *vita civile* as equally valid constituents of the medieval world.

Abbreviations to Bibliographies and References

Annales	*Annales: Économies, Sociétés, Civilisations,* formerly *Annales d'Histoire Économique et Sociale*
ASI	*Archivio Storico Italiano*
ASL	*Archivio Storico Lombardo*
BISI	*Bollettino dell'Istituto Storico Italiano*
CDG	*Codice diplomatico della Repubblica di Genova,* ed. C. Imperiale di Sant'Angelo, FSI (Rome 1936–42).
EcHR	*Economic History Review*
EHR	*English Historical Review*
FSI	Fonti per la Storia d'Italia (Rome, 1887–)
JEH	*Journal of Economic History*
MGH SS	Monumenta Germaniae Historica, Scriptores
NAV	*Nuovo Archivio Veneto*
PL	*Patrologia Latina*
RIS	Rerum Italicarum Scriptores
RSDI	*Rivista di Storia del Diritto Italiano*
RSI	*Rivista Storica Italiana*

Bibliographies

Introductory Note

More than that of any other country, the writing of Italian medieval history is an international enterprise; among those making significant contributions during the last seventy years or so have been Germans, Englishmen, Frenchmen, Americans, Spaniards, Roumanians, Russians both Soviet and émigré, and Danes as well as Italians. Clearly, in an introductory book such as this, a detailed bibliography would be out of place. Instead, there is a list of further reading in English which includes as well as recent and significant works of scholarship, a selection of more popular or older books and articles where these go some way to filling a gap not covered by other material in English. This is followed by a bibliography of works in languages other than English. Of necessity, this is much more selective, the aim being to show the beginner in research where the main sources may be found and indicate some of the more significant secondary works through which he can read his way into any particular aspect of the subject. Finally, notes are provided to give specific references supporting views or statements made in the text.

To make cross-reference easier, both parts of the bibliography have been sub-divided on the following plan.

1. ORIENTATION

2. SOURCES

3. POLITICAL AND SOCIAL HISTORY
   (a) General
   (b) The Pre-Communal Period
   (c) The Early Communes 1100–1200
   (d) The Later Communes 1200–1340
   (e) The Signorie
   (f) General Histories of Individual Cities
   (g) The Empire, the Papacy and the South

4. ECONOMIC HISTORY
   (a) General
   (b) The Countryside, Towns and Cities
   (c) Commerce and the Merchant Class
   (d) The Economic Crisis of the Fourteenth Century

5. THE CHURCH, CULTURE AND SOCIETY
   (a) The Church, Heresy and Society
   (b) Education and Learning
   (c) The Arts, Literature and Society
   (d) Historiography and Political Thought

I SELECT BIBLIOGRAPHY OF WORKS IN ENGLISH

1. ORIENTATION

An introduction to the problems of writing Italian history of the medieval and Renaissance periods can be found in the early chapters of D. Hay, *The Italian*

Renaissance in its Historical Background (Cambridge 1961, paperback 1966). The only up-to-date survey of the Italian communes in English is D. P. Waley, *The Italian City-Republics* (London 1969).

2. SOURCES

U. Balzani, *Early Chroniclers of Italy* (London, 1883) provides an old-fashioned introduction. The only complete translation of an Italian civic chronicle is E. C. M. Benecke and A. G. Ferrers Howell's version of Dino Compagni, *Cronica* (London, 1906), but G. G. Coulton, *From St Francis to Dante* (London 1906), contains the greater part of Salimbene. The *Selections from the First Nine Books of the Croniche Fiorentine of Giovanni Villani*, translated by R. E. Selfe and edited by P. H. Wicksteed (London 1896) concentrate on passages of interest to Dante students. The *Works* of Luitprand of Cremona, trans. F. A. Wright (London 1930); *The Deeds of Frederick Barbarossa* by Otto of Freising and Rahewin, trans. C. C. Mierow and R. Emery (New York 1953); and *The Writings of Leo, Rufino and Angelo, Companions of St Francis*, trans. R. B. Brooke (Oxford 1970), all throw light on Italian conditions.

3. POLITICAL AND SOCIAL HISTORY

(a) General

Before the appearance of D. P. Waley's *Italian City-Republics*, the most recent general study of the Italian communes in English was W. Boulting's thoroughly revised version of Sismondi's *History of the Italian Republics* (London, n.d. 1905?); W. F. Butler, *The Lombard Communes* (London 1906) covers the whole communal period for the regions north of the Apennines. Both these books convey a fair picture of the findings of late-nineteenth century research; the Italian sections of M. V. Clarke, *The Medieval City State* (London 1926, reprinted 1966) are not so satisfactory.

J. C. L. Sismondi's *History of the Italian Republics in the Middle Ages*, trans. D. Lardner (London 1830) remains a great classic; a drastically shortened version was last reprinted in the Everyman's Library series in 1907.

G. Falco, *The Holy Roman Republic*, trans. K. V. Kent (London 1964) surveys a wide area of medieval history from the point of view of Rome; while some of the chapters are fresh and stimulating, the attempt to establish a new perspective is not entirely successful.

(b) The Pre-Communal Period

On the Roman imperial administration there is A. H. M. Jones's masterly *The Later Roman Empire 284–602*, 2 vols (Oxford 1964); the same author's 'The Cities of the Roman Empire: Political, Administrative and Judicial Institutions', *Receuils de la Société Jean Bodin*, iv (1954), 135–76 is a useful summary on the administration of the *civitates*.

As a full scale history of the barbarian period, T. Hodgkin, *Italy and her Invaders*, 8 vols (Oxford 1880–99) has not yet been superseded, but for an up-to-date view see the contributions of D. A. Bullough to *The Dark Ages*, ed. D. Talbot Rice (London 1965).

On pre-communal Rome, see P. Llewellyn, *Rome in the Dark Ages* (London 1971). On Milan in the eleventh century, see H. E. J. Cowdrey, 'Archbishop Aribert of Milan', *History*, li (1966), 1–15; *idem*, 'The Papacy, the Patarines and the Church of Milan', *Transactions of the Royal Historical Society*, 5th ser., 18 (1968), 25–48; and J. P. Whitney, *Hildebrandine Essays* (Cambridge, 1932), 143–57.

(c) *The Early Communes up to 1200*
The only general treatment remains C. W. Previté-Orton, 'The Italian Cities
till *ca* 1200', *Cambridge Medieval History*, v (Cambridge 1926), 208–41. See
also F. C. Hodgson, *The Early History of Venice* (London 1901) and W. Heywood, *A History of Pisa: Eleventh and Twelfth Centuries* (Cambridge 1921).

(d) *The Later Communes 1200–1340*
The best introduction is B. S. Pullan, *A History of Early Renaissance Italy*
(London 1973). There are a number of recent books on particular cities or
regions, i.e. D. P. Waley, *Medieval Orvieto* (Cambridge 1952); *idem, The Papal
State in Thirteenth Century* (London 1961); J. Larner, *The Lords of the Romagna* (London 1965); J. K. Hyde, *Padua in the Age of Dante* (Manchester 1966).
M. B. Becker's *Florence in Transition*, 2 vols (Baltimore 1967–8), supported
by numerous articles listed in the bibliography of vol. 2, attempts a major
reassessment of Florentine history centred on the contrast between the period
before and after 1343. Both Becker's accuracy in detail and the validity of his
interpretations have been questioned – see, for example, reviews by L. Martines
in *Speculum*, xliii (1968), 689–92 and P. J. Jones in *EHR*, lxxxv (1970), 563–7.
However, his work remains important and some of his ideas are stimulating.
W. M. Bowsky has in hand a full-scale study of Siena; until its appearance,
there is his article 'The *Buon Governo* of Siena 1287–1355: a Medieval Oligarchy', *Speculum*, xxxvii (1962), 368–81.
    Particular aspects of communal government and society in this period:
    On taxation: D. Herlihy, 'Direct and Indirect Taxation in Tuscan Finance,
ca 1200–1400', *Finances et Comptabilité Urbaines du XIIIe au XVIe siècle*,
Colloque international, Blankenberge (Brussels 1964), 384–405; C. de la Ron-
cière, 'Indirect Taxes or "Gabelles" at Florence in the Fourteenth Century'
in *Florentine Studies*, ed. N. Rubinstein (London 1968), 140–92; W. M. Bowsky, *The Finance of the Commune of Siena 1287–1355* (Oxford 1970).
    On military service: D. P. Waley, 'The Army of the Florentine Republic
from the Twelfth to the Fourteenth Century', in *Florentine Studies*, ed. Rubinstein, 70–108 and W. M. Bowsky, 'City and Contado: Military Relationships
and Communal Bonds in Fourteenth-Century Siena', *Renaissance Studies in
Honour of Hans Baron*, ed. A. Molho and J. A. Tedeschi (Florence 1971),
75–98.
    On class, party and civil disorder: M. B. Becker, 'A Study in Political
Failure: The Florentine Magnates 1280–1343', *Medieval Studies*, xxvii (1965),
246–308; W. M. Bowsky, 'The Medieval Commune and Internal Violence:
Police Power and Public Safety in Siena, 1287–1355', *American Historical
Review*, lxxiii (1967), 1–17; L. Martines, 'Political Conflict in the Italian City
States', *Government and Opposition*, iii (1968), 69–91; and the volume *Violence and Civil Disorder in Italian Cities 1200–1500*, ed. L. Martines (Berkeley
and Los Angeles 1972).

(e) *The Signorie*
Although practically all the works listed in the last section throw some light
on at least one aspect of the rise of the *signorie*, there is no modern study of
the subject as a whole in English. P. J. Jones, 'Communes and Despots: the
City-State in Late Medieval Italy', *Transactions of the Royal Historical
Society*, 5th ser., xv (1965), 71–96 and D. M. Bueno de Mesquita, 'The Place
of Despotism in Italian Politics' in *Europe in the Late Middle Ages*, ed. J. R.
Hale, J. R. L. Highfield and B. Smalley (London, 1965), 301–31 both discuss
some of the salient problems.

(f) General Histories of Individual Cities
These books are old and aimed at a wide readership, and they therefore reflect the views and prejudices of the time when they were written. They should be used with caution. A. M. Allen, *A History of Verona* (London 1910); W. Heywood, *A History of Perugia* (London 1910); F. Schevill, *Siena: The Story of a Medieval Commune* (London 1909); *idem, History of Florence from the Founding of the City through the Renaissance* (New York 1936, re-published 1961).

(g) The Empire, the Papacy and the South
On Frederick I, P. Munz, *Frederick Barbarossa* (London 1969,) gives a much clearer view of the Italian setting than M. Pacaut's book of the same title, trans. A. J. Pomerans (London 1970). With the appearance of T. C. Van Cleve, *The Emperor Frederick II of Hohenstaufen: Immutator Mundi* (Oxford 1972), the English reader needs to rely no longer on the exciting but wildly biased E. Kantorowicz, *Frederick II*, trans. E. O. Lorimer (London 1931). Still useful are the relevant chapters of G. Barraclough, *The Origins of Modern Germany* (2nd edn, Oxford 1947), especially for the short but crucial reign of Henry VI (1190–7). On Henry of Luxemburg there is an excellent modern study, W. M. Bowsky, *Henry VII in Italy* (Lincoln, Nebraska 1960); see also his supporting articles 'Clement V and the Emperor-elect', *Medievalia et Humanistica*, xii (1958), 52–69 and 'Florence and Henry of Luxemburg, King of the Romans. The Rebirth of Guelfism', *Speculum*, xxxiii (1958), 177–203.

P. Partner, *The Lands of St Peter* (London 1972) covers the temporal power of the papacy throughout the Middle Ages. T. S. R. Boase, *Boniface the Eighth* (London 1933) deals fairly fully with his Italian policies.

As introductions to the history of the South there are two attractive popular books by J. J. Norwich, *The Normans in the South* (London 1967) and *The Kingdom in the Sun 1130–1194* (London 1970), and D. Mack Smith, *Medieval Sicily 800–1713* (London 1968) summarises the period up to *c.* 1350 in about a hundred pages. E. M. Jamison, *Admiral Eugenius of Sicily: His Life and Work* (London 1957) gives a broader view of the twelfth-century Norman kingdom than the title might suggest. Frederick II's legal code, *The Liber Augustalis*, has been translated by J. M. Powell (Syracuse, New York 1971). S. Runciman, *The Sicilian Vespers* (Cambridge 1958) places the rising of 1282 in the wide setting of European and Mediterranean diplomacy.

4. ECONOMIC HISTORY

(a) General
G. Luzzatto, *An Economic History of Italy from the Fall of the Roman Empire to the Beginning of the 16th Century*, trans. P. J. Jones (London 1961), with a very full bibliography by the translator, is the best introduction.

Among recent surveys, R.-H. Bautier, *The Economic Development of Medieval Europe* (London 1971) is more successful than R. S. Lopez, *The Commercial Revolution of the Middle Ages 950–1350* (Englewood Cliffs 1971) in placing the Italian economy in the wider European context.

F. Braudel, *The Mediterranean and the Mediterranean World in the Age of Philip II*, trans. S. Reynolds (London 1972) is a fascinating study of the interaction between geography and history, most of which is valid for the medieval period.

On population, J. C. Russell, 'Late Ancient and Medieval Population',

Transactions of the American Philosophical Society, ns. 48, Pt. 3 (1958), is a valuable review of the evidence; on the other hand, his *Medieval Regions and their Cities* (Newton Abbot 1972) is a Procrustean effort to make the inadequate medieval evidence fit in with theories of rank-size derived from the modern period.

(b) The Countryside, Towns and Cities
The best starting point is the excellent chapter by P. J. Jones in the *Cambridge Economic History of Europe*, i (2nd edn, Cambridge 1966), 340–431.

On the agrarian side, see P. J. Jones, 'An Italian Estate, 900–1300, *EcHR*, vii (1954), 18–32; D. Herlihy, 'The History of the Rural Seigneury in Italy 751–1200', *Agricultural History*, xxxiii (1959), 58–71; *idem*, 'Treasure Hoards in the Italian Economy', *EcHR*, x (1957), 1–14.

On cities, see D. A. Bullough, 'Urban Change in Early Medieval Italy: the Example of Pavia', *Papers of the British School at Rome*, xxxiv (1966), 82–130; D. Herlihy, *Pisa in the Early Renaissance* (New Haven 1958) and *Medieval and Renaissance Pistoia* (New Haven 1967). Both are concerned with demographic and economic aspects of the city and its contado.

(c) Commerce and the Merchant Class
The best introduction to the medieval revival of commerce is the chapter by R. S. Lopez, 'The Trade of Medieval Europe: the South' in the *Cambridge Economic History of Europe*, ii (Cambridge 1952), 257–534, and that by R. de Roover, 'The Organisation of Trade' in the same publication, iii, 42–104. Both have full bibliographies. H. Pirenne's well-known *Medieval Cities* (Princeton 1925), while still stimulating, presents an over-simplified view of the relationship between cities and commerce.

On the Mediterranean, while the fundamental secondary works are in German and French, A. R. Lewis, *Naval Power and Trade in the Mediterranean, A.D. 500–1100* (Princeton 1951) is a useful guide to the early period; see also A. O. Citarella, 'The Relations of Amalfi with the Arab World before the Crusades', *Speculum*, xlii (1967) 299–312, and 'Patterns in Medieval Trade – The Commerce of Amalfi before the Crusades', *JEH*, xxviii (1968), 531–55. For the crusading period there is, on Pisa, W. Heywood, *A History of Pisa, Eleventh and Twelfth Centuries* (Cambridge 1921); on Genoa, E. H. Byrne, 'Genoese Trade with Syria in the Twelfth Century', *American Historical Review*, xxv (1920), 191–219; H. C. Krueger, 'Genoese Trade with Northwest Africa in the Twelfth Century', *Speculum*, viii (1933), 377–95, and 'Wares of Exchange in Twelfth-century Genoese–African Trade', *ibid.* xii (1937), 57–71. The gaps in the secondary material are, however, largely made good by the storehouse of original documents in translation with valuable introductions and bibliography provided by R. S. Lopez and I. W. Raymond, *Medieval Trade in the Mediterranean World* (London 1955). S. D. Goitein, *A Mediterranean Society*, 3 vols. (Berkeley and Los Angeles 1967) gives a comprehensive picture of the Jewish traders who circulated in the Arab half of the Mediterranean from the tenth to the mid-thirteenth centuries.

On trading and other contacts with the Far East, see L. Olschki, *Marco Polo's Asia* (Berkeley and Los Angeles 1960); R. S. Lopez, 'European Merchants in the Medieval Indies: the Evidence of Commercial Documents', *JEH*, iii (1943), 164–84; and I. de Rachewiltz, *Papal Envoys to the Great Khans* (London 1971). The original narratives for the thirteenth-century missions to the East are to be found in *The Mongol Mission*, ed. and trans. C. Dawson (London, New York 1955). Marco Polo's *Milione* has been translated by A.

Ricci, *The Travels of Marco Polo* (London 1931) using the revised text of L. F. Benedetto.

Perhaps the best approach to the Italians in northern Europe is R. de Roover, *Money, Banking and Credit in Medieval Bruges* (Cambridge, Mass. 1948). On particular aspects see R. L. Reynolds, 'The Market for Northern Textiles in Genoa, 1179–1200', *Revue Belge de Philologie et de l'Histoire*, viii (1929), 831–51; *idem*, 'Merchants of Arras and the Overland Trade with Genoa, Twelfth Century', *ibid*. ix (1930), 495–533; J. Henneman, 'Taxation of Italians by the French Crown, 1311–1363', *Medieval Studies*, xxxi (1969), 15–43; J. R. Strayer, 'Italian Bankers and Philip the Fair', in *Economy, Government and Society in Medieval Italy: Essays in Memory of R. L. Reynolds*, ed. D. Herlihy, R. S. Lopez and V. Slessarev (Kent, Ohio 1969), 113–21; W. E. Rhodes, 'The Italian Bankers in England and Their Loans to Edward I and Edward II', in *Historical Essays*, ed. T. F. Tout and J. Tait (London 1902), 137–68; R. J. Whitwell, 'Italian Bankers and the English Crown', *Transactions of the Royal Historical Society*, ns. xvii (1903), 175–233.

The important but forbidding subject of commercial techniques is best approached through the relevant sections in Lopez and Raymond; see also R. D. Face, 'The Techniques of Business in the Trade between the Fairs of Champagne and the South of Europe in the Twelfth and Thirteenth Centuries' and 'The *Vectuarii* in the Overland Commerce between Champagne and Southern Europe', *EcHR*, x (1958), 427–38, and xii (1959), 239–46 respectively. Some of his conclusions are questioned by R. K. Berlow, 'The Development of Business Techniques Used at the Fairs of Champagne from the End of the Twelfth Century to the Middle of the Thirteenth Century', *Studies in Medieval and Renaissance History*, viii (1971), 3–23.

A. Sapori, *The Italian Merchant in the Middle Ages*, trans. P. A. Kennen (New York 1970) is a brief introduction. On Genoese merchants there is in English: M. W. Hall, 'Early Bankers in Genoese Notarial Records', *EcHR*, vi (1935), 73–9; H. C. Krueger, 'Genoese Merchants, their Associations and Investments, 1155–1250', *Studi in onore di A. Fanfani* (Milan 1962), I, 413–26; *idem*, 'Genoese Merchants, their Partnerships and Investments, 1155–64', *Studi in onore di A. Sapori* (Milan 1957), i, 255–72; R. L. Reynolds, 'In Search of a Business Class in Thirteenth-Century Genoa', *JEH*, suppl. v (1945), 1–19; R. D. Face, 'Symon de Gualtero: A Brief Portrait of a Thirteenth-Century Man of Affairs', *Essays in Memory of R. L. Reynolds* (Kent, Ohio, 1969), 75–94. On non-Genoese merchants one many consult the introduction to A. Evans's edition of Pegolotti's *Pratica della Mercatura* (Cambridge, Mass. 1936); see also R. S. Lopez, 'Stars and Spices: The Earliest Italian Manual of Commercial Practice', *Essays in Memory of R. L. Reynolds*, 35–42. For an introduction to another important source for economic and social history, see P. J. Jones, 'Florentine Families and Florentine Diaries of the Fourteenth Century', *Papers of the British School in Rome*, xxiv (1956), 183–205.

(d) The Economic Crisis of the Fourteenth Century

The main points at issue among historians are outlined in an exchange between R. S. Lopez, H. A. Miskimin and C. M. Cipolla, 'The Economic Depression of the Renaissance', *EcHR*, xiv (1962), 408–26, and xvi (1964), 519–29.

On specifically Italian problems, see W. M. Bowsky, 'The Impact of the Black Death upon Siennese Government and Society', *Speculum*, xxxix (1962), 1–34; D. Herlihy, 'Population, Plague and Social Change in Rural Pistoia', *EcHR*, xviii (1965), 225–44; *idem*, 'Santa Maria Impruneta: A Rural

Commune in the Late Middle Ages', in *Florentine Studies*, ed. Rubinstein, 242–76; P. J. Jones, 'From Manor to Mezzadria: A Tuscan Case-Study in the Medieval Origins of Modern Agrarian Society', *ibid.* 193–241.

5. THE CHURCH, CULTURE AND SOCIETY

(a) The Church, Heresy and Society

There is very little for the English reader on these subjects for the period before 1340. For the eleventh century and earlier, see the books and articles on Rome and Milan listed above, p. 201. On a political heretic of the twelfth century, there is G. W. Greenaway, *Arnold of Brescia* (Cambridge 1931); some of the atmosphere of the thirteenth century can be caught from G. G. Coulton, *From St Francis to Dante* (London 1906). R. Brentano, *Two Churches: England and Italy in the Thirteenth Century* (Princeton 1968) is a pioneering impressionistic survey which raises all kinds of questions about Italian society; C. E. Boyd, *Tithes and Parishes in Medieval Italy* (Ithaca, New York 1952) is a specialised study. Much of M. Reeves, *The Influence of Heresy in the Later Middle Ages* (Oxford 1969) is relevant. The first part of J. N. Stephens, 'Heresy in Medieval and Renaissance Florence', *Past and Present*, 54 (1972), 25–60 relates to the period before 1340, as do some of the interrelations proposed by M. B. Becker, 'Some Economic Implications of the Conflict between Church and State in Trecento Florence', *Medieval Studies*, xxi (1959), 1–16.

(b) Education and Learning

Although not entirely up to date, the English reader can gain a fair picture of the development of higher education in Italy from the relevant parts of H. Rashdall's classic *The Universities of Europe in the Middle Ages*, ed. F. M. Powicke and A. B. Emden, 2 vols (Oxford 1936); C. H. Haskins, *The Renaissance of the Twelfth Century* (Cambridge, Mass. 1927); and P. Vinogradoff, *Roman Law in Medieval Europe* (2nd edn, Oxford 1929). On the university as a typical Italian *societas*, see J. K. Hyde, 'Commune, University and Society in Early Medieval Bologna', in *Universities in Politics*, ed. J. W. Baldwin and R. A. Goldthwaite (Baltimore 1972), 17–46.

On the study of rhetoric, see: 'The Early *Artes Dictandi* in Italy' in C. H. Haskins, *Studies in Medieval Culture* (New York 1929), 170–92; H. Wieruszowski, 'Ars Dictaminis in the Time of Dante', *Medievalia et Humanistica*, i (1943), 95–108.

On early humanism, see: R. Weiss, *The Dawn of Humanism in Italy* (London 1947) and the early chapters of *The Renaissance Discovery of Classical Antiquity* (Oxford 1969); P. O. Kristeller, *Renaissance Thought, the Classic, Scholastic and Humanist Strains* (New York 1961); B. Smalley, *English Friars and Antiquity in the Early XIV Century* (Oxford 1960), 265–98.

There are two articles which survey education and learning in a local setting: H. Wieruszowski, 'Arezzo as a Center of Learning and Letters in the Thirteenth Century', *Traditio*, ix (1953), 321–91 and C. T. Davis, 'Education in Dante's Florence', *Speculum*, xl (1965), 415–35.

(c) The Arts, Literature and Society

For the period 1290–1340, the starting point is J. Larner, *Culture and Society in Italy 1290–1420* (London 1971) with extensive bibliographies. On painting, see: F. Antal, *Florentine Painting in its Social Background* (London 1947);

and N. Rubinstein, 'Political Ideas in Siennese Art: the Frescoes by Ambrogio Lorenzetti and Taddeo di Bartolo in the Palazzo Pubblico', *Journal of the Warburg and Courtauld Institutes*, xxi (1958), 179–207. On communal patronage, see: H. Wieruszowski, 'Art and the Commune in the Time of Dante', *Speculum*, xix (1944), 14–33.

(d) Historiography and Political Thought

There is no modern general study on Italian historiography of this period, but for particular aspects see C. B. Fisher, 'The Pisan Clergy and an Awakening of Historical Interest in a Medieval Commune', *Studies in Medieval and Renaissance History*, iii (1966), 144–219; N. Rubinstein, 'Some Ideas on Municipal Progress and Decline in the Italy of the Communes', *Fritz Saxl Memorial Essays*, ed. D. J. Gordon (London 1957), 165–83; J. K. Hyde, 'Medieval Descriptions of Cities', *Bulletin of the John Rylands Library*, xlviii (1966), 308–40 and 'Italian Social Chronicles in the Middle Ages', *ibid.* xlix (1966), 107–32; C. T. Davis. 'Il Buon Tempo Antico', *Florentine Studies*, ed. Rubinstein, 45–69, and The Malispini Question', in *Studi Medievali*, ser. III, x (1969), 215–54.

On Florentine political thought and Dante, see: N. Rubinstein, 'The Beginnings of Political Thought in Florence', *Journal of the Warburg and Courtauld Institutes*, v (1942), 198–227; Dante's *Monarchy and Three Political Letters*, trans. D. Nicholl and C. Hardie (London 1954); A. P. D'Entrèves, *Dante as a Political Thinker* (Oxford 1952); C. T. Davis, *Dante and the Idea of Rome* (Oxford 1957); B. H. Sumner, 'Dante and the "Regnum Italicum" ', *Medium Aevum*, i (1932), 1–23; C. T. Davis, 'An Early Florentine Political Theorist: Fra Remigio de' Girolami', *Proceedings of the American Philosophical Society*, civ (1960), 662–76; *idem*, 'Brunetto Latini and Dante', *Studi Medievali*, 3rd ser. viii (1967), 421–50.

On Marsiglio of Padua, see: A. Gewirth, *Marsilius of Padua*, 2 vols (New York 1951–6), vol. 2 being a translation of the *Defensor Pacis*; C. W. Previté-Orton, 'Marsilius of Padua: Doctrines', *EHR*, xxxviii (1923), 1–18; N. Rubinstein, 'Marsilius of Padua and the Italian Political Thought of his Time', *Europe in the Late Middle Ages*, ed. Hale *et al.*, 44–75. For discerning observations of Marsiglio's views on the Church, see G. Leff, *Heresy in the Later Middle Ages* (Manchester 1967), ii, 413–22.

II SELECT BIBLIOGRAPHY OF WORKS IN OTHER LANGUAGES

1. ORIENTATION

A recent personal view of the present state of work on medieval history by Italians is O. Capitani, 'Dove va la storiografia medioevale italiana?', *Studi Medievali*, 3rd ser., viii (1967), 617–62. Co-operative volumes summarising the state of knowledge and suggesting future lines of research, with select bibliographies, are *Questioni di storia medioevale*, ed. E. Rota (Milan 1948), and *Nuove questioni di storia medioevale*, publ. Marzorati (Milan 1964). L. A. Muratori, *Antiquitates Italicae Medii Aevii*, 6 vols (Milan 1738–42). though obviously dated, is still unsurpassed in the inspiring breadth of its approach .

Recent bibliographies include E. Dupré-Theseider, 'Literaturbericht über Italienische Geschichte des Mittelalters; Veroffentlichungen 1945 bis 1958', *Historische Zeitschrift, Sonderheft*, i (1962), 613–725 and N. Rubinstein,

'Studies on the Political History of the Age of Dante', *Atti del Congresso Internazionale di studi Danteschi, Relazioni* (Florence 1965), i, 225–47.

2. SOURCES

The main source collections for the history of medieval Italy are the *Rerum Italicarum Scriptores*, original edition, ed. L. A. Muratori, 25 tomes in 27 vols (Milan 1723–51) and the new edition initiated by G. Carducci and V. Frorini (Città di Castello, later Bologna 1900) with additional volumes containing supplementary material, still far from complete. It is published by the Istituto Storico Italiano per il Medioevo, which is also responsible for the series *Fonti per la Storia d'Italia* (Rome 1887–), of which 100 volumes have now appeared. Medieval archive material is published by the Ministero dell'Interno, Pubblicazioni degli Archivi di Stato (Rome 1951–) with 78 volumes so far. Narrower in scope, but not restricted to any particular region, are the *Corpus Statutorum Italicorum*, general editor P. Sella (Rome 1912–) and the *Regesta Chartarum Italiae*, published by the Istituto Storico Italiano (Rome 1914–). It should not be forgotten that the various series which make up the *Monumenta Germaniae Historica* contain a great deal of material relating not only to imperial affairs but to many other aspects of Italian history.

Just as medieval Italy was a land of city-states, so medieval history in Italy is largely the preserve of innumerable local societies, and it is among their publications that the scholar must search for the sources relating to particular regions. Two collections of exceptional scope and importance are the *Historiae Patriae Monumenta* published by the Deputazione Subalpina di Storia Patria, 30 tomes (Turin 1836–99) for Lombardy, and the *Documenti di Storia Italiana* published by the Deputazione Toscana di Storia Patria, 15 vols (Florence 1869–1952) for Tuscany.

3. POLITICAL AND SOCIAL HISTORY

(a) General

Despite the problems involved, multi-volume political histories of Italy continue to be sponsored by several Italian publishers, notably Montadori's *Storia d'Italia Illustrata* and Vallardi's *Storia Politica d'Italia*, relevant volumes of which will be mentioned in the appropriate sections below. The whole medieval period is covered in the *Storia d'Italia I*, ed. N. Valeri, UTET (2nd edn, Turin 1965). Much more selective in approach is Y. Renouard, *Les Villes d'Italie de la fin du Xe siècle au début du XIVe siècle*, ed. P. Braunstein, 2 vols (Paris 1969); based on lecture notes and incomplete at the author's death, this is still a very good introduction to the subject.

(b) The Pre-Communal Period

G. Romano and A. Solmi, *Le dominazioni barbariche in Italia*, 2 vols (Milan 1940–5) and C. G. Mor, *L'età feudale* (Milan 1952), both in the Vallardi *Storia Politica d'Italia*, provide general coverage of the period. On the cities, the best recent survey is G. Fasoli, *Dalla 'civitas' al comune nell'Italia settentrionale* (Bologna 1969). Older, but still of value, are L. Chiappelli, 'La formazione storica del comune cittadino in Italia', *ASI*, 7th ser., v, ii (1926), 3–59; VII (1927), 177–229; X (1928), 3–89; XIII, i (1930), 3–59 and ii, 3–56; and G. Mengozzi, *La città italiana nell'alto medioevo* (Florence 1931).

For the social background to the rise of the cities, C. Violante, *La società milanese nell'età precomunale* (Bari 1953) is fundamental; for legal aspects see P. Vaccari, *Dall'unità romana al particolarismo giuridico del medio evo* (Pavia 1936). On Pavia as capital and the emergence of the commune, see: A. Solmi, *L'amministrazione finanziaria del regno italico nell'alto medioevo* (Pavia 1932) and *Atti del 4 Congresso Internazionale* published by the Centro italiano di studi sull'alto medioevo (Spoleto 1969), especially the contribution by C. Brühl, 'Das Palatium von Pavia und die Honorantie civitatis Papie', 189–220.

(c) The Early Communes 1100–1200

The generally accepted view of the nature of the Italian communes is based on that of Gioacchino Volpe, which he expressed most succinctly in his review of the *Liber Maiolichinus, ASI*, 5th ser., xxxvii (1906), 93–114, reprinted in his *Medio evo italiano* (Florence 1951), 189–210 and further developed in his essay 'Questioni fondamentali sull'origine e svolgimento dei comuni italiani', *ibid.* 87–118. See further N. Ottokar, 'Il problema della formazione comunale', in *Questioni di storia medioevale*, ed. E. Rota, 355–84; E. Sestan, 'La città italiana nei secoli XI–XIII nelle sue note caratteristiche rispetto al movimento comunale europeo', *Rapports du XIe Congrès International des Sciences Historiques* (Uppsala 1960), 75–95; and G. Fasoli 'Gouvernants et Gouvernés dans les Communes Italiennes du XIe au XIIIe Siècle', *Receuils de la Société Jean Bodin*, xxv (1965), 47–96.

On the origins of the communes in particular cities: for Genoa, see F. Niccolai, *Contributo allo studio dei più antichi brevi della compagna genovese* (Milan 1939); for Milan, see G. Zanetti, 'Il comune di Milano dalla genesi del consolato fino all'inizio del potere podestarile', *ASL*, lx (1933), 74–133, 290–337, and lxii (1935), 227–80; for Rome, see L. Halphen, *Etudes sur l'Administration de Rome au Moyen Age* (Paris 1907); for Verona, see L. Simeoni, 'Le origini del comune di Verona', *NAV*, xxv (1913), 49–143; for Venice, see G. Fasoli, 'Comune Veneciarum' in *Venezia dalla prima crociata alla conquista di Costantinopoli*, published by the Fondazione Cini (Florence 1965), 73–102.

Among collections of documents throwing light on the early communes are: the Genoese consular oaths, *CDG*, nn. 128, 285; C. Manaresi, *Gli atti del comune di Milano* (Milan 1919); R. Soriga, 'Il memoriale dei consoli del comune di Pavia 1192–1206', *Bollettino della Società Pavese di Storia Patria* (1913), 103–18; A. Solmi, 'Le legge più antiche del comune di Piacenza', *ASI*, 2nd ser., lxxiii (ii) (1915), 3–81; F. Bonaini, *Statuti inediti della città di Pisa*, 3 vols (Florence 1854–7); and F. Berlan, *Statuti di Pistoia del secolo XII* (Bologna 1882). Brief selections from the sources up to about the mid-twelfth century are in P. Brezzi, *I comuni cittadini italiani: origine e primitiva costituzione* (Milan 1940).

On the *podestà*: V. Franchini, *Saggio di ricerche sull'istituto del podestà nei comuni medievali* (Bologna 1912); G. Hanauer, 'Das Berufspodestat im 13. Jahrhundert', *Mittheilungen des Instituts fur Oesterreichische Geschichtsforschung*, xxiii (1902), 378–426.

The basic studies of the *Consorterie* are: F. Niccolai. 'I consorzi nobilari ed il comune nell'alta e media Italia', *RSDI*, xiii (1940), 116–47, 292–341, 397–477; P. Santini, 'Le società delle torri in Firenze', *ASI*, 7th ser., xx (1887), 25–58, 178–204; and on the nobility: F. Cusin, 'Per la storia del castello medievale', *RSI*, 5th ser., iv (1939), 491–542.

On guilds and confraternities, see: G. M. Monti, *Le corporazioni nell'evo antico e nell'alto medio evo* (Bari 1934); *idem, Le Confraternite dell'alta e media Italia*, 2 vols (Venice 1927); P. Valsecchi, *Comune e corporazione nel medio evo italiano* (Milan 1949); P. S. Leicht, 'L'origine delle "Arti" nell' Europa occidentale' and 'La corporazione italiana delle arti nelle sue origini e nel primo periodo del comune' in *Scritti vari di storia del diritto* (Milan 1943), i, 297–308, 431–48.

(d) The Later Communes 1200–1340

A textbook for the whole communal period up to 1340 is L. Salvatorelli, *L'Italia comunale dal secolo XI alla metà del secolo XIV*, Storia d'Italia illustrata, Montadori (Milan, 1940).

For the *popolo*, see: G. de Vergottini, *Arti e popolo nella prima metà del secolo XIII* (Milan 1943); idem, 'Note sulla formazione degli statuti del popolo', *RSDI*, xvi (1943), 61–70; I. Ghiron, 'La credenza di S. Ambrogio', *ASL*, 3rd ser., iv (1876), 583–609; U. Gualazzini, *Il 'Populus' di Cremona e l'autonomia del comune* (Bologna 1940); A. Gaudenzi, *Statuti delle società del popolo di Bologna*, FSI, 2 vols (1889, 1896); G. Fasoli, 'Le compagnie delle armi a Bologna', *L'archiginnasio*, xxviii (1933), 158–83, 323–40; idem, 'Le compagnie delle arti a Bologna', *ibid.* xxx (1935), 237–80 and xxxi (1936), 56–80; W. Montorsi, 'Plebiscita Bononiae', *BISI*, lxx (1958), 181–298. G. Masi, 'Il popolo a Firenze alla fine del dugento', *Archivio Giuridico*, xcix (1928), 86–100.

On particular aspects of communal politics and society: for taxation, see E. Fiumi, 'L'imposta diretta nei comuni medioevali della Toscana', *Studi in onore di A. Sapori* (Milan 1957), i, 327–53; for food policy, see H. C. Peyer, *Zur Getreidepolitik Oberitalienischen Städte im XIII. Jahrhundert* (Vienna 1950); on relations with the contado, see G. de Vergottini, 'Origini e sviluppo della comitatinanza', *Studi Senesi*, xliii (1929), 347–481; E. Fiumi, 'Sui rapporti tra città e contado nell'età comunale', *ASI*, cxiv (1956), 18–68.

On the vendetta, see I. Del Lungo, 'Una vendetta in Firenze il giorno di S. Giovanni 1295' *ASI*, 4th ser., xviii (1886), 355–409; and A. M. Enriques, 'La vendetta nella vita e nella legislazione fiorentina', *ASI*, 7th ser., xix (1933), 85–146, 181–223. On magnates, see G. Fasoli, 'Ricerche sulla legislazione antimagnatizia nei comuni dell'alta e media Italia', *RSDI*, xii (1939), 86–133, 240–309; G. Pampaloni, 'I magnati a Firenze alla fine del dugento', *ASI*, cxxix (1972), 387–423. On parties see R. Davidsohn, *Forschungen zur älteren Geschichte von Florenz* (Berlin, 1896–1908), iv, 29–67; R. Caggese, 'Sull' origine della Parte Guelfa e le sue relazioni col comune', *ASI*, 5th ser., xxxii (1903), 265–309; G. Fasoli, 'Guelfi e Ghibellini di Romagna 1280–1', *ASI*, xciv (i) (1936), 157–80; G. Masi, 'Sull'origine dei Bianchi e dei Neri', *Giornale Dantesco* 30 (1927), 124–32; E. Orioli, Documenti bolognesi sulla fazione dei Bianchi', *Atti e Memorie di Storia Patria per le Provincie di Romagna*, 3rd ser., xiv (1896), 1–13; G. Masi, 'La struttura sociale delle fazioni politiche fiorentini ai tempi di Dante', *Giornale Dantesco*, xxxi (1930), 1–28; idem, 'I banchieri fiorentini nella vita politica della città sulla fine del dugento', *Archivio Giuridico*, cv (1931), 57–89.

Books which deal at length with nobles, magnates, the popolo and parties in particular Italian cities are: G. Salvemini, *Magnati e popolani in Firenze* (Florence 1899, reprinted without valuable appendix of documents, Turin 1960), modified in important respects by N. Ottokar, *Il comune di Firenze alla fine del dugento* (Florence 1926; 2nd edn 1962); B. Stahl, *Adel und Volk im Florentiner Dugento* (Cologne 1965); E. Cristiani, *Nobiltà e popolo nel comune di Pisa dalle origini del podestariato alla signoria dei Donoratico* (Naples 1962); and G. Cracco, *Società e stato nel medioevo veneziano* (Florence 1967).

(e) The Signorie

The basic constitutional study is still E. Salzer, *Uber die Anfänge der Signorie in Oberitalien* (Berlin 1900). F. Ercole, 'Comuni e signori nel Veneto', *NAV*, xix (1910), republished in *Dal comune al principato* (Florence 1929), 53–118, remains of value, though the criticisms of G. B. Picotti, 'Qualche osservazione sui caratteri delle signorie italiane', *RSI*, ns. iv (1926), 7–30 should be noted. On the legalising role of the Empire, see G. de Vergottini, 'Vicariato imperiale e signoria', *Studi di storia e diritto in onore di A. Solmi* (Milan 1941), i, 43–61; G. Sandri, 'I vicariati imperiali perpetui di Enrico VII di Lussemburgo', *Atti dell'Istituto Veneto di scienze, lettere ed arti*, civ (1944–5), 151–90; P. Torelli, 'Capitanato del popolo e vicariato imperiale come elementi costitutivi della signoria bonacolsiana', *Atti e Memorie della R. Accademia Virgiliana di Mantova*, ns. xiv–xvi (1921–3), 73–166.

Among general studies of the rise of *signorie*, see L. Simeoni, 'La formazione della signoria scaligera', *Atti e Memorie dell'Accademia di Agricoltura, Scienze e Lettere di Verona*, cviii (1926), 117–67; idem, 'L'elezione di Obizzo d'Este a signore di Ferrara', *ASI*, xciii (1935), 165–88; W. Montorsi, 'Considerazioni intorno al sorgere della signoria estense', *Atti e Memorie della Deputazione di Storia Patria per le Provincie Modenesi*, 8th ser., x (1958), 31–43; M. Rapisarda, *La signoria di Ezzelino da Romano* (Udine 1965); *Studi ezeliniani*, ed. G. Fasoli et al. (Rome 1963).

For openings towards fresh approaches to the *signoria*, see F. Cognasso, 'Le origini della signoria lombarda', *ASL*, lxxxiii (1956), 1–19; E. Sestan, 'Le origini delle signorie cittadine: un problema storico esaurito?', *BISI*, lxxiii (1962), 41–69; and F. Diaz, 'Di alcuni aspetti istituzionali dell'affermarsi delle signorie', *Nuova Rivista Storica*, l (1966), 116–44.

(f) General Histories of Individual Cities

A selection of the more important recent books on the leading cities is all that can be attempted here:

R. Davidsohn, *Geschichte von Florenz*, 4 vols (Berlin 1896–1927), Italian translation, 8 vols (Florence, 1956–68); Fondazione Treccani degli Alfieri, *Storia di Milano* (Milan 1953–); idem, *Storia di Brescia* (Brescia 1963–); T. O. De Negri, *Storia di Genova* (Milan 1968); *Mantova: la Storia*, ed. G. Coniglio (Mantua 1958); Società Editrice Storia di Napoli, *Storia di Napoli* (Naples 1967–); Istituto di Studi Romani, *Storia di Roma* (Bologna 1938–); Centro Internazionale delle Arti e del Costume, *Storia di Venezia* (Venice 1957–); R. Cessi, *Storia della Repubblica di Venezia* (Milan–Messina 1944–6); H. Kretschmayr, *Geschichte von Venedig* (Gotha–Stuttgart 1905–34).

(g) The Empire, the Papacy and the South

The main sources for the Empire in Italy are in the Monumenta Germaniae Historica: official *acta* in Legum Sectio IV, *Constitutiones* I–VI (up to 1330) and many Italian chronicles in *Scriptores*. J. Ficker, *Forschungen zur Reichsund Rectsgeschichte Italiens*, 4 vols (Innsbruck 1874; reprinted Aalen 1961) has a useful collection of documents in vol. iv. The main documents on the Lombard League are in C. Vignati, *Storia diplomatica della Lega Lombarda* (Milan 1867; reprinted Turin 1966). For documents on the Papal States, see A. Theiner, *Codex Diplomaticus Dominii Temporalis Sanctae Sedis*, 3 vols (Rome 1861–2; reprinted Frankfurt am Main 1964).

An excellent textbook covering the period from the twelfth century up to 1276 is E. Jordan, *L'Allemagne et l'Italie au XIIe et XIIIe Siècles*, Histoire du Moyen-Age, ed G. Glotz, IV, 1 (Paris 1939); idem, *Les Origines de la Domina-*

tion Angevine en Italie (Paris 1909), besides dealing in great detail with the period 1250–68, includes a survey of the first half of the thirteenth century in its lengthy introduction. P. Brezzi, 'I comuni cittadini italiani e l'Impero medioevale', in *Nuove questioni di storia medioevale*, ed. Marzorati, 177–207 provides a useful introduction. G. Pepe, *Lo stato ghibellino di Federico II* (2nd edn, Bari 1951) is very hostile to the emperor.

On individual popes, see L. Gatto, *Il pontificato di Gregorio X* (Rome 1959); G. Levi, 'Bonifazio VIII e le sue relazioni col comune di Firenze', *Atti della Società Romana di Storia Patria*, v (1882), 365–474; and T. Bottagisio, *Bonifazio VIII e un celebre commentatore di Dante* (Milan 1926). A comprehensive study of the most turbulent part of the Papal States is A. Vasina, *I romagnoli fra autonomie cittadine e accentramento papale nell'età di Dante* (Florence 1965).

On the Angevins, see E. G. Léonard, *Les Angevins de Naples* (Paris 1954) and R. Caggese, *Roberto d'Angiò e i suoi tempi*, 2 vols (Florence, 1922 and 1931).

4. ECONOMIC HISTORY

(a) General

A. Doren, *Wirtschaftsgeschichte Italiens im Mittelalter* (Jena 1934; Italian translation by G. Luzzatto, Padua 1937) is still useful.

An important collection of sources and studies on Italian economic history is *Documenti e Studi per la Storia del Commercio e del Diritto Commerciale Italiano*, published under the direction of F. Patetta and M. Chiaudano (Turin Genoa 1933–), of which some 20 volumes have now appeared, including a number of early notarial registers which are an indispensable source for the history of Italian commerce and business in the twelfth and thirteenth centuries.

On population, K. J. Beloch, *Bevolkerungsgeschichte Italiens*, 3 vols (Berlin 1939–61) has been criticised for the inaccuracy of some of its medieval statistics and should be used with caution. For Florence, see E. Fiumi, 'La demografia fiorentina nelle pagine di Giovanni Villani', *ASI*, cviii (1950), 78–158, and for two small towns and rural areas in Tuscany, *idem*, 'La popolazione del territorio volterrano-sangimignanese e il problema demografico dell'età comunale', *Studi in onore di A. Fanfani*, i, 249–90.

(b) The Countryside, Towns and Cities

To an even greater extent than in other countries, agrarian history has been a neglected subject in Italy. The *Rivista di Storia dell'Agricoltura*, founded in 1960, provides information about the latest research; the best statement of the present state of knowledge and the problems awaiting investigation is P. J. Jones, 'Per la storia agraria italiana nel medio evo: lineamenti e problemi', *RSI*, lxxvi (1964), 285–348. E. Sereni, *Storia del paesaggio agrario italiano* (Bari 1961) is a stimulating essay on a subject which cries out for more thorough investigation.

On the late Roman and early medieval period, some new ideas are advanced by L. Ruggini Gracco, *Economia e società nell' 'Italia annonaria': rapporti fra agricoltura e commercio dal secolo IV–VI* (Milan 1961) and *idem*, 'Vicende rurali dell'Italia antica dall'eta tetrarchica ai Longobardi', *RSI*, lxxvi (1964), 261–86.

There is as yet no comprehensive work on the agrarian revival of the eleventh and twelfth century, so its outline must be pieced together from particular studies such as C. Violante, *La società milanese nell'epoca precomunale*

(Bari 1953); P. Torelli, *Un comune cittadino in territorio ad economia agricola*, 2 vols (Mantua 1930 and 1952); G. Volpe, *Studi sulle istituzioni comunali a Pisa* (Pisa, 1902), 1–118; V. Fainelli, 'Intorno alle origini dei comuni rurali veronesi', *NAV*, xxv (1913), 381–444; L. Simeoni, 'Il commune rurale nel territorio veronese', *NAV*, xlii (1921), 152–200.

On various aspects of the thirteenth century there is R. Romeo, 'La signoria dell'abate di S. Ambrogio di Milano sul comune rurale di Origgio nel secolo XIII', *RSI*, lxix (1957), 340–77, 473–507; G. Fasoli, 'Ricerche sui borghi franchi dell'altra Italia', *RSDI*, xv (1942), 139–214. J. Plesner, *L'Emigration de la Campagne à la Ville Libre de Florence au XIII Siècle* (Copenhagen 1934) is still the essential starting point on this subject, but see G. Luzzatto, 'L'inurbamento delle popolazioni rurali in Italia nei secoli XII e XIII', *Studi in onore di E. Besta* (Milan 1938), ii, 183–203. The ideas in J. Plesner, 'Una rivoluzione stradale nel dugento', *Acta Jutlandica*, x (1938), 1–101 have not yet been followed up. E. Fiumi, *Storia economica e sociale di San Gimignano* (Florence 1961) is a model study of a small town, mainly concerned with the 'golden age' of the thirteenth century. On major inland cities there is A.-E. Sayous, 'Dans l'Italie, à l'Interieur des Terres: Sienne de 1221–1229', *Annales*, iii (1931), 189–206 and E. Fiumi, 'Fioritura e decadenza dell'economia fiorentina', *ASI*, cxv (1957), 385–439; cxvi (1958), 443–501; and cxvii (1959), 427–502.

(c) Commerce and the Merchant Class

By far the best book on the Mediterranean trade is W. Heyd, *Histoire du Commerce du Levant au Moyen-Age* (Leipzig 1885, reprinted Amsterdam 1967). For the early period there is also A. Schaube, *Handelsgeschichte der Romischen Völker des Mittelmeergebiets bis zum Ende der Kreuzzüge* (Munich and Berlin 1906).

For Venice, see G. Luzzatto, *Storia economica di Venezia dall' XI all'XVI secolo* (Venice 1961). There is no equivalent outline history of Genoa, but E. Bach, *La Cité de Gênes au XIIe Siècle* (Copenhagen 1955) provides a useful summary for the twelfth century, and there is much information on the next two centuries in the introduction to R. Doehaerd, *Les Relations Commerciales entre Gênes, la Belgique et l'Outremont d'après les Archives Notariales Génoises*, 3 vols (Brussels and Rome 1941). A short study on Pisa is E. Rossi-Sabatini, *L'espansione di Pisa nel Mediterraneo* (Florence 1935).

On particular aspects of international trade: P. Vaccari, 'Da Venezia a Genova. Un capitolo di storia delle relazioni commerciali nell'Alto Medioevo', *Studi in onore di G. Luzzatto* (Milan 1950), i, 88–95; J. Heers, 'Urbanisme et Structure Sociale à Gênes au Moyen-Age', *Studi in onore di A. Fanfani* (Milan 1962), i, 369–412; R. S. Lopez, 'L'attività economica di Genova nel marzo 1253 secondo gli atti notarili del tempo', *Atti della Società Ligure di Storia Patria*, lxiv (1935), 163–270; *idem*, 'I primi cento anni di storia documentata della banca a Genova', *Studi in onore di A. Sapori* (Milan, 1957), i, 215–53; A.-E. Sayous, 'Les Opérations des Banquiers Italiens aux Foires de Champagne pendant le XIIIe Siècle', *Revue Historique*, clxx (1932), 1–31; R.-H. Bautier, 'Les Foires de Champagne', *Receuils de la Société Jean Bodin*, v (1953), 97–147; C. Piton, *Les Lombards en France et à Paris*, 2 vols (Paris 1892); G. I. Bratianu, *Recherches sur le Commerce Génois dans la Mer Noire au XIIIe Siècle* (Paris 1929); *idem*, *Les Vénetiens dans la Mer Noire au XIVe Siècle* (Bucharest 1939); G. Pistarino, 'Genova medievale tra oriente e occidente', *RSI*, lxxxi (1969), 44–73.

On merchants, the best guide is A. Sapori, *Le Marchand Italien au Moyen Age* (Paris 1952) – short essays with extensive bibliographies. Other general surveys are Y. Renouard, *Les Hommes d'Affaires Italiens du Moyen Age* (2nd edn, Paris 1968) and J. Lestocquoy, *Aux Origines de la Bourgeoisie: Les Villes de Flandre et d'Italie sous le Gouvernement des Patriciens* (Paris 1952).

For the great Italian banks and trading companies see A. Sapori, *Una compagnia di Calimala ai primi del trecento* (Florence 1932); *idem, La crisi delle compagnie dei Bardi e dei Peruzzi* (Florence 1926); *Studi di storia economica medievale* (3rd edn, Florence 1953).

On the merchant class, see R. S. Lopez, 'Aux Origines du Capitalisme Génois', *Annales*, ix (1937), 429–54; A.-E. Sayous, 'Aristocratie et Noblesse à Gênes' *ibid.* 366–81; G. Luzzatto, 'Les Activités Economiques du Patriciat Vénetien', *ibid.* 25–57. For a unique merchant–admiral–statesman, see R. S. Lopez, *Genova marinara del duecento, Benedetto Zaccaria* (Messina 1933).

(d) The Economic Crisis of the Fourteenth Century

An optimistic view of the late medieval Italian economy is presented by G. Miani, 'L'Economie Lombarde au XIVe et XVe Siècles: un exception à la regle', *Annales*, xix (1964), 568–79; a pessimistic one by R. Romano, 'L'Italia nella crisi del XIV secolo', *Nuova Rivista Storica*, l (1966), 580–95. A detailed local study is E. Carpentier, *Une Ville devant la Peste: Orvieto et la Peste Noire de 1348* (Paris 1962).

5. THE CHURCH, CULTURE AND SOCIETY

(a) The Church, Heresy and Society

There is, surprisingly, no up-to-date history of the Church in Italy, though there are innumerable local studies which it is impossible to list here. New research may be followed through the *Rivista di Storia della Chiesa in Italia*; the publications of the Centro di Studi sulla Spiritualità Medioevale at Todi should also be noted. The volume *Vescovi e diocesi in Italia nel medioevo sec. IX–XIII*, Atti del II Convegno di Storia della Chiesa in Italia, Italia Sacra V (Padua 1964) contains some valuable contributions. See also S. Mochi Onory, 'Vescovi e città', *RSDI*, iv (1931), 245–329, 555–600; v (1932), 99–179, 241–312; vi (1933), 199–238 for the 4th–6th centuries.

Older historians were chiefly interested in the contacts between Church and State at the constitutional level, e.g. 'Le lotte fra stato e chiesa nei comuni italiani durante il secolo XIII' in G. Salvemini, *Studi Storici* (Florence 1901), 39–90, and S. Pivano, *Stato e chiesa negli statuti comunali italiani* (Turin 1904).

H. C. Peyer, *Stadt und Stadtpatron im Mittelalterlichen Italien* (Zürich 1955) opens up a large and important topic.

On heresy, the contributions of C. Violante and R. Manselli to *Hérésies et Sociétés dans l'Europe Pre-Industrielle*: Colloque de Royaumont, ed. J. Le Goff (Paris 1968) raise some interesting speculations on the social significance of heretics in Italy up to the end of the thirteenth century. On the twelfth century, see R. Manselli, *Studi sulle eresie del secolo XII* (Rome 1953) and *L'eresia del male* (Naples 1961); also A. Frugoni, *Arnaldo da Brescia nelle fonti del secolo XII* (Rome 1954). G. Volpe, *Movimenti religiosi e sette ereticali nella società medievale italiana* (Florence 1922) remains useful.

(b) Education and Learning

On the pre-communal period, see D. A. Bullough, 'Le scuole cattedrali e la cultura dell'Italia settentrionale prima dei Comuni', *Vescovi e diocesi in Italia*, 111–43; A. Viscardi, *Le origini, Storia letteraria d'Italia*, i, publ. F. Vallardi (4th edn, Milan 1966).

The best introduction to the revival of law and rhetoric is S. Stelling-Michaud, *L'Université de Bologne et la Pénétration des Droits Romain et Canonique en Suisse au XIIIe et XIV Siècles* (Geneva 1955). For the Bolognese law school and university, the series *Studi e Memorie per la Storia dell'Università di Bologna* (Bologna 1907-) should be consulted, especially Volume I of the new series (1956), with important contributions by G. De Vergottini, U. Gualazzini, P. S. Leicht, C. G. Mor and G. Rossi. See also G. Cencetti, 'Studium fuit Bononie: note sulla storia dell'università di Bologna nel primo secolo della sua esistenza', *Studi Medievali*, 2nd ser., vii (1966), 781–833. F. C. von Savigny, *Geschichte des Römischen Rechts im Mittelalter*, 6. Bd (Heidelberg 1815–31) is still valuable for the lives of the Bolognese jurists; the main sources are in the *Chartularium Studii Bononiensis*, published by the Commissione per la storia dell'Università di Bologna (Bologna 1909-) and M. Sarti and M. Fattorini, *De Claris Archigymnasii Bononiensis Professoribus*, ed. C. Albicinius and C. Malagola, 2 vols (Bologna 1888–94).

On the Bolognese rhetoricians, A. Gaudenzi, 'Sulla cronologia delle opere dei dettatori bolognesi da Boncompagno a Bene di Lucca', *BISI*, xiv (1895), 85–174 provides essential groundwork. The most important texts are in L. Rockinger, *Briefsteller und Formelbücher des Elften bis Vierzehnten Jahrhunderts* (Munich 1863, reprinted New York 1961) and *Biblioteca Juridica Medii Aevi*, ed. A. Gaudenzi and J. B. Palmieri, 3 vols (Bologna 1888–1901). On Boncompagno, C. Sutter, *Aus Leben und Schriften des Magisters Boncompagno* (Freiburg and Leipzig 1894) is still unsuperseded. On Guido Fava, G. Vecchi, 'Le Arenge di Guido Fava e l'eloquenza d'arte, civile e politica duecentesca', *Quadrivium*, iv (1960), 61–90; on Brunetto Latini, E. Wieruszowski, 'Brunetto Latini als Lehrer Dantes und die Florentiner', *Archivio Italiano per la Storia della Pietà*, ii (1959), 169–98 and B. Ceva, *Brunetto Latini, l'uomo e l'opera* (Milan and Naples 1965). *Li Livres dou Trésor* has been edited by F. J. Carmody (Berkeley 1948). The handbooks for civic magistrates are discussed by F. Hertter, *Die Podestaliterature Italiens in XII. und XIII. Jahrhunderts* (Berlin and Leipzig 1910) and A. Sorbelli, 'I teorici del Reggimento comunale', *BISI*, lix (1944), 31–136.

For the early humanists, see R. Weiss, *Il primo secolo dell'umanesimo* (Rome 1949); G. Billanovich, *I primi umanisti e le tradizioni del classici latini* (Freiburg 1953); and Guido Billanovich, 'Veterum vestigia vatum' nei carmi dei preumanisti padovani', *Italia Medioevale e Umanistica*, i (1958), 155–243.

(c) The Arts, Literature and Society
This is not the place to list the many books on the history of the arts and literature in Italy. The most interesting attempts to place the arts in their social setting have been made by writers in English (see above, p. 206); an important exception is W. Braunfels, *Mittelalterliche Stadtbaukunst in der Toskana* (Berlin 1953). Examples of the results of communal patronage of architects are illustrated in N. Rodolico and G. Marchini, *I palazzi del popolo nei comuni italiani del medio evo* (Milan 1962); on lay patronage of church building, 'Intorno ai reciproci rapporti fra Chiesa ed organizzazioni cittadine nel medio evo italiano' in N. Ottokar, *Studi comunali e fiorentini* (Florence 1948), 163–78.

(d) Historiography and Political Thought
On the Florentine chronicles see O. Hartwig, *Quellen und Forschungen zur ältesten Geschichte der Stadt Florenz*, 2 vols (Marburg 1875; Halle 1880);

A. del Monte, 'La storiografia fiorentina dei secoli XII e XIII', *BISI*, lxii (1950), 175–282; G. Villani, *Cronica*, 1st edn, I. Moutier, 4 vols (Florence 1823; reissued 1844–7), 2nd edn, F. Dragomanni, 4 vols (Florence 1844–5); Dino Compagni, *Cronica*, ed. I. Del Lungo, *RIS*, ix, ii (1907–16) and many other editions; I. Del Lungo, *Dino Compagni e la sua Cronica*, 3 vols (Florence 1878–87).

For north-eastern Italy in the thirteenth century, see G. Arnaldi, *Studi sui cronisti della Marca Trevigiana nell'età di Ezzelino da Romano* (Rome 1963).

References

1. THE SOCIAL FOUNDATIONS OF MEDIEVAL ITALY (pp. 10–37)

1. Rothari's *Edict* of 643, MGH, *Fontes Iuris Germanici separatim editi*, ii, cl. 134–5.
2. D. A. Bullough, 'Europae Pater – Charlemagne and his Achievement in the light of Modern Research', *EHR*, lxxxv (1970), 92–6.
3. Migne, *PL*, cxxxiii, col. 658; English translation by Dom Gerard Sitwell, *St Odo of Cluny* (London 1958), 117–18. See also F. L. Ganshof in *Mélanges N. Iorga* (Paris 1933), 295–307.
4. MGH, *Leges*, iv, 196–7; trans. R. S. Lopez and I. W. Raymond, *Medieval Trade in the Mediterranean World* (London 1955), n. 9.
5. D. A. Bullough, *The Age of Charlemagne* (London 1965), 198; also R.-H. Bautier, *The Economic Development of Medieval Europe* (London 1971), 39.
6. MGH, *Poetae Latini*, i, 142–4.
7. *Ibid.* 22–6, 118–22; J. K. Hyde, 'Medieval Descriptions of Cities', *Bulletin of the John Rylands Library*, xlviii, ii (1966), 311–13.
8. Abu al-Qasim Muhammed ibn Hawqal, *The Book of the Routes and the Kingdoms*, Italian trans. M. Amari, *Biblioteca Arabo-Sicula*, i (Turin and Rome 1880) 24–5; short extracts in English, Lopez and Raymond, nn. 16–18.
9. P. Jaffé, *Regesta Pontificum Romanorum*, n. 3308; C. Cahen, 'Un texte peu connu relatif au commerce oriental d'Amalfi au Xe siècle', *Archivio Storico Napolitano*, xxiv (1955), 61–6.
10. A. Gloria, *Codice Diplomatico Padovano* (Venice 1877), 12–16; trans. in Lopez and Raymond, n. 10.
11. *Honorancie Civitatis Papie*, MGH. SS, XXX, ii, 1444–60; partial trans. in Lopez and Raymond, n. 20.
12. *Mutinensis Urbis Descriptio*, RIS (old edn), II, ii, 687–92; F. Patetta, 'Note sopra alcune iscrizioni medievali della regione modenese', *Memorie dell'Accademia di Scienze di Modena*, iii, 6 (1906), 485–550; M. Roncaglia, 'Il canto delle scolte modenesi', *Cultura Neolatina*, viii (1948), 1–46.
13. R. Davidsohn, *Geschichte von Florenz* (Berlin 1896–1927), i, 136–7; P. Torelli, *Un comune cittadino in territorio ad economia agricola* (Mantua 1930–52), i, 118.
14. C. Violante, *La società milanese nell'epoca precomunale* (Bari 1953); D. Herlihy, 'Treasure Hoards in the Italian Economy, 960–1139', *EcHR*, x (1957), 1–14.
15. *De servis libertatem enhelantibus*, MGH, *Constitutiones*, i, n. 21; Leo of Vercelli cited in Violante, *Società milanese*, 157.
16. V. Fainelli, *Codice diplomatico veronese* (Venice 1940–63), ii, n. 187.
17. MGH, *Constitutiones*, i, n. 45.
18. Cited in H. Pérès, *La Poesie Andalouse en Arabe Classique au XIe siècle* (Paris 1937), 216.
19. *Vita Mathildae*, MGH. SS, XII, 379; *Vita S. Anselmi*, MGH. SS, XXX, ii, 1248 *et seq.*
20. *Tetralogus*, MGH. SS, XI, 251.
21. Cited in D. B. Zema, 'The Houses of Tuscany and of Pierleone in the Crisis of Rome in the Eleventh Century', *Traditio*, ii (1944), 170.

22. A. Hofmeister, 'Der Übersetzer Johannes und das Geschlecht Comitis Mauronis in Amalfi', *Historische Vierteljahrschrift*, xxvii (1932), 225–83, 493–508, 831–33. The surviving bronze doors are illustrated in H. Leisinger, *Romanesque Bronzes* (London 1956).

2. THE EMERGENCE OF THE COMMUNES (pp. 38–64)

1. See above, pp. 21–2.

2. A. Solmi, *L'amministrazione finanziaria del regno italico* (Pavia 1932), 187 ff.

3. Guibert de Nogent, *De vita sua*, iii, 8, trans. J. F. Benton, *Self and Society in Medieval France* (New York 1970), 174.

4. Muratori, *Antiquitates*, iv, 19.

5. 'Carmen in victoriam Pisanorum', in E. Du Méril, *Poésies Populaires Latines au Moyen-Age* (Paris 1847), 239–51.

6. *Liber Maiolichinus de Gestis Pisanorum Illustribus*, ed. C. Calisse, FSI, 28 (Rome 1904).

7. *CDG*, i, n. 8.

8. *CDG*, i, nn. 128, 285.

9. L. Savioli, *Annali bolognesi*, i, ii (Bassano 1784), nn. 96, 109; A. Hessel, *Geschichte der Stadt Bologna* (Berlin 1910), 51–85; L. Simeoni, 'Bologna e la politica italiana di Enrico V', *Atti e Memorie Dep. Storia Patria per l'Emilia e la Romagna*, ns. ii (1937), 147–66.

10. For example, in 1211 the Modenese council met in the bishop's tent outside the castle of Bazzano (Savioli, *op. cit.* n. 397).

11. C. Manaresi, *Gli atti del comune di Milano* (Milan 1919), n. iii; Jaffé, *Regesta Pontificum*, nn. 5354–6.

12. F. Bonaini, *Statuti inediti della città di Pisa* (Florence 1854–7), i, 16–18.

13. *Ibid.* i, 18–19.

14. *Libellus de Situ Civitatus Mediolani*, ed. G. and A. Colombo, RIS, 1, 2 (1942); *Mutinensis Urbis Descriptio*, RIS, II, ii (old edn), 687–92.

15. Plate II. G. Fasoli, *Dalla civitas al comune*, 157–8, suggests that this sculpture represents the peace between the *milites* and the citizens from which the commune was born. This is an attractive idea, but it must be regarded as not proven, since there is no firm evidence that the knights and citizens formed separate bodies at Verona at this period, though they did in contemporary Milan. All one can say with certainty is that the bishop is presenting only one standard, and he is giving it to the *populus*, which must signify the whole active membership of the newly formed commune.

16. See C. B. Fisher, 'The Pisan Clergy and an Awakening of Historical Interest in an Italian Commune', *Studies in Medieval and Renaissance History*, iii (1966), 141–219.

17. G. Cremaschi, *Mosè del Brolo e la cultura a Bergamo nei secoli XI e XII* (Bergamo 1945).

18. Edited many times, e.g. R. Valentini and G. Zucchetti, *Codice topografico della città di Roma*, FSI (1940–6), iii, 1–65.

19. P. Jaffé, *Biblioteca Rerum Germanicarum* (Berlin 1864–9), i, 539–43.

3. THE CENTURY OF GROWTH, 1150–1250 (pp. 65–93)

1. E. Bach, *La Cité de Gênes au XII Siècle* (Copenhagen 1955), 50–2.

2. *Annali genovesi*, ed. L. T. Belgrano and C. Imperiale di Sant'Angelo, FSI (1898–1929), i, 62.

3. *CDG*, i, n. 22.

4. *Ibid.* i, nn. 81–5, 126.

5. *Ibid.* i, nn. 253–7; Savioli, *Annali bolognesi*, I, ii, n. 302.

6. P. Santini, *Documenti dell'antica costituzione del comune di Firenze*, Documenti di Storia Italiana, x (Florence 1895), 17–18, 191, 365, xlvii.

7. A. Fumagalli, *Delle Antichità Longobardico-Milanesi*, 4 vols (Milan 1792–3), ii, 133–146; also G. Biscaro, 'Gli antichi "Navigli" milanesi', *ASL*, 4th ser., xxxv (1908), 285–326.

8. M. Zucchini, 'Di un documento pomposiano sulla "laboreria" ', *Rivista di Storia dell'Agricoltura*, v (1965), 95–101.

9. M. Lecce, 'Una bonifica in territorio veronese alla fine del XII secolo', *Economia e Storia*, ii (1954), 193–7.

10. Savioli, *Annali bolognesi*, I, ii, n. 380.

11. D. Herlihy, *Medieval and Renaissance Pistoia* (New Haven and London 1967), 55–64; E. Fiumi, 'La popolazione del territorio volterrano-sangimignanese ed il problema demografico dell'età comunale', *Studi in onore di A. Fanfani* (Milan 1962), I, 277, 283.

12. J. Plesner, *L'Emigration de la Campagne à la Ville Libre de Florence* (Copenhagen 1934), 20–1.

13. *Ibid.* 177.

14. L. Simeone, 'II documento ferrarese del 1112 della fondazione dell'arte dei calegari', *Rendiconto della Reale Accademia di Scienze di Bologna*, 3rd ser., vii (1932), 56–71.

15. V. Licitra, 'La "Summa de arte dictandi" di maestro Goffredo', *Studi Medievali*, 3rd ser., vii (1966), 890.

16. Extracts from the *Rhetorica Antiqua* are in Rockinger, *Briefsteller und Formelbücher*, i, 128–74; a complete edition is at present being prepared by G. Vecchi and V. Pini.

17. *Rhetorica Novissima*, Biblioteca Juridica Medii Aevi, ed. A. Gaudenzi and J. B. Palmieri, ii, 249–97; *Cedrus* in Rockinger, *op. cit.* i, 121–7.

18. *Liber de Obsidione Ancone*, ed. G. C. Zimolo, RIS, VI, ii (Bologna 1913).

19. Published in the Appendix to A. Gaudenzi, *I suoni, le forme, e le parole dell'odierno dialetto della città di Bologna* (Bologna 1889).

20. *Oculus Pastoralis*, ed. D. Franceschi, *Memorie dell'Accademia delle Scienze di Torino: Classe di Scienze Morali, Storiche e Filologiche*, 4th ser., xi (1966).

4. THE CONSOLIDATION OF THE COMMUNES (pp. 94–123)

1. See above, p. 52.

2. Bonaini, *Statuti di Pisa*, ii, 822.

3. *CDG*, i, n. 128.

4. *CDG*, i, 158; Bonaini, i, 4–5.

5. A. Solmi, 'Le legge più antiche del comune di Piacenza', *ASI*, lxxiii (1915), 3–81.

6. Manaresi, *Atti del comune di Milano*, nn. xc, cviii, cxv, cxx; Bonaini, i, 4.

7. See A. Franceschini, *I frammenti epigrafici degli statuti di Ferrara del 1173* (Ferrara 1969).

8. Adalberto Samaritano, *Praecepta Dictaminum*, ed. F.-J. Schmale, MGH, Quellen zur Geistesgeschichte, iii, 60–1.

9. G. Rabotti, 'Contributo alla storia dei podestà prefedericani: Guido da Sasso, podestà di Bologna 1151–5', *RSDI*, xxxii (1959), 249–66.

10. *Oculus Pastoralis, ed. cit.* 26.

11. *Annali genovesi*, iii, 45; *Liber Consuetudinum Mediolani*, ed. E. Besta and G. L. Barni (Milan 1949).

12. Santini, *Documenti dell'antica costituzione di Firenze*, 51. The well-known destruction of the town of Semifonte and the resettlement of the inhabitants by the Florentine commune in 1202 was an exceptionally drastic measure.

13. Rockinger, *Briefsteller und Formelbücher*, i, 122.

14. *Liber Consuetudinum*, 125.

15. *Annales Placentini Guelfi, Annales Placentini Gibellini*, MGH. SS, XVIII, 403–581.

16. I. Ghiron, 'La credenza di S. Ambrogio', *ASL*, 4th ser., iv (1876), 583–609.

17. Gerardi Maurisii, *Cronica dominorum Ecelini et Alberici fratrum de Romano*, ed. G. Soranzo, RIS, VIII, 4 (1913–14). See G. de Vergottini, 'Il "popolo" di Vicenza nella cronaca ezzeliniana di Gerardo Maurisio', *Studi Senesi*, xlviii (1934), 354–74 and G. Arnaldi, *Studi sui cronisti della Marca Trevigiana nell'età di Ezzelino da Romano* (Rome 1963), 27–66.

18. A. Gaudenzi, *Statuti del popolo di Bologna del secolo XIII* (Bologna 1888); *idem, Statuti delle società del popolo di Bologna*, FSI, 2 vols (Rome 1889–96).

19. *Cronica Marchie Trivixane*, ed. A. Bonardi, RIS, VIII, i (1906), 67.

5. POLITICS AND THE AGE OF DANTE (pp. 124–52)

1. *Annales Placentini Ghibellini*, MGH. SS, XVIII 565; *Chronicon Parmense*, ed. G. Bonazzi, RIS, IX, 9 (1902–4), 32.

2. For an invaluable collection of data concerning the parties, see R. Davidsohn, *Forschungen zur Geschichte von Florenz* (Berlin 1896–1908), iv, 29–67.

3. *Chronicon Parmense*, 25–85.

4. *Gli statuti veronesi del 1276*, ed. G. Sandri (Venice 1940), i, 53.

5. MS. Archivio di Stato, Florence, Capitani di Parte 25, f. 32 r.

6. Quoted by C. T. Davis, 'An Early Florentine Political Theorist', *Proceedings of the American Philosophical Society*, civ (1960), 667.

7. Johannes de Cermenate, *Historia*, ed. L. A. Ferrai, FSI (1889), 23; Nicolai episcopi Botronensis, *Relatio de Itinere Italico Henrici VII*, in Stephanus Baluzius, *Vitae Paparum Avenionensium*, ed. G. Mollat (Paris 1921), 525–9.

8. L. A. Muratori, *Delle Antichità Estensi ed Italiane* (Modena 1717–40), ii, 25–7; for the circumstances, see L. Simeoni, 'L'elezione di Obizzo d'Este a signore di Ferrara, 1264', *ASI*, xciii (1935), 165–88.

9. *Chronica Parva Ferrariensis*, RIS (old edn), VIII, coll. 487–8.

10. *Chronicon Parmense*, 108–88.

11. *Ecerinide*, ed. L. Padrin (Bologna 1900).

12. Bonvesin della Riva, 'De Magnalibus Urbis Mediolani', ed. F. Novati, *BISI*, xx (1898), 155–6.

6. THE FLOWERING OF THE 'VITA CIVILE' (pp. 153–77)

1. *De Magnalibus, ed. cit.*; translation in Lopez and Raymond, n. 64–6, abbreviated and slightly adapted.

2. Davis, *art. cit., Proceedings of the American Philosophical Society*, civ (1960), 667–8.

3. Abbreviated from Lopez and Raymond, 67.

4. *Visio Egidii Regis Patavii*, ed. G. Fabris, *Bollettino del Museo Civico di Padova*, ns. x–xi (1934–9), 17–19; 'Le Proprietà del Mercato Vecchio', *Delizie degli Eruditi Toscani*, ed. Ildefonso di San Luigi (Florence 1780), vi, 269.

5. G. Villani, *Cronica*, ed. I. Moutier (Florence 1823), Bk. ix, chs 91–4; partial translation in Lopez and Raymond, n. 24. See A. Frugoni, 'Giovanni Villani "Cronica" XI. 94', *BISI*, lxxvii (1965), 229–55.

6. *Chronicon*, MS. Ambrosiana cod. B. 24 Inf. Lib. XIV, ch. 117.

7. Dino Compagni, *Cronica*, ed. I. Del Lungo, RIS, IX, ii (1907–16), 135.

8. Ed. A. Evans (Cambridge, Mass. 1936). Pegolotti's intention seems to have been practical, though some of his information has been proved to have been out of date. See P. Grierson, 'The Coin List of Pegolotti', *Studi A. Sapori*, i, 483–92.

9. Lopez and Raymond, n. 193.

10. Davis, 'Il buon tempo antico' in *Florentine Studies*, ed. N. Rubinstein (London 1968), 66–7.

11. Dante, *Paradiso*, xvi; Otto of Freising, *Gesta Friderici Imperatoris*, MGH. SS, XLVI, 115–17.

12. Folgore da San Gimignano, *I sonetti*, ed. F. Neri (Turin 1917).

13. Lopez and Raymond, nn. 205, 208.

14. Dino Compagni, *op. cit.* 55 ff.

15. L. Cerri, 'Alberto Scotto, signore di Piacenza 1290–1318', *Archivio Storico per le Provincie Parmensi*, ns. xii (1912), 1–36; *Chronica Tria Placentina*, Monumenta Historica ad provincias Parmensem et Placentinam pertinentia III (Parma 1859); Johannes de Mussis, *Chronicon Placentinum*, RIS (old edn), xvi, cols 447–560.

16. *La Bataille des Sept Ars*, quoted by C. Piton, *Les Lombards en France et à Paris* (Paris 1892), i, 9.

17. I. Del Lungo, *Dino Compagni e la sua cronica* (Florence 1879–87), i, 366–7.

7. THE END OF AN ERA (pp. 178–98)

1. Plesner, *L'Emigration de la Campagne à la Ville de Florence*, 163–5, 226–9; E. Fiumi, *Storia economica e sociale di San Gimignano* (Florence 1961), 122; D. Herlihy, *Medieval and Renaissance Pistoia* (New Haven and London 1967), 62–6, 180–91. Unfortunately, the discussion of contado taxation in W. M. Bowsky, *The Finance of the Commune of Siena* (Oxford 1970), 225–55, reaches no conclusions on these questions.

2. For an admirable survey of present views on communal finance and debt, see Bowsky, *op. cit.* 279–97.

Index